THEOLOGY AS NARRATION

A Commentary on the Book of Exodus

THEOLOGY AS NARRATION

A Commentary on the
Book of Exodus

GEORGE A. F. KNIGHT

WILLIAM B. EERDMANS PUBLISHING COMPANY
Grand Rapids, Michigan

Published in the U.S.A. by
Wm. B. Eerdmans Publishing Company,
Grand Rapids, Michigan

222.14
K69t

First published 1976

© 1976 George A. F. Knight

Library of Congress Cataloging in Publication Data

Knight, George Angus Fulton, 1909-
   Theology as narration.
   Includes index.
1. Bible. O.T. Exodus—Commentaries. I. Title.
BS1245. 3. K58 1977   222'. 12'06 76-20463
ISBN 0-8028-3489-2

Printed in Great Britain by
R. & R. Clark Ltd., Edinburgh

CONTENTS

ABBREVIATIONS

AV or KJV	The Authorized Version of the Bible
ET	English Translation
EVV	English Versions
Ex	Author of the Book of Exodus
ftn	footnote
IB	Interpreter's Bible
IDB	Interpreter's Dictionary of the Bible
JBL	Journal of Biblical Literature
Jer. Bib.	Jerusalem Bible
KJV or AV	King James Version of the Bible
LXX	The Septuagint, the Greek Version of the Old Testament
MT	Massoretic Text, Biblia Hebraica, ed. Rudolf Kittel, 7th ed., 1951
NEB	New English Bible
NT	New Testament
OT	Old Testament
RSV	Revised Standard Version of the Bible
Sam. Pent.	Samaritan Pentateuch
Syr	The Syriac Version of the Old Testament
Targ	Targum, Aramaic Version of the Old Testament

Targ. Onk.   Targum Onkelos

Targ. Ps. Jon.   Targum Pseudo-Jonathan

Tor   The Torah, the Five Books of Moses, the
                    Jewish Publication Society of America,
                    1962

VVS   The Versions of the Old Testament

INTRODUCTION

The book of Exodus is a theological essay in the form of narrative. Its theme is Revelation. As narrative its form is very different from that employed by an Aquinas or a Karl Barth or a Tillich. It could be compared rather with the work of the author of the Fourth Gospel. For it expresses revelation by recounting a series of dialogues, dialogue between Moses and Pharaoh, between Moses and Israel, between Moses and God, and describes even the dialogical thinking that goes on in the mind of Moses. This occurs when we meet the phrases 'The Lord said to Moses', and 'Moses said to the Lord'. These dialogues are then set within a framework which also is narrative, a narrative of events. These events are not necessarily factual; for the author regards their interpretation (which for him is now Revelation) as more important than 'mere' happening. This revelation, then, is not expressed in philosophical form, as a mystically minded Asian or a theosophically minded westerner might chose to write, but in terms of history writing and of man's experience of space and time. The result is to produce for us an 'incarnational' theological essay, one that is revelatory in terms of man's experience of what it means to be a human being under God.

This second book of the Bible is known, with the other four books of the Pentateuch, as *Torah*. This word means both Revelation and Instruction at the same time. Following on from the narrative found in Genesis, Exodus begins by introducing the reader to the People of Israel, living then as slaves in Egypt. Thereafter appear the two chief characters of the book. The one is Moses, the other is God, although Moses is never depicted in heroic terms. He is great only in so far as he is the servant of God, and as the intermediary between God and

Israel. Yet in reality the chief character in the book is God.
The book of Exodus is virtually a chapter in the history of God.
Right at the beginning of the story God makes himself known
to Moses as 'I AM WHO I AM'. As such he is the transcendent
author and creator of both nature and history. But in the course
of the same dialogical situation the same God also declares
himself to Moses as 'I AM with you'. As such he becomes in our
story immersed in history himself in and through his relationship with the historical people of Israel.

The book of Exodus is a human composition. We are inevitably concerned to discover how it came into being. In this
regard, however, we are largely in the area of supposition,
although biblical scholarship has provided us with vastly more
information than scholars possessed even a century ago. Today,
for example, few would question the basic historicity of the
man Moses, although no trace of him has as yet turned up in
contemporary extra-biblical literature or from the reports of
archaeologists working in Egypt or Sinai. The so-called
biblical sciences have advanced our knowledge of the Mosaic
period and of the cultures of Israel's neighbours to a surprising
degree. No one, again, would today question the statement
that Moses *wrote*, though his ability to do so was virtually
denied as recently as in the period of my youth. But how his
material was transmitted over the years, orally or in written
form, is another matter. And how much of the contents of
Exodus are from hands other than his are issues still wide open
to scholarly investigation. But a detailed examination of such
issues does not belong in a commentary. It belongs in the area
of Introduction, of which there are many examples in the
English language.

That is why in the limited space at our command we have
little to say on matters of form-criticism, or about the hypothesis of a Kenite source within Exodus; nor do we analyse the
various strands lying behind the J tradition. We make little
reference to either source criticism or to tradition criticism;
and we have little to say about the problems relating to the
date of the Exodus, or about the identity of the Pharaoh of the
oppression.

I do not agree with those Old Testament scholars, again, who
speak as if the book of Exodus 'grew' over the centuries, even

as E was conjoined with J and as both were woven into P's material. I am of course compelled to accept the hypothesis of the existence of these several traditions and more, for no other hypothesis has as yet, I believe, so successfully provided answers to the innumerable problems that biblical criticism raises. Yet some *one* person, I would claim, *wrote* Exodus, in the same sense that some *one* person wrote Matthew's Gospel. The latter obviously made use of Mark, the Testimonies, and other sources. The Gospel of Matthew, in fact, did not *grow*. Some one person finally wrote it.

I would therefore offer the reader my own, of course debatable, hypothesis, which is that some one person (whom I call in this Commentary Ex for convenience – Mr X?) *wrote* the book we examine here, and produced it in the form almost that we have today (for there could indeed have been small additions after his day), and that he did so about the year 515 B.C. We are justified in speaking of 'Ex' in this way, moreover, if we believe we are justified in calling the editor of 1 and 2 Chronicles, Ezra and Nehemiah, 'The Chronicler'. The latter undoubtedly gathered up themes discussed long before his day and then put the stamp of his theological outlook upon them.

I proffer this hypothesis because we can assume today that the Priestly material in the Pentateuch had been compiled and nearly completed during the Exile. Any accretions that were made in later centuries do not affect the issue. Through Deutero-Isaiah's teaching on the meaning of the Covenant, I would maintain, Ex had become deeply aware of his heritage as a member of Israel, the people *in whose midst*, as Deutero-Isaiah proclaimed (cf. Isa. 45: 14–15), Yahweh was to be found, hidden. Moreover, this latter prophet had regarded the Return from Exile in 538 B.C. as no less than a Second Exodus. What then exactly had the First Exodus meant to the Israel of Moses' day? Haggai and Zechariah had recently been urging their contemporaries to set to and rebuild the Temple, on the site of Solomon's earlier edifice. Yet, as men might ask, what was the *theological significance* of this new Temple now that it was being recognized as the successor, not just of Solomon's Temple, but also of the Tabernacle of Moses' day? And since the completion and dedication of the new Temple was now being marked, in 515 B.C., by the holding of the solemn rite of a special Passover, a ceremony whose like had not now been seen for centuries, what had the original Passover in Moses' day meant to the People of God, *then*?

Ex was not a scholar writing for scholars; he was clearly a believing man writing for a believing community and for the sake of posterity. We his readers are now that posterity whether we call ourselves Jews or Christians; for both of us now accept the book of Exodus as nothing less than Holy Scripture.

The book of Exodus is not legendary, for it tells of God's actions and not man's. Legends are stories that enlarge upon human activities and put them into some form of narrative. Neither is the book of Exodus to be classified as myth, for its contents are set in history. Nor is it to be dismissed as fairy tale, for its basis is so expressed that the story is to Israel's discredit. Much of the narrative in Exodus, however, is best described as saga. Saga preserves historical memories of events that aroused the emotions of the people that underwent the experiences in question, so that saga says more than does mere reportage. As Martin Buber puts it, saga becomes the 'mythization' of history. Thus Exodus is not merely history. We do not even know when it all happened. On the other hand, neither is it theology. We do not find here a 'Theology of the Old Testament'. Rather, it is *kerygma*, it is 'Good News about God', news to which Jews, Christians and Muslims alike must pay close attention.

Exodus is a Jewish book, even although the word Jew does not occur in it, because it is Torah; and from Torah there has developed the Talmudic faith, in which we find the whole Jewish way of life. And it tells the story of the People of God, who, from the period of the Second Temple onwards came to be known – by foreigners – under the name of Jews.

Exodus is a Christian book, because it deals with the activity of the Word of God. Christians recognize that this activity was not only confirmed (*pleroun*) in the person of Jesus, but also that Jesus himself spoke of the exodus as that which he himself would *pleroun* (absolutize? finalize? render *eph hapax*, Heb. 10: 2?) in Jerusalem, Luke 9: 31.

Exodus is a Muslim book. Moses and Aaron are referred to frequently in the Qoran. These sacred Scriptures accept moreover the reality of the activity of the *kalima*, the Word of God which has been working in history from Abraham onwards, through Moses and in Jesus; in fact the Qoran accepts the role of the biblical prophet right up to the advent of Mohammed. For the Qoran was sent to 'confirm the book which was before it', and to act as 'a protector over it' (Qoran 5, 52/48).

In his *Theology of the Old Testament*, I, ET 1961, p. 31, Walter Eichrodt writes: 'It is high time that the tyranny of historicism in Old Testament studies was broken and the proper approach to our task rediscovered. This is no new problem, certainly, but it is one that needs to be solved anew in every epoch of knowledge – *the problem of how to understand the realm of Old Testament beliefs in its structural unity, and how, by examining on the one hand its religious environment and on the other its essential coherence with the New Testament, to illuminate its profoundest meaning.*'

It used to be taken for granted that the great prophets preceded the Torah, in that much of the material found in the Torah 'grew' only because of the deep insights of the prophets into the ways of God. Today however that hypothesis is untenable. We now recognize that the prophets were acquainted with at least the basic material to be found in the Pentateuch. Thus any writer who sets down in his own words the story of the Mosaic period, making liberal use of whatever material has come down to him through history, must go beyond what the earliest traditions and documents wanted to express. I may say that when I first read Runciman's *History of the Crusades* I became aware that he possessed a much deeper insight into the moods and passions of both parties to the quarrel than can be discovered merely from a reading of the contemporary Latin and Arabic texts which comprised elements in his source material.

To say that the book of Exodus is 'revelation', however, is not to suggest that what we meet in it is final for both Jews and Christians, and even Muslims. There are elements in the Law, for example, which are unacceptable in the light of further revelation. The Jew, in this technological age, does not feel called upon to build either a Tabernacle or its successor, the Temple. The Christian, in the light of Jesus' self-giving on the Cross, and of his teaching about forgiving an enemy 'seventy times seven', does not regard the Lex Talionis (Ex 21: 24) as God's final word. Yet here we have revelation that was right for the period in which it took place, and which was presented in such pictorial categories that men both then and today can grasp what God means them to understand. Thus, by their very nature these pictorial categories remain open to indefinitely new possibilities of interpretation. It is the task of the modern commentator therefore to show how alive, how explosive the work of this sixth century theologian is.

Today we are blessed with a number of good translations of Exodus. I refer in the text to just three of these: (1) the Revised Standard Version, which is (a) common to Protestants and Roman Catholics in the Common Version, and (b) is American in origin; (2) the New English Bible, which is (a) a *de novo* translation from the MT, and (b) is British in origin; and (3) the excellent and often realistic Jewish publication, *The Torah, the Five Books of Moses* (the Jewish Publication Society of America, 1962).

If Revelation is indeed the revelation of Truth or Reality, then the book of Exodus is as much a challenge to the Synagogue as it is to the Church. Let our conjoint study of it bring us into those deep waters which flow around the roots of our common heritage in the Covenant made at Sinai.

CHAPTER 1

THE PEOPLE OF GOD

————

1–4   This first chapter unashamedly speaks of God as having a special relationship to Israel, even though he associates himself with every nation of men.

According to tradition Israel was the name that God himself had given to Jacob, the grandson of Abraham after the former had struggled for a whole night against God's offer of a gracious plan for his life, Gen. 32: 24–30. The new orientation that Jacob had then received was the sign that the objectionable, self-centred Jacob, who had contemptuously cheated his brother and barefacedly tricked his dying father, was still beloved of God. The 'new' Jacob had therefore become known as 'Israel', because as a forgiven man he had now become a new personality. So he needed a new name, a new description. The tradition thus tells us something important about God. It is that the descendants of Abraham, of whom Jacob was a good example, through whom all the families of the earth were to be blessed (or bless themselves), Gen. 12: 3, by their rebellion against God ought to have invalidated this promise that God had made. But God's action in turning the objectionable Jacob into the new man, Israel, was a revelation of how his gracious promise would work out.

We notice that Ex (the name that we give to the author of our book) supposes that the word 'Israel' means 'God rules', rather than the translation found at Gen. 32: 28. By beginning his book, then, with this emphasis upon Jacob and his name-change Ex is doing two things at once. First, he is expressing the God-centredness of his tale. While his interest is naturally in man, especially Israelite man, he is even more interested to show how 'God reigns' in human history. Yet, secondly, as we shall learn in chapter 3, Ex plans to show how God reigns *in* and *through* Israel. Israel is thus in a special sense the People of God. By 520 B.C. Ex would have heard or read Deutero-Isaiah's famous double couplet, Isa. 45: 14c–15:

> 'God is *in* you only, and there is no other. . . .
>   Truly thou art a God who hidest thyself, O God
>   of Israel, the Saviour'.

The book of Exodus, then, tells us how God both hides himself and reveals himself *in* Israel.

Ex picks up the story of God's grace that had already been told by a priestly colleague in the book we now call Genesis by recording the names of those persons, descended from Abraham (as later generations firmly believed) with whom God had entered into covenant, Gen. 17: 1–21. These persons had later emigrated from Canaan down to Egypt. Yet they had not done so by mere chance. In the customary biblical manner the 'theology' of history is, as here, made evident through the experience of individuals. Joseph had glimpsed only that one area of the divine plan which affected himself, Gen. 45: 5; 50: 20, but from it he could make wider generalizations. Ex now begins his book at Scene 2 of the divine drama by explaining what happened to God's plan while Jacob's descendants were still in Egypt.

We note that 'the names of the sons of Israel' here correspond with the list found in Gen. 35: 23–25. The name 'Abraham' occurs in Babylonian records contemporary with the period in which the biblical Abraham lived, where it occurs as the name both of an individual and of his clan. The name 'Jacob' appears in the eighteenth century Babylonian records. The credibility of our biblical material is thus enhanced.

5–7   The number 70 is a specially significant number in biblical thinking rather than a mere mathematical count of Jacob's offspring. 70 is the multiple of the basic number 7 whose importance Israel had learned from the Babylonians. As participants in the culture of the ancient Near East Israel had accepted the count that there were 70 nations in the known world of men. Gen. 10, a composite of the P and J traditions, names these nations as they were known to Israel. Yet we note that the name Israel is not recorded in Gen. 10 along with those of the nations, even though Ex singles Israel out for special attention. We have to search under the name Arpachshad in Gen. 10: 24 to discover an ancestor of the Hebrews.

That is to say, unlike the tables of nations recorded by the
royal scribes elsewhere, which included a 'most favoured
nation clause' for the nation to which the writer happened to
belong, Israel had no special place in the world of men.

Again, the myths of other nations sought to establish that
the king of the 'most favoured nation' had originated from the
gods. But Israel thought otherwise.

> 'When the Most High gave the nations their inheritance,
>   When he separated the sons of men,
> He fixed the bounds of the peoples,
>   According to the number of the children of Israel.'
>
> Deut. 32: 8.

That is to say, this early poem expresses the view that each
family within Israel owed its existence to a plan in the mind of
God. This was not that God had chosen Israel merely for
himself, but rather that Israel was chosen for the sake of the
nations of the earth. The Greek text of the above passage reads,
interestingly enough, '. . . he fixed the bounds of the peoples
according to the number of the angels of God'. This reading
gave rise at the end of the Old Testament period to the thought
that there was a guardian angel for each of the nations, as
seen in Dan. 10: 13, 20, 21; Ben Sira 17: 17. This seems to be
a pictorial description of Israel's task in the world. Jesus
would have this theology in mind when he sent 70 disciples to
take the Gospel, symbolically, to the whole world, and thus
carry on the mission of Israel.

In the seventh century Jeremiah recognized that the Israel
of his day, that is to say, the 70, had failed to uphold the Covenant that God had made with them in the days of Abraham
and Moses. Ex would have access to the memoirs of Jeremiah
two centuries later. Because of Israel's unfaithfulness, he would
read at Jer. 25: 3–29 how Jeremiah was to hand the cup of
God's wrath to all the 70 nations of the earth; cf. I Cor. 11:
27–29. But first Israel had to suffer the judgment of God
upon herself for a period of 70 years, 29: 10. Again, we note,
the very name LXX, Septuagint, may have been chosen to
express the plan of God for the whole world, when the Hebrew
text of the OT, a foreign tongue to all other men, was translated into Greek with a missionary purpose. From all this we

see that the election of Israel within the Covenant for God's employ in his plan is a basic theme of the book of Exodus.

v. 5 speaks of 70 *persons*. The Hebrew word is *nephesh*. The Greek way of thinking that has imbued western culture all down the centuries accepted as axiomatic that the world is divisible in two, into spirit, and into matter, into the ideal and into the actual. Man too, said the 'Greeks', is a dual creation, a body in which there dwells a soul. This soul could, of course, be immortal and thus continue to exist when the body dies. This view of creation however was never accepted by Israel, when they met echoes of it in Babylonian, Egyptian and Canaanite culture. The whole OT proclaims (and this is unique in the world's thought) that creation, that is to say, the heavens and the earth, and man within it, is not two, but one. What is more, man is not a mere individual identity. Throughout the OT a family, or even a whole nation regarded as one, may be a *nephesh*. This is an idea that the East and the Pacific can grasp when it sounds foreign to Western man. Here then the *nephesh* is something like the 'extended family' of Asia, Africa and Polynesia. In such a grouping of people three or four generations live together in the one village, in fact the family *is* the village; and all of them together work, share life, think and plan for the future unto the third and fourth generation. Their guiding mind is the chief – possibly the great grand-father of the village; he is the 'head' of the 'body' of the family. In such terms therefore Ex can say that 70 *persons*, 70 extended families of Hebrews, were to be found in Egypt when our story begins. And in accordance with the promise of God to Abraham, these families had by now multiplied even as God had said they would.

The Hebrews were 'fruitful', that is to say, God had given them many babies, cf. Gen. 1:28; and so they 'increased greatly'. The verb found here, cf. Gen. 9:7, is applied to the swarming of insects; evidently the Egyptians regarded Israel as something like a plague of lice, and so a threat to their superior way of life. God uses their thoughts in the later 'plagues'. Actually seven expressions for 'increase' occur in v. 7 alone. 'The land' mentioned is the area known as Goshen in the north east corner of the Nile Delta, the nearest area of Egypt to the land of Canaan, cf. Gen. 47:1.

8–10   Rameses II figures in history as a bully and a bombast. He may be the new king referred to here. For example he returned to Egypt with a stricken army from an encounter with the Hittites in Qadesh while still a young man, having come off only second best in the campaign; yet we possess an inscription in which he records his victory! If we wonder why no inscription is extant recording the exodus of the Israelite people, we are just to recall the destruction of his army at the Sea. Such a 'victory' could not be recorded under any circumstances! On the other hand we possess the name 'Israel' on a list of conquered nations from an Egyptian inscription dating from the following generation – when it was safe to speak of Egypt's 'victory' without attracting the scorn of neighbouring peoples!

To the immediate east of Goshen lay the desert area called Shur. This word means 'wall'. This may be why, at v. 10, we find the words 'go up' (or, with the RSV, 'escape') over the wall, and so 'up' to the hill country of Canaan.

The death of Joseph is not, however, the end of everything, as that generation of Hebrews might well have supposed. Joseph's God is he who gives life and who makes all things new. God can take up and subsume within his ongoing purpose even the lash of the taskmasters and the weary burden of the slaves. As *Exodus Rabba* (a second century A.D. Jewish commentary) 1:1 puts it: 'Because God loved Israel, he multiplied sufferings for him'.

The Israelites now 'burst out', as the Hebrew puts it. No wonder the Egyptians developed a superstitious fear of their 'supernatural' vitality. In response, therefore, they forced the Hebrews to spend this strange vitality on the hardest tasks. A vivid memory preserved in Deut. 11:10 reveals Israelites sowing seed and watering it with the ancient shadoof, a waterwheel turned by a kind of bicycle pedal. And of course there are many wall-pictures extant showing slaves in Egypt carrying bricks and building walls.

15   It is interesting to note that Ex was wise enough to weave into his narrative old folk-tales that had come down over the centuries to his day. It is only in a folk-tale that two midwives could have sufficed for the hundreds of births amongst this 'lively' people. Here they are called 'Beauty' and 'Radiant'.

And we read how these two foreigners could hold a casual conversation with the great king! This little story, told with a real touch of humour, also exemplifies how God was with his people, sustaining and increasing them despite all evil opposition. In passing we note at v. 16 that 'birthstool', RSV, is actually 'the two stones'. Some think this means the male sex organs, Jer. Bib.; others that it means two stones (how were they placed?) on which women sat or kneeled for labour. In v. 16 also 'Hebrew' is not the early name of Israel. All over the Near East in the second millenium B.C. the *Apiru*, whom we meet later (written in Hebrew as *'abiru*, developing into *'ibhri* 'Hebrew') were a stateless people of heterogeneous origin. The Biblical Hebrews came to be classified along with them.

Pharaoh's order to choke the male babies at birth seems reasonable to natural man, especially today when millions in the West insist on abortion on demand. Population control has been a problem at various periods in history. The modern demand is consonant with what became accepted custom in ancient Greece before the time of Christ. The name Eve, however, means 'life-giver', Gen. 3: 20. In Genesis she is the mother of all nations, thus including even the Egyptians. In the view of Israel, therefore, all women, believers or unbelievers, are 'life-givers' to the world. The word translated by 'they let (the boy-babies) live', v. 17, is a form of the name Eve, even as is the word rendered by 'vigorous' in v. 19, RSV. In biblical thinking Eve's calling is to 'build a house'. She does so by producing (lit. building) babies. Here then God gives the midwives 'houses' (another form from the same Hebrew root). We recall that in the centre of the Garden of Eden there stood the Tree of Life. That is to say, God's first gift of life is central to all else. Jesus too regards life as basic. Man cannot have the 'more abundant life' that Jesus speaks of unless he first possesses physical life.

We are not told why Pharaoh did not punish the midwives for their disobedience. The story is too good to be spoiled by an 'unhappy ending'. Enough misery is suggested in the historical note that Pharaoh ordered his Egyptian subjects to throw any new-born Hebrew boy they came across into the Nile. What a deep biblical insight we have here. In the cosmic war between the purposes of God and the arrogant selfish planning of man who is it that suffers most? It is always, as we can see in every age, the 'little children', cf. Matt. 2: 16. But God is in this war. From this point on throughout the Bible he is always to be found on the side of the weak, the poor and the oppressed.

Historical note. Ramses I and Sethos I were the builders of the fortress called Pithom (meaning House of the god Tum or Atum), and of the fortress called Raamses. Ramses II afterwards continued to develop these two store cities, v. 11. Ramses was known as Son of the Sun, and as the Son of Heron. The sun deity itself was Atum. Atum's successor at On, or Heliopolis (i.e. Sun City, near the present Cairo) was Re, 'father of all mortal kings of Egypt'. The spade has uncovered a temple of Ramses II painted in brilliant red, yellow and blue. On its front is a sculptured relief showing Ramses himself smiting an Asian immigrant to Egypt. In the store cities they kept food against famine years, Gen. 41: 26, and arms for use against incursions of bedouin from the Sinai desert. Raamses was also called Zoan, Ps. 78: 12; it lay quite near to the Mediterranean Sea. The city had been the old capital of the Hyksos dynasty in Joseph's time. Ramses' capital was now Memphis. Ramses II is usually dated 1292–1225.

CHAPTER 2

MOSES

———

1–3   Moses, born at the nadir of Israel's fateful story, in God's plan is to be the instrument that will unite God and Israel in an indissoluble relationship with each other. Moses himself epitomises this nadir. He is a total orphan, has no parents, no possessions, no home. More than usually so, he is a helpless baby, as helpless as a foetus. We find here no fancy stories about his birth and education, though Josephus has much apocryphal matter to offer about Moses' upbringing in Pharaoh's court. Josephus assures us that Moses became an army general, fought and won Pharaoh's wars against the Sudanese, married the beautiful daughter of his conquered foe, and returned to receive a triumphant welcome. Polyhistor has another story about Moses, how at the age of 24 he was betrothed to Hatshepsut's pretty younger daughter. Wherever the truth lies, we find at v. 14 that Moses was in some kind of supervisory position, so that, mixing only with Egyptians, he was not given the chance to 'see' his brethren. Josephus offers us still other information. It parallels our biblical account in that he tells how the Pharaoh came to hate and fear Moses, and eventually tried to kill him.

Of one thing we can be sure. Whatever Moses' social position, if he had remained on as a member of Egyptian society, all we would know of him now would be as a name on a mummy in the British Museum! The point is, of course, that the biblical narrative is not primarily about Moses; it is primarily about God. And so we are given the minimum of information about Moses as a person. We do not know whether he was tall or short, blue-eyed or dark, handsome or ugly, just as is the case when we meet with the figure of Jesus in the Gospels. For the Gospels are just as much *not* primarily about Jesus either; they too are primarily about God as he makes himself known *in* his Word.

Scholars have pointed to the fact that a number of ancient heroes had stories told about them and their birth similar to that told of Moses. Thus the cases of King Cyrus, Perseus, and Romulus and Remus come to mind. The most obvious instance in relation to Moses is that told about Sargon I of Mesopotamia. Yet Sargon lived hundreds of years before Moses and a thousand miles from Egypt. The story goes that Sargon's mother had to hide her new-born baby and then had to entrust him to the mercy of the river Euphrates in a basket sealed with bitumen. The semi-divine figure Akki then found the baby and reared him as his own son. Thereupon when he grew up Sargon married Ishtar, the goddess of love.

Coincidences are possible. A story woven around one birth does not necessarily occasion a story around another. Again, it is not likely that the details of the story of the baby Moses are an accurate record of events. The embellishing power of the story-teller over the centuries is to be allowed for before the story assumes its final form. Clearly however we are meant to note the main intention of the story. It accounts for the fact that, though he belonged to the people that was virtually condemned to a programme of genocide, Moses grew up actually within the court of Pharaoh (Acts 7: 22), that is to say, in the very bosom of the serpent that was seeking to destroy his people.

As he tells his story Ex reveals still further his interest in the purposes of God. When he chose the word *tebhah* to describe Moses' floating cradle (for he might have chosen one of a number of other Hebrew words for 'basket') Ex was linking the fate of Moses with that of Noah. The word *noah* means 'rest'. In the story of Noah's Ark, despite the universal catastrophe that overwhelmed creation, we see how God's purpose 'rested' calmly in that little ship on the waters. Not even the watery chaos out of which God created order and life, Gen. 1: 2, could hinder the advance of God's cosmic plan. So too, once again, at the nadir, as we have called it, of the fate of Israel, right within the overwhelming blackness of chaos that Israel's slavery, pain and disillusionment signified, the plan of God still sailed insouciantly along the waters of the Nile. And yet, as Ex wants us to see, and this is important in all matters of divine revelation, God could not have advanced his plan, humanly speaking, had not this simple woman entrusted her baby absolutely to the waters of a river which, though believed by the Egyptians to be divine, she as a Hebrew knew to be the creation of the living God.

Notes on two words

(1) The word Ark here, *tebhah*, is not to be confused with the word *aron*, the Ark of the Covenant, Ex. 25. This was a wooden box about the size of a coffin. People were in the habit of dropping overboard little duplicates of shrines as votive offerings to a temple, letting them float along in just such little papyrus baskets as Moses was in.

(2) 'Reeds' is an Egyptian word. Thus it was a puzzle to the Versions which were unacquainted with that language. Targum Ps.–Jon., e.g., has 'sea-weed'; Targum Onk. has 'thicket'; the LXX has 'ooze'. But the word is understood by Isaiah (19: 6), who certainly met with Egyptians during his lifetime, as 'papyrus'.

The uniqueness of the OT way of presenting truth is to concretize the question at issue. Job does not ask, 'Why does God allow evil to exist?' Rather he asks, 'Why does God let evil happen to *me*?' In the same way Ex tells us a story, not about faith in general, but about the faith of one particular woman. And that man or woman might, of course, be me.

4–10   Again, as often happens in a folk-tale, both the sister and Pharaoh's daughter are left unnamed. Big sister is, however, called Miriam at 15: 21 and at Num. 12: 1; 26: 59. Now, would Ex have us suppose that Miriam just happened to be on the spot by chance? And that it was only a coincidence that she was able to fetch Moses' mother without the princess guessing at the truth? Ex emphasizes that pity and compassionate love for helpless babies are natural human emotions, and not the monopoly of an Israel that is living close to God under the Covenant. Again, the suggestion is made that love, even amongst pagans, is a creative thing. The princess' compassion for a lost baby energizes the hearts of her servants to love him too. Yet we note that before the princess finally decides to do the *right* thing, she must have experienced a battle between fear of her father and compassion for the child. [There was a very strong-minded Egyptian princess

before Moses' day who defied her father and eventually
ruled as a female Pharaoh. She was the Hatshepsut mentioned above, and she appears on the list of Pharaohs who lived
between Thutmose I and Thutmose II.]

Our story presses home three points. First, that God takes up
Pharoah's own pagan daughter into the plan that is to work
out for the world through Israel. So we watch God's agent
upsetting her father's plan. Second, that the child is to become
the enemy from within. And third, that the boy Moses from
now on is to imbibe unwittingly the religion and culture of his
own people; for even while he dwelt in the royal court he was
being fed his own mother's milk. A Hebrew baby was not
weaned till he was some three years old. And, as the psycho-
logist assures us today, these early years in a child's life are all-
important; cf. Ps. 22: 10. Pharaoh then is unaware of the
reality so clear to Shakespeare: 'There is a divinity that shapes
our ends, rough hew them how we will'.

In his history writing Ex makes a creative change from the
weaving of myths that was common to the ancient Near East.
What he does in story form is to show that 'the foolishness of
God is wiser than men, and the weakness of God is stronger
than men', 1 Cor. 1: 25. What he relates is that Pharaoh becomes unwittingly the saviour of Moses, even as pagan king
Cyrus was later used by God, in 538 B.C. to let his people go
free from Babylon.

The name *Moses* cannot derive from the root *mashah*, 'to
draw out', v. 10. In the OT we are frequently offered a meaning for a name based on assonance rather than on derivation.
Anyway, an Egyptian princess would not give a Hebrew name
to her foundling. 'Moses' derives from the Egyptian for 'son
of ...' as we see in such a name as Thutmose, son of Thut,
or Ra-mses, son of Ra. So when the princess adopted the baby
she may have named him son of a particular god. Using half
of a name seems improbable to us, but it is common practice
in Polynesia.

By now, in God's providence, Moses is able to speak and
write Egyptian, Hebrew, Aramaic (the lingua franca of
diplomacy, culture and commerce of the Near East), and,
once he is called to take over leadership, Moabite as well.
Knowing the last of these languages he would be able to make

himself understood by any Semitic tribe that moved about the Sinai peninsula.

But now a transforming event takes place. Moses 'looks at' his blood-brethren; he 'sees' them suddenly as if for the first time. It was their suffering that induced this traumatic change in him. Did he glimpse what he saw clearly later, that God works *in* human suffering, ever bringing good out of evil? Moses now becomes the 'angry young man', the youthful activist. It is hard to believe Rashi, the Jewish commentator, when he suggests that Moses was only 12 years old at this point. But we should compare Luke 2: 41–51. The 40 years of age mentioned in Acts 7: 23 is probably part of a schema that divided Moses' life into three periods of 40 years each.

Moses now 'empties himself' in readiness to become one with a nation of slaves. He makes a choice that has eschatological significance, as all our choices have, though at the time naturally he could not know it. If he had remained a 'prince' (possibly a vizier, as at Gen. 44: 18) he could not have represented his people nor won their confidence. Even yet they are unwilling to accept him. First he must enter the desert. Clearly God looks for total emptying before he can use a man as his instrument. Moses continues to be the egotist however who supposes that he can change the state of affairs by himself, and by using violence, for now he commits murder. We read of no external divine judgment upon him for his act. But internally Moses clearly knows God's judgment for he flees in fear from the scene of his violence. The question, 'Why are you striking your neighbour?' thus echoes God's primal question to Cain in the face of mankind's original sin, Gen. 4: 9. Then, like Cain, Moses flees to 'a land of wandering' also with the mark of God's mercy on his brow.

The way of violence in producing the death of a bystander is obviously not the will of God, for God is he who gives life, not death. It is not for man to 'play God'. ' "Vengeance is mine, I will repay", says the Lord'. Yet God *uses* Moses' egotism and ruthless anger, for from it he brings forth a greater good than, humanly speaking, would have developed without Moses' deed. Ex, that great theologian, thus puts in story form the theological reality that the grace of God works in and through all things, through both man's co-operation and its opposite, man's rebellious egotism. 'Situation ethics' is not in harmony with the mind of the God whom we meet in the book of Exodus.

The story that follows must be rooted in a true historical memory, since in later years Israelites and Midianites were mortal enemies. No Israelite would ever suggest that a Midianite would befriend a Hebrew. The picture of the incident at the well reminds us that in those days the well was the centre of social life, that every community produces its young bullies, that an angry young man, the adrenaline in whose system is running strong, would act just as Moses did. For he would be re-enacting within himself time and time again the fight he had conducted in Egypt, followed by the humiliation of flight. So he would find himself furiously punching the heads of the interloping shepherds, as he rationalized within himself what he had done to those other bullies. There follows an act of hospitality typical of the wilderness community. For in the Arab heritage it is required that hospitality to strangers should rank even before the duties required by blood relationship. Incidentally we read that Moses spoke and dressed like one of those hated Egyptians, v. 19. But now he finds peace in the shelter of a kindly home, in the joy of his wife's love, and in occupying himself with creative work.

23–25   Behind the innocent language of this passage lies a depth of insight into the ways of God. Apparently the mills of God grind slowly. The suffering of Israel goes on 'for many days'. According to one tradition some sixty (!) years have to pass, 7: 7, while Israel continues to suffer in pain and degradation. But to God 60 years are but a brief moment, as Deutero-Isaiah had said, Isa. 54: 7, a generation before Ex put pen to paper. This then is our strange God, as Isaiah of Jerusalem declared of him before 720 B.C. ('Strange is his deed; and his work – alien is his work', Isa. 28: 21, RSV), a God whose activity Martin Luther called God's *opus alienum*. God continues to live in the silence while Egypt continues to be 'religious', goes on praying to its gods, never ceasing to ill-treat the men, women and children whom it has now enslaved. We wonder, then, how Moses could continue to live in peace in a strange land.

Then Pharaoh dies. A new king takes his place. But there is

no immediate change in Israel's condition. But Ex will later show us that it is not just Israel but the whole of creation that is now waiting for God's *kairos*, God's 'moment' (if we might borrow a NT term at this point – see chap. 14); so now we find ourselves trembling on the threshold of that eschato-logical moment.

'Their cry came up to God'; the gravity of the 'scream' is produced by a pile up of three synonyms for this word. Man in his misery is on earth, but God is exalted above all his creation. Despite that fact, however, the cry of the Israelites crossed the gap; 'and God heard their groaning'. That is to say, we do not find here a kind of deism, a God who is merely the power behind all things, the ground of all being of man and nature. Rather Ex gives us a theistic picture of God, of a God whom the OT calls consistently, not, as we would want to say, a 'personal' God, but rather the 'living' God. Since life is God's precious gift to man, rendering him able to hear, see, feel and act, so also God, in whose image man is made, can hear the cry of the slaves and act upon it. 'And God remembered his covenant with Abraham, Isaac and Jacob': cf. Ps. 105: 8; 106: 45. That is to say, every event in Israel's history, in-cluding the suffering of his people in Egypt, is rooted in the eternal *'etsah* of God, his *plan*, his *ḥephets*, his *will* or *purpose* (to use the language of Deutero-Isaiah), so that Israel's present sufferings have now become part of the plan initiated when God first made covenant with Abraham. It is clear that Ex now expresses in his narrative the theological insights of the great prophets who preceded him. As the German language expresses the idea of 'remember', God has 'er-inner-n' what he has seen, appropriated it into himself. v. 25 reads literally: 'And God saw the children of Israel and God *knew*', with no object to the verb. When used theologically this verb means 'to share an experience with another'. And so we have a glimpse, even as early on in Exodus as this, of a God who is not only transcendent but who is also immanent, who is not only Creator of Israel, but who is also Lover of that people with whom he has entered into covenant, the God who is utterly loyal to the people of his choice.

This then is a God who suffers. We are now in a different theological world from that of the Egyptian priests, of present-

day eastern religions such as Buddhism with its Nirvana, and
of the majority opinion in Christendom throughout the Middle
Ages. This hint about the nature of God is enlarged upon in
the following chapter.

Notes on four names

(1) *Reuel*, v. 18. Ex may have inserted this name into the
original J material he was handling. Elsewhere this priest of
Midian has two names, Jethro, 18: 1, and Hobab, Jud. 4: 11.
The E tradition calls him Jethro (Iothor in the Greek). In Num.
10: 29 (J) we have 'Hobab the son of Reuel'. So Reuel seems
to have been originally the name of the father of the priest of
Midian. In the LXX the name is spelled Raguel, because Greek
cannot represent the Hebrew guttural. The name *Re'um-el*
appears in the Mari Letters where it means 'El is a Shepherd'.

(2) *Zipporah*, v. 21, Hebrew for 'little bird', perhaps 'sparrow'.
Bird and animal names would have had a totemistic connection
in very early days. But in biblical times such names were
obviously given to children in all innocence. Zipporah was
evidently a strong-minded woman, as we read at 4: 24–26.
When Moses returned to Egypt she seems to have stayed with
her father, caring for her two boys, 18: 2–5. Num. 12: 1 tells
us that Moses later married a black woman. Evidently Moses
did not know about the modern colour bar.

(3) *Gershom*, v. 22, reveals the ache in Moses' heart as he
longs to be at peace and settle down in his new home. For
then he might wash his hands of the fate of his brethren in
Egypt. Popularly *ger shom* was read as *ger sham*, 'a (mere)
resident alien there'. What *gershom* means no one has discovered. This son is mentioned at Jud. 18: 30.

(4) *Pharaoh*. This name means 'great house' in a sense similar
to our 'White House'. If a statement issues from the White
House we do not expect to hear the name of the incumbent
president responsible for it. In this sense we are not told the
name of the various Pharaohs.

CHAPTER 3

THE BUSH

In this chapter Ex draws upon both J and E as his sources.
'The Bush' is the name given to this section of the book of
Exodus in NT times, as we know from the Greek of Mark
12: 26. Chapter and verse divisions were of course only introduced in later centuries.

Moses now makes his living in a fine tradition, that of being
a good shepherd, a calling that the Egyptians despised. The
word 'wilderness' offers two levels of interpretation to the
Hebrew mind. The wilderness was first, literally, the arid area
we understand by the word, such as the Wilderness of Judea
known to both John the Baptist and to Jesus. But the wilderness
was also the physical sign of the idea of desolation, as it was
the place of the vampire and the night-hag, the place, theologically speaking, of 'non-being'. The Hebrews were acutely
aware that it lay just 'behind' (the one word in Hebrew serves
for both 'west' and 'behind') the ordered life of God's creation;
cf. Gen. 1: 2. Moreover, the literal meaning of Horeb, one of
the peaks in the Sinai range, is 'desolation'. On the other
hand, while Mount Horeb is indeed a bare, desolate, arid
peak, yet it is also, we are told 'God's mountain'. That is to
say, the living God can be present even in such negative
conditions. We must admit, however, that the name 'God's
mountain' may mean merely 'god of a mountain', i.e. 'a
very high mountain'.

It is fitting that we do not know – nor need to know – the
exact location of the mountain, even as we do not know the
site of the Mount of the Transfiguration in the NT. There is
not even agreement between the sources on its name. J prefers
Sinai and E and D prefer Horeb. Its very indefiniteness may
tell us that God can step out of his holiness anywhere and
speak with man wherever he may be. Moreover, v. 3 attests
that Moses saw nothing more than a bush; that is to say, he

saw no 'form' of God. Yet Moses 'hid his face' from the presence of God. Contrariwise, Ex reveals to us step by step in his book how God wills to reveal *his* Face to Moses. In fact, one commentator calls the book of Exodus 'The Book of the Presence' (Hebrew *panim*, 'face') of God. Various forms of the word for 'seeing' occur seven times here. Clearly the emphasis is that 'hearing' the Word is not the only vehicle of revelation.

2–4 *The Burning Bush.* Ex is not interested to tell us how Moses would interpret this wonder as a natural phenomenon. Actually it may have been an occurrence of St. Elmo's Fire, commonly seen at sea, where it leaps along the sails and masts of ships. 'It is a kind of brush lightning ... harmless ... the ancient Romans called it Castor and Pollux' (Thomas King, *Water, Miracle of Nature*, 1953, p. 73). Such a ball of fire may possibly have rested behind the bush as viewed from Moses' stance.

In v. 2 we read that 'an *angel* of *Yahweh* (not 'God') appeared to him out of the midst of the bush'. Then at v. 4 we read that '*God* called to him out of the bush'. This is not just an unfortunate discrepancy as Ex puts J and E together. It is Ex's way of expressing theological truth in pictures. We have here three different words in use to describe the moment when the divine Being makes himself known in his actions. Firstly, to translate the Hebrew into English by the word 'angel' is a case of modern eisegesis. The word in Hebrew simply means 'a sending'. This Hebrew word and its Greek equivalent, *angelos*, may thus describe the human messenger that men send to each other. But God's message must be alive, even as God himself is alive. So we are encouraged to envisage the living message as some kind of 'extension of Yahweh's personality', as a *projection* of the living God into our human situation. The messenger is in effect the living Word of God reaching through to us in a thought-pattern that the human mind can grasp.

To show that he is not thinking in terms of myth like the Canaanites and Babylonians, Ex, along with other biblical writers, portrays the angel as a man. Never, until we reach the book of Revelation, is the angel a supernatural being with wings. The modern theologian inclines to the use of abstract theological terms. He speaks of God, for example, as *Deus Absconditus* and *Deus Revelatus*. Ex, on the other hand, quite simply speaks of the God who is silent for 60 years and then of the God whose Word becomes visible and audible to a chosen individual.

God accosts Moses on a working day, not at a festival, not at a moment of worship within the cult. So the God of whom Ex writes is the God of secular human experience, of a working man, of life lived without ecstatic abnormal insights or visions. Thus, instead of this being a shocking and traumatic experience, when the 'other world' suddenly impinges on his consciousness, Moses is not at all upset.

The holy God now steps out of his holy place and directly confronts a sinful man. No one would expect an Egyptian god to do such a thing. The Egyptian god stayed within the *temenos*, the holy place, where alone he was to be encountered. More than that, all matters relating to the divine were handled by priestly intermediaries. Yet, despite his Egyptian cultural background Moses answers God *at once*. It would seem that in a flash he is aware that the living God respects him as a man, and addresses him on a person-to-person level; cf. Ezek. 2: 1.

'The Lord said unto Moses' is a phrase occurring about 90 times in the book of Exodus. It strikes the ordinary reader as a rather simplistic thing to say. But Exodus is no ordinary book; for it deals with the mystery of the divine Word coming into human life. The two extant Targums on Exodus, Onkelos and Pseudo-Jonathan, are pregnant with awareness of the significance of 'the Word'. At this verse they both translate by 'The *memra* (Aramaic for "word") of Yahweh said . . .'. This is because human language must struggle to find terms to express the reality that the Word of God is alive, in that it issues from the mouth of the living God.

Moses is made aware that any place can be holy since God may be in any place. Certain types of rabbinical literature even call God 'The Place', out of respectful awe for this fact of revelation. At Gen. 28: 17 Jacob exclaims of the locale of his dream: 'How awesome is this place; this is none other than the house of God, and this is the gate of heaven', RSV. In John 1: 51 the Son of man is likewise identified with the 'place' upon which angels ascend and descend.

6–9   The divine Being now identifies himself to Moses in at least five ways, each and all of which is most surprising.

First, he reveals himself as the God of the individual. No ancient man could have invented this idea, for in itself it is a blasphemous thought. Secondly, the spiritual experience that we see Moses undergoing opens his mind to recognize that the divine Being has been pressing himself upon the spirit of each of Moses' forefathers, howbeit under various forms. Thirdly, the concepts of 'the Fear of Isaac' (almost the 'uncanny', Gen. 31: 42), and of 'the Bull of Jacob', Gen. 49: 24, under which the Patriarchs had thought of the divine Being, now take on a new dimension, for, as we shall see presently, the God of the Fathers is a God who makes himself known through pain and suffering. How strange it is (and who could invent such an idea?) that the point at which God meets man most nearly is no less than the point of pain; cf. Gen. 22.

Fourthly, the God of Nature has now become the God of Revelation. Fifthly, the God who confronts Moses at this one moment in history must be the same God as he was yesterday in Abraham's day, and as he will be tomorrow in Israel's unknown future. No wonder Moses 'was afraid to look at God'.

But God's response is to confront Moses with a word of grace. Moses had fled from his kith and kin, believing himself to be outlawed by all his Hebrew folk, and therefore alienated also from the God of this people. It is in this frame of mind that an interpretation of the physical phenomenon of the Burning Bush strikes him. He hears the words 'I have seen the affliction of my people'. The words 'my people' imply the concept of election, and so they refer back, first, to the choice of the Fathers and second, forward to the divine act of Israel's election that is described in chap. 19.

'I have seen', I have totally seen, I have taken to heart. . . . This naive anthropomorphic language is put into the mouth of God. Yet it reveals what the modern Jewish scholar Abraham Heschel has called 'the pathos of God'. 'I have heard their cry', virtually, 'their scream'. The vast gap between man and God is crossable by God, though not in the reverse direction, cf. Gen. 3: 24, a reality incomprehensible to the religions of the East. 'To hear' means more than to use the ears. It includes a response to the hearing as well, a response in action. God is aware that the scream arises as the result of human cruelty. God is affected by the cry. 'I know their sufferings'.

This verb, as we have seen, means to enter in sympathy into the mind and experience of another. God then had *come down* into the chaos of Egypt, out of the realm of the holy, in order to rescue his people *from* suffering and to *bring them up* into a wholly new situation.

The descent of other gods in the Near East was for their own glory. This descent and then ascent, however, of which Moses now learns, is being made in order to rescue a bunch of slaves! This 'up and down' language again is our natural human way of speaking of the divine activity. But Moses has evidently demythologized the 3-decker universe of his day, and then remythologized the physical up and down movement in terms of historical action. He gives us a picture of grace, no less, *coming down* into the misery of the human predicament.

This is no 'establishment' theology. It is not merely radical in the human and political sense; it is radical in the revelatory sense. Where else in the world's religions do we have language such as this? No wonder this passage meets the needs of oppressed peoples everywhere, of all colours, black, brown, yellow and white.

The oft-recurring phrase 'A land flowing with milk and honey' is actually pre-Israelite in origin. But Israel adopted it to express a theological reality. Milk and honey were the food of the gods in early Near Eastern mythologies. This choice of phrase is thus another example of Israel's ability to re-mythologize pagan thought to the glory of God. Ex refers to the geographic area that was then occupied by the Canaanites. Yet he virtually calls this land then occupied by a number of very real people Paradise, the Garden of Eden restored. The phraseology has therefore now become a picture of the *theological* interpretation of God's coming action of grace. God is about to rescue his people, Moses discovers, not by a wave from an almighty hand from outside of the tragic situation, but by entering *himself into* the situation. Having come down he will then, not *send* them, but personally *bring* them up, into complete fellowship with himself in 'paradise'. In this way the book of Exodus becomes the basic revelation of the pattern of divine salvific activity in all ages.

10–12   God's action takes place in history. It needs the help of persons living in history. 'Come, I will send you to Pharaoh'. But Moses replies: 'Who am I that I should go to Pharaoh?' It seems that Moses has understood the reality of the first element of revelation given through the Burning Bush, that God was calling him to join with himself in the pain (the fire) of the Egyptian situation. Evidently, however, he has not yet grasped the second element in the vision, the fact that the Bush was not consumed. The living God is in the Bush. The fires are part of his creation. Naturally then God is not consumed by his own Bush. God is bound to win in the end over all the evils known to man. Moses has now to learn that if only he commits himself to God in total surrender and obedience, he too will win out by sharing in the victory of God.

In his grace, however, God does not leave Moses to think through this tremendous reality in a vacuum. Instead he proceeds to let him hear the most important affirmation about himself that any of the OT writers has been able to record. God now, v. 12, makes a declaration to Moses in three simple Hebrew words: 'That, I-will-be, with-thee'.

(1) The Hebrew particle *ki*, like *hoti* in Greek, introduces a subordinate clause. It follows after a verb, oftenest of speech. So *ki* means 'that' as in the common phrase 'He said that. . . .' But if no verb is written before the *ki* we are to understand a 'speaking' word of strong asseveration, such as 'I declare', 'I swear', or 'I promise'. So we are to translate, not by 'but', as RSV, but as 'I declare that I will be with thee'; cf. Ps. 95: 3, 7.

(2) The Hebrew language possesses no verb corresponding exactly with the English 'to be'. The verb used in this declaration leans towards the idea of 'take place', 'come to pass', 'happen', etc., since it is not static, but potent with movement. Perhaps 'become' is its nearest English equivalent. We find it at Hosea 1: 1, 'The Word of Yahweh which (be-) came to Hosea'. Applied to the living, active God of the Bible, this verb must represent movement of some kind; and so it means, perhaps, 'I will become with thee'. For God is only beginning to reveal himself to Moses at this point; he will go on 'becoming with' him through the experience of the plagues, the delivery from the Sea, the revolt of Israel in the wilderness, and in the giving of the Covenant.

So Ex's view of God is wholly other than the neo-Platonic

or Aristotelian God of past Christian centuries. Finally we note that, since Hebrew does not make use of tenses, this verb can be expressed equally well by the English present or future.

(3) The concept of individuality is a modern one. Here Moses is about to become Israel's leader. As such he will stand in a special relationship to Israel. He will be 'father' of the extended family of that name. He will be the 'head of the body', the 'pinnacle of the triangle' whose broad base is the people of Israel. He is thus representative of Israel and as such will speak to God. Thus when God 'becomes with' Moses, *ipso facto* he 'becomes with' all Israel. Thus 'with thee', v. 12, means 'with, in, and through thee, Moses, to all my people'. In later centuries Isaiah (7: 14) turns the first personal utterance into the third person, with *'immanu'el*, meaning 'God is with us'. Thus from this point onwards we watch God's becoming involved in the life of his people, Israel, and through them with all humanity.

God constantly provides man with 'signs' to help him believe. The word 'sign', *oth*, in the OT is virtually conceived in sacramental terms. That is to say, the *thing* referred to becomes the medium through which is revealed that which the thing represents. The *oth* may be anything at all, either an ordinary phenomenon, or else strange and incomprehensible happenings such as we meet in chap. 4; cf. 1 Sam 2: 34; Isa. 7: 11.

The sign that the promise 'I will become with you', is real is to be a series of factual situations in the near future. At the moment the mere idea of entering Egypt and of bringing out the Hebrews from under the nose of almighty Pharaoh is to Moses quite preposterous. But later on, the implication is, 'You, Moses, will stand on this very mountain where you are now, and will worship me on it. You will then look at the rescue as a fact of history. You will see it as the sacramental sign of my grace'. Since God is the living God, his Word, or his Promise, is as truly alive as he is, and will therefore inevitably perform his will; c.f. Isa. 55: 9–11. The words of God 'Truly I will (be)come with you' are thus the expression of God's saving will. The latter will become visible, sacramentally speaking, in the form of his cosmic redemptive plan for all mankind working out throughout the whole history of the human race; cf. Deut. 30: 11 ff; Isa. 44: 25 ff; 48: 13; 50: 2;

59: 21; Ps. 104: 7; 147: 4. The promise therefore is that the sending and the sign are one. The medium is now the message.

13–14   Moses' question, expressed in English, is 'What is your name?' But for Moses that means 'Who are you?', 'What is your nature, character, essence?' The answer comes as Moses contemplates the task he is to perform *with* God, and this is now expressed in three Hebrew words, I-AM WHO I-AM. So Moses becomes the apostle (cf. 'sent') of the Name. What he is to witness to will be expanded at 33: 19, then universalized at Joel 2: 32. There we read: 'Everyone who invokes the Lord by *name* is to be saved'. And since this 'salvation', 14: 13, comes from *I AM with you*, the theological significance of the Name becomes apparent even at this early moment in the story of God's saving love.

There is no scholarly unanimity on the meaning of I AM. All are agreed, however, that the translation of the LXX is misleading. It has *ego eimi ho ōn*, 'I am the existing One', 'I am the Being'. The translation was made about 300 B.C. in the Hellenistic city of Alexandria. The translators were evidently unwittingly conditioned by their culture and education (as we all are) and supposed that divinity could only be represented in terms of pure philosophical Being. The Vulgate then copied the LXX (under the influence of Aristotle?) and put *ego sum qui sum*. And finally the AV/KJV translated the Vulgate literally with I AM THAT I AM.

God himself interprets the I AM, *ehyeh*, by speaking of himself in the third person, under the name of YHWH, and links his own name, in retrospective grace, with that of the deity or deities worshipped by the Patriarchs. 'This is my name for ever' must mean therefore that in the days of Abraham God had a like concern for the family that had wandered from Mesopotamia to Canaan, and that he had continued to be 'with them' when they 'burned' in their particular bush, revealing himself to them there also by being *in* their life and thoughts. Now he would do and be the same for Israel in all the days to come. The Pharaohs of Egypt, each and all, had a secret name, as well as a throne name, one that was known only to the gods. Here however God is 'emptying himself' before Moses by revealing to him his essential nature. From now on, in consequence, Yahweh's Name becomes Israel's source of power. Without the Name revealed here to Moses Israel's history would be unthinkable.

The name YHWH has four consonants. Both ancient Israel and the later Jew reverentially forebore from uttering the sound of the divine name. So they vowelled the Sacred Tetragrammaton with the vowels that fit the word 'lord'. They then preferred to address the living God as LORD. There is as little scholarly unanimity on the derivation and meaning of YHWH as there is of I AM. Perhaps we should just accept what Proksch wrote in his *Theology of the Old Testament*, 1950, p. 437: 'Yahweh is God's name for Israel only'; and what Martin Noth wrote in his *Exodus*, ET 1962; 'I AM may be summed up best by the words "being (or) becoming for" Israel'. The name Jehovah, NEB, is of course to be disregarded. This word was invented by those who were responsible for the first printing of the Bible as late on as the fifteenth century A.D. They did so on the basis of the vowel sounds used with the consonants that form the Hebrew word for God.

Isa. 43:2 brings together in a few lines of verse the main theological concepts handled so far in chap. 3. The words quoted come out of that other 'fire', the Babylonian exile:

> 'When you walk through fire, you shall not be burned,
>   And the flame shall not consume you.
> For I am Yahweh your God, the Holy One
>   Of Israel, your Saviour.'

It is clear that the idea conveyed by the Hebrew words: 'I am to be remembered', RSV, is parallel with that of Name. The meaning is that to 'remember' Yahweh in days to come Israel is to think back to the time when God revealed himself to Moses in the manner describable by the words 'I will become with you', and in that way to bring the past into the present moment. The present moment will then take on new meaning and will be seen as the latest step in that plan for mankind which Yahweh began in the days of Moses; cf. Ps. 30:4, where the Name recalls the event; and Vincent Taylor, *Mark*, p. 545, on I Cor. 11:24.

'In his Word', says Brunner, 'God says *what* he is; in his Name he says *who* he is. The Word reveals the fullness of the content, the Name reveals the unity, the uniqueness of the divine Being – the one who makes himself known. In the Name we meet with a wonderful union of holiness as the self-affirmation and the self-giving of God'.[1] This giving of the Name is the fundamental fact in the whole history of revelation; consequently we are not surprised to find that it is surrounded by signs and wonders.

The Hebrew word for 'word' or 'thing' comes from the root 'to turn the back', or 'go behind' in other Semitic languages. When Ex tells us that Moses heard the Word, he is expressing in a picture a theological reality. We human beings experience life only from the point of view of one side of the coin, that which we call 'space and time'. But the OT theologians were not satisfied to remain at that point. From the root *ahar*, 'back', these men built and made use of another noun, viz. *aharith*. By its use they mean that every moment and event in this life has its 'back-side' (of the coin), its 'end', or as we would say today, its eschatological significance, 33: 23; cf. Ps. 37: 37–38; Prov. 23: 18; 24: 14, 20; Eccles. 7: 8; Isa. 46: 10; Jer. 29: 11; Dan. 12: 8. The ultimate reality behind the divine Name is thus 'incarnationally' related to the experience Moses knew in the words 'I will become with you'.

The Word of God is not exhausted in words, for the Word is itself the purpose and plan which God is revealing in words and events. It possesses, like the Name, both a dianoetic and a dynamic element. Each 'word-event' of God contains within it its own meaning and its own power. It is only when we grasp the significance of the vitality of the Word that we see why the biblical faith is not interested in 'another world' or with the concept of the immortality of the soul. In fact the NT claim for the resurrection of the body is the only ultimate and logical development of the insistence we find on the eschatological significance of such factual realities as the land of Canaan, the Burning Bush, and par excellence, the embodiment of the Word in the person of Israel.

18 God 'met' with the elders of Israel only through the man Moses. This is the first intimation we receive of a reality that Ex deals with later, that 'ordination to the ministry', as we would call it, sets a man in a special position, so that he becomes

[1] *Revelation and Reason*, p. 89; and cf. D. Bonhoeffer, *Christology*, ET 1966, p. 47: 'God is not God in himself, but in his relation to me'.

the channel of divine grace to others. His 'ordination', in other
words, has a sacramental value.

This projected visit to Pharaoh reads almost like an extract
from a comic opera; but then we are now hearing the divine
laughter at the stupidity of tyrants, Ps. 2: 4. We are meant to
envisage a mob of ragged serfs pushing their way past armed
guards and politicians and arriving unhindered in the mystical
presence of the Son of the Sun! And they are saying naively,
'Yahweh, the God of the Hebrews has met with us!' However,
Pharaoh would fully understand the idea of a *hajj* with sacrifice at the end of it. This Arabic word represents to this day
what Moses was asking for, a pilgrimage like that made to
Mecca by the faithful Muslim. *Three days* is a phrase used
frequently to represent a time sequence which completely
separates one set of circumstances from another, even when
there is no suggestion that 72 hours must necessarily elapse.

19–20   The God who is already in the future knows of
course that Pharaoh will not let his people go. Yet God tells
the visiting group to pose their request; for by doing so they
are activating the first step in the divine plan. Pharaoh must
first be given the chance to say No. God's subsequent actions
will then appear to Pharaoh like the occurrence of mere natural
phenomena, for Pharaoh knows of only one side of the coin.
On the other hand, Israel will know from now on that these
phenomena, with their own special *aharith*, will actually be
expressing the vitality of the Word. These will then be known
as 'wonders', 7: 3, the working out in the here and now of the
power of the Word in the there and then of the ultimate
purpose of the living God.

There is an obvious parallel drawn here between Pharaoh's
mighty hand and God's mighty hand. The first reads, 'No, not
even by a mighty hand', v. 19. The second reads, 'But *I* will
stretch out *my* hand', v. 20. 'And after that Pharaoh will be
glad to be rid of you'. The passage thus insists on speaking of
God in *personal* terms, consonant with the Being whom his
revealed Name exhibits: 'I will (be)come with you'.

When the Christian reads this passage he should open his
heart sympathetically to realize how the Jew thrills to recall
his ancestry, his unique story, his special relationship to the
living God, the I AM. When the Jew reads this chapter he

should enter sympathetically into the joy the Christian discovers when he realizes that his Faith is not a new cult two thousand years old, just one of the latest of the world's 'religions'; but that, along with the Jew, he shares in commitment to the God who made heaven and earth, to that Yahweh on whose Name men have called since the dawn of human history, Gen. 4: 26.

21–22 'I will give this people favour in the sight of the Egyptians', RSV. God can make even the wrath of man to praise him. He will make the Hebrews an object of pity, compassion and good-will on the part of the Egyptians. He will move their corporate conscience to make reparation for all the suffering the Hebrews have undergone. The jewelry and the gold are obviously handed over willingly and represent the equivalent of the income the Israelites ought to have received over the years as a living wage. 'Thus you shall seek restitution from the Egyptians', for Yahweh is the God of justice.

So now the Hebrews will merely 'go' from Egypt, not flee, for this is the work of Yahweh and need involve no secrecy. Pharaoh will only 'send' them away. When they go, they will take with them the wisdom and technology of Egypt and use these to the glory of God in the construction of the Tabernacle and the priestly vestments. Thus even the 'science' of the heathen, and the artifacts of pagan artisans, take their place in the totality of the divine plan as elements in the will of the God of *justice*.

CHAPTER 4

GOD PREPARES MOSES

Moses faces a new problem. 'My people will simply say that my experience at the Bush was an illusion'. The manner in which God handles this latest of Moses' questions becomes the catalyst by means of which much subsequent revelation validates itself to the human mind.

2 The rod in Moses' hand would probably be the crook he used to lead and rescue his sheep. He now learns that God is guiding him not primarily by what he is saying to him, but through actions performed before his eyes. Curiously enough, his genuine calling to be a shepherd of sheep now serves as a subtle temptation to shut his eyes to God's new call, for he would have preferred to remain quietly with his sheep in Midian. God orders him to pick up from the ground the staff he has thrown down. Lying there it had become a snake. Theologically speaking, *tiamat* the watery chaos of the Babylonians which to the Hebrew mind was *tehom*, 'negation', mentioned in Gen. 1 : 2, was real to the mind of Moses in the form that the ancient world conceived of the Mistress of Chaos, a snake, a serpent, a sea-serpent, a monster. God must shake Moses out of his selfish rationalizings. Moses must learn that it is God who is calling him to do the absurdly difficult thing. The natural place to grasp a snake is at the back of the neck, so that it cannot whip round and bite. So the command to take it by the tail appears to court disaster. But Moses must discover that God is in earnest when he commands him to go right in to the very fountain-head of all evil, to go right into the presence of Pharaoh. It may well be that Moses had looked at his staff from an odd angle, or contemplated the horror should his staff actually be a snake. But God made use of Moses' mental illusion, if it was such, to his glory.

3-4 But we spoke of a sacramental sign, and not just of an inner experience of sudden awareness of the loathesomeness of evil. Moses grasped the snake, and as he did so, he learned that he could grip evil itself by the tail. He found that by trusting in God he was doing what God does, that is to say, he was making use of evil to bring about a new creative act of good.

5   The good in this case is 'in order that Israel may believe'. The price of gaining this purpose is indeed high, as we have seen. But even as he swayed on the edge of the abyss of unreason, he found that God is Lord even there.

6   The second symbolic act strikes right home to Moses' physical being. Never again could he dare declare 'My body is my own'. It may be that he slipped and fell on the rocks, to find his arm numb and turned white. For a moment he may have imagined that he was smitten with the dread disease of leprosy. It is not important for us to know what happened to Moses, medically speaking. What is important is to discover what this second shocking experience meant to him psychologically. The answer is bound up with the ancient view of leprosy. Leprosy destroys not only the flesh, it also cuts a man off from his kind; it even cuts him off from God. For a leprous body was the outward sign of a leprous heart. Leprosy was the mark of the judgment and wrath of God. God now orders Moses to infect his torso with the horrible disease.

This is a radical test of Moses' faith, like that of Abraham. The latter believed he must sacrifice his only son, the boy through whom God should carry on the promise. But Moses was to learn that God is he who both smites with sickness and then makes whole again, Deut. 32: 39; cf. 4: 23; 15: 26. God is also stronger than all cultic impurities and physical plagues. And so, when the flesh of Moses' arm returns to its normal colour, Moses gives a deep sigh of relief. God had accepted him even as he was in all his filthiness of heart, and was still determined to use him as his instrument to rescue his people of Israel from slavery.

8   This verse makes clear that the actions of Moses are not to be confused with those of the local magicians. The latter have learned how to make people believe that they can manipulate nature. Moses does actions similar to theirs, but even as he performs them he invokes the Word to declare that these are but 'signs' of a mighty purpose working in

human life (see v. 5). In the same way the Christian sacraments have at times in history sunk to the level of mere magical
acts (in the eyes of simple folk) when they became divorced
from the preaching of the Word.

9   The third 'sign' does not happen as merely the third
of three. For it is more in the nature of a promise that God will
continue to use sacramental actions once Moses begins his
mission. It forms a kind of 'preview' of what God will do to
Egypt and the Nile, once Moses returns there. And by hinting
at its life and death nature it indicates the total or eschatological act of God about to take place. Ahead lies no bed of
roses, but disease, revolution and the shedding of blood.

10–11   Moses is still obsessed by his personal problems.
Man's sinfulness springs ultimately from his self-centredness.
Moses supposes that God is calling *him* to speak to Pharaoh.
He has not yet grasped that he is merely to be the servant of
the Word. He will not even be in control of the words that
must be spoken; rather the Word will control him. Ex expresses this idea by his phrase: 'The Lord *said* to Moses, "Thus
you shall say to Pharaoh"'. God will in fact 'teach' him what
to say. This verb is from the root that produces the noun
Torah. So Torah (ineptly translated by 'Law') is both the
teaching of God and simultaneously the revelation of the mind
of God.

12–13   Moses' reply is, as one commentator calls it, a
mere querulous colloquialism. To it however God graciously
repeats the deeply significant promise he had made at 3:12,
'I will become with you'; we now hear it as 'I will become
with your mouth' or, as the Targ. Onk. interprets it, here and
at v. 15, 'My Word will go with your mouth'. This must
mean that the Word, in its boundless humility, is to become
integrated with the very words that issue from the heart, the
brains and the lips of sinful Moses. The majesty of this divine
offer is too great for Moses to grasp; for once again he suggests that God should *send* someone else. Clearly a minister is
one who is *sent*.

14   The modern reader only too casually expects the OT
to say what he thinks it should. Thus he is often shocked when
he meets with the anger of Yahweh. The OT, however, is
revelation, not 'religion'. It reveals to us a God who loves.

The opposite of love, man imagines, should be hate. But in the Bible the opposite of love is indifference. Moses' God so loved Moses that he could not be indifferent to Moses' insolence; his love therefore showed itself as wrath – because to God Moses *mattered*.

God's election of Aaron springs from this part-rejection of Moses in anger at Moses' self-centredness. We note at 15: 20 that Aaron is called the brother of Miriam, with no mention of Moses. At 32: 22; Num. 12: 11 Aaron addresses Moses as 'sir'. At Num. 26: 59 all three are regarded as a family. At 4: 14 he is called a Levite, as was Moses, 2: 1. Yet in chap. 32 Aaron is set against the Levites. In the P tradition Aaron joins with Moses to confront Pharaoh; at 7: 2, however, Aaron meets him alone. Ex reconciles this at 7: 7 in the light of 4: 15. At 2: 2 one is led to believe that Moses is the first-born. Yet Aaron is three years older than Moses, 7: 7. At 2: 7 Moses' sister is nameless, yet she is named at 15: 21. Aaron dies at Mount Hor, Num. 20: 25–26; 33: 38, aged 123. Yet Moses dies the same year on Mount Nebo, 'to the top of Pisgah', Deut. 34: 1, aged 120. We are to recall, however, that Ex is not writing a definitive history of Moses, but a history of God.

The purpose of God, then, cannot be thwarted. God is quite able to 'change his plan'. He does not throw Moses aside because of his obduracy; what he does is to make use of Aaron in addition. Aaron now becomes God's calculated risk, even as Judas Iscariot was to Jesus. 'Aaron', we read, 'will be glad in his heart', a note by Ex to show with hindsight how the Aaronic priestly line did later rejoice in its special vocation. For the service of God is embedded in joy.

15   On the other hand, Moses still remains the chosen mouthpiece of God and Aaron is merely his echo. Here we have the classic explanation of the nature and function of a prophet. Though the word *nabhi* does not occur here, later generations applied the term to Moses, just as they did to 'the great prophets', cf. Deut. 18: 15. Most modern Bible readers take for granted that the office of the prophet was to foretell the future. Some of the prophets did undoubtedly have unusual powers of mind, that is to say, they possessed *insight, ḥazah*, into the meaning of events, with the result that they could declare what God would certainly bring to pass as the outcome of events; on the other hand, the English word comes from the Greek *pro-phemi*, 'to speak on behalf of', 'to be a spokesman'. That is to say, the word 'prophet' is an exact rendering of what God here summons Moses to do.

Here it is the Word which is all-important, not a man, not a priest, not even a sacrament, and so not a mere staff. As minister of the Word Moses still has the primary task to perform in God's plan, despite his weakness and unfaith. The cult, the sphere of the priest, the area of Aaron's responsibility, is secondary to the preaching of the Word. The minister is not even primarily the minister of the sacraments; he is primarily the minister of the Word. He is minister of Word and Sacraments only because the sacraments are sacraments, not of the 'church' or of the cult, but of the Word. Yet the presence of the Word simpliciter is clearly not enough. The man who merely possesses a Bible does not discover his exodus, his liberation, his salvation from sin. The Bible always needs an interpreter, whether human or divine, for without him the Word does not authenticate itself to man. The minister, as the necessary mediator of the Word, is thus himself actually a part of the divine plan of redemption. The ordained ministry is bound up with the revelation of the Word and does not exist apart from the Word. Thus the ministry is not a profession in the human sense of the word. The minister has no calling apart from the Word that he announces. He is an empty barrel unless he mediates, not his own thoughts and ideas (for he is dumb and blind, 4: 11) but the very mind of the eternal Word; cf. Jer. 1: 4–10; 15: 19; John 14: 26. No wonder then that Ex can say that Moses was called to 'be God' to his brother Aaron.

17   That magic is not associated with Moses' staff is clear from 18: 10–11. Elsewhere a staff is the symbol of authority, Gen. 38: 11; 49: 10, and of royalty, Ps. 15: 6.

18–20   We are not reading a 'biography of Moses'. Ex is not concerned to give us details about this 'descent into Egypt'. The emphasis is upon the guidance that God gives to Moses, and, particularly, on the fact that the staff, now called 'God's staff', goes too.

21   Moses does not 'do' these miracles. It is God who does them, by making use of Moses, his staff, or his mouth. Moses is not a wonder-worker, even if he seemingly 'does'

what Egyptian magicians can do. In this chapter the difference between religion and magic becomes clear. Naturally we
dismiss discussion of any mere sleight of hand. There are
clever tricksters in all generations. But we are now to meet
with Egyptians who claim to be magicians, that is, men who
are able to work wonders beyond the grasp of the human
mind. These men believed themselves to be so deeply en
rapport with their favourite god that they could influence
him to do what they willed. 'Magic', says the sociologist, 'is
man's constraining of the unseen'. But Moses approached the
issue in reverse of this. His was an attitude of 'obedience to the
unseen'. Paganism controls its gods. Moses learned to be
controlled by God.

Unlike the magicians, Moses is deeply reluctant to be the
instrument of God's power, as is Isaiah (chap. 6), and Jeremiah
(chap. 1). These men experienced the reality that the Word of
God is effective and 'does not return to God empty', Isa. 55: 11,
but must inevitably complete the divine revelation. So to be
an instrument of the Word could well be a terrifying experience.

Three words occur here, sign, miracle and wonder.

(1) the word 'sign', *oth*, occurs 79 times in the OT, 25 of
them referring to the plagues in Exodus. The mark on Cain,
Gen. 4: 15, is not a 'mark'; it is an *oth*, even as was Rahab's
cord, Josh. 2: 12, as was the Rainbow, Gen. 9: 12, and as was
the blood on the lintel, Ex. 12: 13. Circumcision is an *oth*,
Gen. 17: 11, and so is the Sabbath, Ex. 31: 13, 17, and so is
the baby named Immanuel, Isa. 7: 11, 14. When it is 'a sign
for ever' it refers to an event of eschatological significance.

(2) The word 'miracle', *mopheth*, leans to the idea of 'portent'.
It describes something extraordinary, beyond human reckon-
ing, suggesting mystery and the incursion into human life of
the divine. It occurs 19 times in the OT, nearly all with reference to the plagues.

(3) The word 'wonder' or 'marvel', *pele*, in its noun or verbal
forms occurs 43 times in the OT. Its usage hints that on occasions one may just glimpse 'the back of the coin'. We shall meet
with a surprising use of the term at 33: 16; see also at 3: 19.

The fact that God names Israel his first-born son has great
theological significance. In the first place, that which opened
the womb belonged to the Lord, 13: 12. The first-born animal,

however, could be redeemed as could the first-born child, 11: 13. The position of Israel vis-à-vis the other peoples of the earth is therefore a very special one, as we shall see at 19: 6; and cf. 1: 5. Before Ex's day Hosea had called Israel God's son, Hos. 11: 1, and Jeremiah had added to this term 'first-born', Jer. 3: 22; 31: 9. The first-born was set apart for the service both of God and of God's other sons and daughters. When God adopted Israel, all other nations of men ipso facto became God's children too. Again, God did not choose as his first-born son and heir one of the great powers. Egypt with its scholarship was already three thousand years old in Moses' day. Babylon the 'wise' was equally old. God did not wait to choose the Greeks 800 years later, the philosophers and scientists of the ancient world. Nor did he elect the practical empire-building qualities of the Romans, and their genius for law and order. Strangely he chose a slave-nation, and for no reason save one – 'Because the Lord loved your fathers'; see Deut. 4: 32–37; 1 Cor. 1: 19–21, 25. This then is the illogicality of love.

23   This verse reads shockingly to him who does not think biblically. At 15: 26 God speaks of himself as the divine surgeon, even as at Ps. 103: 3. The modern mental picture of a doctor must not be employed here. In the ancient world the doctor was the surgeon with his knife, of whom, in the days before anaesthetics, the patient could be terrified. His task was to 'cut out the cancer' in order to save the life, Deut. 32: 29. In the area of divine-human relationships there is no such thing as a smooth transition from unbelief and rebellion to belief and obedience. For, as Jesus says, unless a seed falls into the ground and *dies*, it cannot bear fruit. Egypt must undergo God's drastic treatment, because drastic issues are at stake.

24–26   Moses falls dangerously ill. That passive way of expressing what happens here, however, is not being true to Exodus. We read, 'Yahweh sought to kill Moses'. This follows straight after the information that Yahweh was prepared to kill Pharaoh's son. Desperate situations require desperate measures. While God has not *created* evil, Gen. 1: 1–3, yet he allows it to exist. His Spirit broods over evil, always able to employ it for his own ends. Finally, out of the tension between Word and chaos there comes light. So too here.

Circumcision is meant to be the 'sign' of Israel's loyalty to the Covenant. Thereafter it is ultimately significant for the purposes of God. Moses ought to have known this fact, Ex is saying. He would certainly have known the stories about the Patriarchs, 3: 6, and so he must have learned of God's command to Abraham, Gen. 17: 9–14, to circumcise all the males who in any way belonged to the extended family. That is why the Tradition regarded it as shocking that Moses, brought up in Egypt as he had been, where he would not dare be circumcised, should now, safe in Midian, have done nothing to remedy the situation. Not only had he a leprous heart, he had an uncircumcised heart in the matter of doing the will of God in obedience. His Midianite wife, however, is more loyal to the plan of God then he. We note at Gen. 17: 13 how non-Israelites were welcomed into the community of the circumcised. Zipporah, the foreigner, recognizes the hand of God in her husband's sickness. It is the hand of judgment. Judgment begins at home; it is not just for the Pharaohs of this world. Moses is now too ill for her to dare circumcise him. So she circumcises her son instead, as he must some day be circumcised anyway, and since the rite of circumcision always points to the future of Israel through the next generation, and then touches her husband's private parts with the bloody foreskin of her boy, thus making Moses bloody too. Her hope is, of course, that God will accept what she has done as the best thing possible under the critical circumstances.

Had Zipporah argued with her husband before this point about having himself circumcised? And had Moses, with a remnant of Egyptian pride and obstinacy in his soul, postponed the operation even after he had met with God at the Burning Bush? In later centuries, as we know, the Covenant between God and Abraham was understood in terms of Marriage, Hos. 1–2. Did Zipporah even in those old days glimpse this idea about the Covenant more clearly than her husband? Did she believe that the union of a man and a woman under God within the Covenant reflected the significance of the divine Covenant itself, and so had she come to believe that her husband had dishonoured both her and God? Had Zipporah intuitively glimpsed the great reality of revelation that there is no redemption (of the first-born in this case) without the shedding of blood?

Clearly it is not enough for modern philosophic man to declare: 'The Unseen is benign'. Moses discovers that he has been saved from death's door by the loyalty of his wife, who has, in the simple terms of the story, at its primary level, 'placated the wrath of the divinity of the place'. So now he must walk solemnly all the days of his life, cf. Isa. 38: 9–20. For now he has seen that the purpose of God can pick up and use his rebellious frame of mind, his sickness, and even his wife's estrangement for his mighty ends.

The OT, by the way, records three institutions of the rite of circumcision, at Gen. 17: 9 f, Ex. 4: 2 f, Josh. 5: 2 f. All three, we note, are fed into the theology of the covenant relationship between Yahweh and Israel.

27   Aaron, Moses' echo, must now cover the same ground as his brother. He has to leave Egypt and go to find Moses at 'the mountain of God'; thus they meet in the presence of God. Moses, on his part, tells Aaron all that the Word has interpreted to his mind. They rejoice, we can well imagine, in that God has accepted them both, *as they are*, and despite their unbelief, and plans to 'send' them (see at v. 12) forth in brotherly fellowship.

So now the Word is in turn mediated through Aaron, first to the elders, and then to the people. Aaron is thus caught up into the eschatological purpose of God, in that he too is now able to perform the 'signs'. Yahweh is clearly working in Israel's history.

The verb 'to visit' is translated correctly here in the RSV. The NEB develops the idea by saying 'The Lord has shown his concern for the Israelites'. The verb in the original conveys a picture of a literal action, such as when a commanding officer arrives unexpectedly to inspect his troops. He comes, in other words, to see things for himself. Sometimes the verb is rendered by 'judge', and even 'punish'. But these ideas are secondary; they depend on the primary act of visitation.

31   Before the mystery, then, of God's divine condescension into the life of sinful man, there to experience for himself the sufferings of humanity, man can only bow down in awe and wonder.

CHAPTER 5

PHARAOH RESISTS GOD

1   The end of the four centuries-long silence of God has come. God now utters within history the words: 'Let my people go'. Yahweh is now called 'The God of Israel', and Israel is now called '*my* people', or 'the people of Yahweh'. What does God's silence mean? It means two things: (a) that God is utterly other than the gods of men. Men manipulate their gods at will, whether they be the gods of nature, of sex, of nationalism, or of mysticism. These gods represent the human conception of religion. But this God, Yahweh, is silent when men pray to him. (b) God is silent until he wills to make himself known. He does so now, in fact, but in one place only, that is, within the life of Israel. 'Truly thou art a God who hidest thyself', Isa. 45: 15, is an affirmation that is often quoted out of context, and can thus lead to a non-biblical view of God. (See at 1: 1–4). The passage as a unit runs: 'The Egyptians (and others) will make supplication to you (Israel), saying, "God is *in* you only and there is no other, no god besides him. Truly thou art a God who hidest thyself, O God of Israel, the Saviour"', RSV. Yahweh hides himself from the world but reveals himself as he acts within Israel as the Saviour of the world. The people of Israel is therefore the only proof of God that we have. The freeing of Israel ('Let my people go') thus becomes the sacramental sign of God's saving love for all men. On the mere human level Moses' demand of Pharaoh is incredible. But Ex is not telling a mere human tale. Rather he is showing that God demands obedience as his right, and all human problems of faith and action are second to and dependent upon the obedience that God expects.

2   No one knows exactly how many gods the ancient Egyptians worshipped. This is because down the centuries there had been an ongoing syncretistic movement, with gods coalescing or splitting off from each other like living cells.

This happened when various gods were regarded as apotheoses of human traits. In Moses' day probably some 80 gods were listed on Egypt's 'calendar'. Most importantly, the sun was god, for from it all life flowed to man; the reigning Pharaoh was 'son of the sun', and was therefore both *servant* of the sun and *object* of his people's worship at once. How Pharaoh must have laughed therefore at Moses' request. For he would ask: 'Who is this divinity without a name' (for YHWH, of course, is not a name, 3: 14), 'a divinity without identity, without any sphere of influence amongst the gods? Why should the Son of the Sun pay any attention to this divinity at all?' We note the restraint of the narrative. Attention is drawn only to the essential point being made, the fact that the Word has now been uttered. We would be glad to know how Moses and Aaron, unknown desert sheiks as they were, could reach their objective in the court, what distance they had to walk to reach the palace, what problems they encountered on the way, and how they got past the various guards and sentries, so as to be able to penetrate right into the awesome presence of the heritor of three thousand years of royal and virtually divine dignity.

3   Moses is aware that he must be as wise as a serpent when he is dealing with serpents. He is aware that all the Egyptian gods, created as they are in the image of man, were regarded as having human qualities, including those of touchiness, conceit and self-esteem. So his first approach to Pharaoh is on the level he supposes Pharaoh, as a touchy 'god', can appreciate. But Pharaoh is essentially an unbeliever. Like the dictators of all time the real object of his worship is himself. He needs to hold on to the Hebrew workers for the aggrandisement of his own ego; consequently the economics of the situation take priority in his mind. The psychology of Pharaoh is clear to us today. Modern anthropological studies have helped us to categorize the whims and moods of the bully of any period in history once he has climbed to a position of power and authority. It is not Ex's concern, however, to give us a study in human psychology. Rather it is to describe how the Word of God meets the resistance of man's free will. Egypt is 'natural man', represented in this case by the king of his people. And natural man is free, free of God, free of the

gods, free to live as if God were dead, free to turn a deaf ear to an instrument of the Word (in this case Moses), free to fight against the revelation of the Word, free to harden his own heart right on until in the end he damns himself. Yet, and this is what Ex continues to show, even Pharaoh cannot win in the end against the grace of God. The following half dozen chapters reveal this reality in sequence and in detail.

The choice of verb, 'The God of the Hebrews has *met* with us', shows that the meeting was not by chance. 'God happed upon us' by the decision of his own will.

5   'And Pharaoh said . . .' is a common use of the verb. It means 'said to himself', 'thought'. The NEB brings out the real reason for Pharaoh's attitude. A dominant minority must necessarily hold power by force and so deal viciously with the majority it rules, particularly if they belong to another race. Ex is careful to show that God is on the side of the poor and suffering.

6   It is a fact of life that in any bureaucratic situation it is the little man exercising a little authority who most frequently acts the tyrant. The taskmasters were junior Egyptian 'warders'; the foremen were Hebrews set over their fellows, probably because of their willingness to be stooges of the Establishment. Understanding the motives and fears of their fellows, these sycophants refused the slaves the right to strike (though we must not use the word in its modern sense!). Little did they realize that socially they themselves were really no better off than the slaves, for the Egyptian taskmasters would surely despise them for their disloyalty to their own folk, and withdraw from them in contempt, even though these foreman imagined that they had risen in the social scale.

NEB 'lazy' is better than RSV 'idle'. The verb pictures a man's arms hanging down by his sides, and thus not working. 'Lying words', RSV; 'a pack of lies', NEB. This noun describes deliberate lying which does hurt to one's neighbour; cf. 23: 7; Hos. 7: 1; Jer. 6: 13.

10–16   We have a picture here of the complete degradation of masses of men. The last vestige of joy in creative work has now been taken from these workers. Out of sheer spite the Hebrews were required to do the impossible. Moreover, separated and scattered as they were they had lost even the sense of fellowship in misery which previously had borne them up. As individuals without hope, separated from their wives and children, bullied by their own Hebrew foremen, hungry, probably suffering from filariasis (if they were at all like their modern peasant counterparts) which renders a man listless (cf. 'idle'!) and continually weary, their powers of resistance to the evil system in which they were involved were now virtually eroded.

The tragedy of the situation portrayed here is that Israel is no longer ripe for freedom, and no longer worthy of it. 'The People of God' have now accepted servitude as inevitable. This means that God must now operate *against* the will of the people whom he has chosen to liberate. So we are about to see God doing a new thing. In answer to Pharaoh's human dictatorship God institutes his own theocracy. First of all Moses and Aaron are now living and breathing in the atmosphere of this new situation; so it has become possible for the people to learn to *desire* the new revealed way of life of their own free will. For the Kingdom of God now begins to come within Israel's life, through the medium of the Word, which is uttered, paradoxically, through the mouth of Moses even in his un-belief. This basic event in the history of humanity we shall now watch developing with deepening interest.

17   Pharaoh cannot appreciate (or is afraid to recognize the idea) that freedom means freedom to worship God. When a man worships, he is no longer a slave, either to himself or to another. He has been re-orientated to discover the meaning and purpose of human existence. So Pharaoh enunciates a *non sequitur*: 'You are idle, *therefore* you say, "Let us go and sacrifice to Yahweh" '.

18   Why indeed should there be justice on the earth, if in fact man is the measure of all things, as certain of the ancient Greek (and many modern) thinkers declared, or if the gods are made in the image of man? A world in which there is no redress against tyranny can turn men into beasts. Ex is showing us that the concept of a God of Justice is a *sine qua non* if man is to be truly human. Yet curiously enough this same God allows Israel to suffer this almost bestial humiliation. Ex knew, of course, what Moses has still to learn, that Israel's strange God is he who kills and only then makes alive again, who prefaces resurrection with a cross. The story of all this is now told lengthily and repetitiously. The object of its telling, however, is to make clear that if man attempts to live by his own abilities, he fails. The only ultimate reality is the grace of God.

19 Rudolf Kittel once wrote: 'No people could have thought of inventing so ignominious and shameful an origin for itself if it had not been factual'. Israel's shameful origin is remembered in Deut. 26: 7 f; Jud. 6: 13; in a number of Psalms, etc.

20 There is a verisimilitude about this incident also. What we observe here is the original sin of Adam, who put the blame on Eve, who in turn put it upon the serpent, Gen. 3: 12–13.

21 Pharaoh is self-styled 'Lord of the world'. He alone held the power of the sword. The foremen now accuse Moses and Aaron of being inept in their approach to Pharaoh and of contributing to his 'power of the sword'. They probably accepted the ancient view that a god was overcome when his people were overcome, Isa. 36: 18; 2 Chron. 32: 13, 14, 19. They did not understand that which Moses was slowly learning, that Moses had at his command a power greater than that of the sword, viz., the Word.

22 Again we hear words ringing with verisimilitude. No other person would dare attribute such unbelieving ideas to the great hero, Moses. For Moses dares to call God's justice in question and to disbelieve in the promise given to Abraham. Moses has still to learn that God waits for, or even instigates, a crisis before he acts to rescue. And now in addition to the tension of faith involved in waiting comes the anger of Moses' own people against him. Moses, poor man, has not yet heard the stupendous answer of God that we meet at 7: 1, 'See, I make you as God to Pharaoh'.

We observe a simple man, wearing the (to the Egyptian court) smelly clothing of a bedouin shepherd, the representative of the lowest stratum in Egyptian society; these were the mere animated machines on which the economic process ground ahead; and beside him his brother, similarly clad. And we see this plain man, believing as he does that he is called of God to turn the economic machine upside down, now beginning to doubt all that God has said to him. Could it be true, he wonders, that his experience at the Bush had really been an illusion? Had he now misread the ways of Providence? Could it be that God had no plans for his people after all? Were they even his people at all? So far from upholding him when he had uttered the words 'Let my people go', God had let matters go from bad to worse. God had continued to 'do evil to this people' through the might of Pharaoh.

We stand in awe as we witness this great man Moses at the very nadir of both faith and hope. For his experience of despair is a constituent element in God's plan for the redemption of the cosmos; in fact his despair becomes a vehicle of revelation of the nature of Almighty God himself.

Chapter 6

I AM YAHWEH

---

1   This verse completes chap. 5, but it also forms an introduction to 6: 2 ff.

Yahweh says: 'See what I will do . . .' then at once he initiates the action by *saying*, not doing. But we recall that 'word' and 'thing' are one in Hebrew. It is not even a transition for word to become flesh; it is only a change of point of view. But first, however, Yahweh points to what Pharaoh will *do* with 'a strong hand' – to which Yahweh will then reply with 'an outstretched arm', v. 6. The parallelism points to the value of anthropomorphic language, for human activity, which we can understand, interprets for us the divine act. Such anthropomorphic language, common to the whole OT, can clothe a fully-developed doctrine of God, revealing him to be (1) transcendent, (2) empowering, (3) immanent at once, cf. 13: 16. It emphasizes that revelation as I AM is not to be understood in terms of philosophical abstractions, but in terms of personal relationships.

2   6: 2 to 7: 7 is clearly a doublet of 3: 1 to 6: 1. Ex wisely makes use of the Priestly traditions to supplement the J material he has called on before. One scholar has deemed that we are now about to read 'the very heart of P's Gospel'. For here God declares, not 'I AM', but 'I am YHWH' (We recall that the vowels in the Name were added in the Christian centuries), Num. 14: 35; Ezek. 17: 24, etc.

Scholars have sought for the meaning of this divine name amongst the cognate Semitic languages, but with little unanimity. Some suggest that the word arises from the two sounds *ya-hu*, meaning 'Oh, he!' that a man uses as an exclamation when he encounteres the *mysterium tremendum*, others that it means 'He who causes to be', and so 'Creator'. No matter what its origin was, however, Ex obviously wants us to see 6: 2 in the light of 3: 12.

At 3: 12 we saw that the divine Name conveyed the idea of God's *effective* presence. Here now the same reality is in evidence; for the Name does not occur in isolation, but in conjunction with the Patriarchs of the past, v. 3, with Israel in the present, v. 4–6, and with the promise for the future of a new relationship to be entered into in Canaan, v. 7.

3   The Patriarchs, as we saw at 3: 6, knew their divinity under various titles; cf. Gen. 14: 18; 16: 13; 21: 33; 31: 13. One of them, *El Shaddai*, 'God Almighty', RSV, is now mentioned. Its use certainly predates the descent into Egypt. But what it meant in origin is open to question. *El* certainly means 'divine being', for it is the common Semitic root for 'god', and as such is the name of the High God of the Canaanite pantheon in the Ras Shamra tablets. At Gen. 28: 3 and 43: 14 *shaddai* is the divine Being who protects Isaac and Jacob. The consonants could be vowelled as *shedi*, and so mean 'my Lord'. Most scholars, however, prefer the Akkadian word *shadu*, meaning 'mountain'. The Patriarchs would all speak that language. *El Shaddai* would then be the Mountain God. As such he fits with Moses' experience at Mount Sinai. Thus our modern suggestion of Almighty God is as good as any other.

But throughout the centuries Rabbinical circles in particular have sought for a *theological* meaning to this strange name. Aquila, Symmachus and Theodotion, for example, all translators of the OT into Greek, although perpetrating a linguistic solecism, confidently explained *shaddai* as being really *shel dai*, 'He who is for me', on the analogy of the Aramaic *didhi dili*. Thus they created a parallel to 'I shall become with you'. Putting *shaddai* into Greek, then, they used the word *hikanos*, 'sufficient', basing their choice of term on the LXX of Ex 4: 10. By this means they underlined the reality, as they saw it, of God's personal identity with his people Israel.

But v. 3 makes the statement that the name YHWH was not known hitherto. What are we to make of this? One of two things:

(a) The P tradition may honestly have had no knowledge that the Patriarchs called their God YHWH as well as *Shaddai*, even though the J tradition uses it, as we see in the book of Genesis. Ex does not consider it worth while to reconcile the two traditions.

(b) On the other hand P may have been just as aware as J that the name YHWH long preceded the Egyptian period. But to him the revelation of the *meaning* of the Name is so important that its content, described by the word 'name', is now so transformed that to all intents and purposes it might not have existed hitherto. If this is the case, then neither do we need the hypothesis that Moses learned the Name from his father-in-law in Midian (the so-called Midianite or Kenite hypothesis), as many scholars suggest. In fact, P sees no need at all to 'explain' the Name. For its appearance here in the context of revelation is, for his own Hebrew-speaking readers, completely self-explanatory. So the words 'I am Yahweh' are now the signature of the God of *revelation*.

4–6   God had 'set-up', 'erected' his Covenant with the Patriarchs, as if on a basis firm enough to withstand the subsequent long dark night of slavery in Egypt. Now God has 're-membered' (see at 3: 15) *my* Covenant, made with Abraham in the first place, Gen. 17, then renewed with each successive generation, Gen. 26: 4; 35: 11. For *my* Covenant is the one and only Covenant, even if Israel is constantly unfaithful to it, Jer. 31: 32.

It is important for Jews and Christians alike to realize that when, at Jer. 31: 31, a new covenant is spoken of, Jeremiah cannot conceive of the abrogation of *my* Covenant. His word for 'new' is a variant of the word for 'new moon'. Each new moon, is, of course, the same moon as before, but now re-appearing in new glory. This word 'new' is represented by Jesus with the word *kainos*. If he had inferred that his New Covenant had somehow superseded the old, then he would have used the adjective *neos*. Conversely, the NT never speaks of the Old Testament as in any sense outmoded. It calls it *palaios*, which means 'ancient', but *not* 'outdated'. So the 'New Covenant in my blood', 1 Cor. 11: 25, of Jesus is naturally one with God's *my* Covenant mentioned here, although now containing the content that Jeremiah looked for. For Jesus is the Word, John 1: 1–13, the Word that Moses heard. And again, as the Jew should note, the NT never calls the Church the New Israel, as some readers expect to find in its pages. For in the Old and New Testament alike the word for 'Israel' never occurs in a plural form; cf. Rom. 11: 1, 13–32; Ex.

12: 18. Just as there is only one Covenant, so there is also only one Israel of God.

7–8 'You shall know that I am Yahweh your God'. As we have seen, this Hebrew verb is poorly represented in English, whereas French, German and other languages use two separate words to express the idea of knowing, e.g. savoir and connaître. Israel the Son is to *know* that Yahweh is his God by coming to *know* him in a personal sense, in an existential relationship offered within the bonds of the Covenant given by him who has promised to 'become with' Israel as the days go by. vv. 6–8 employ seven clauses, all representing actions of the speaker who is 'becoming' in this way: 'I will bring you out'; 'I will deliver you'; 'I will redeem you'; 'I will take you'; 'I will be your God'; 'I will bring you into . . .'; 'I will give it to you'. All this is in complete contrast to the Greek idea of knowing, which was to contemplate ultimate reality, *to ontōs on*, in its changeless essence.

Finally Israel is to receive the land promised to the Patriarchs as an 'inheritance'. In most cultures the eldest son inherits the family estate. God is here promising to endow Israel with the land, even though he is only his adopted son, 4: 22, just as if Israel were his own eldest boy.

'Behind 6: 4–8 is concealed the thought that People, Homeland, and Faith in God belong together' (Georg Beer, *Exodus*, 1939, p. 43). 'For the history of a people is not a mere waxing and waning process, a rise and fall of fortunes. It is an area for the embodiment of a higher plan to work out and unfold. In Israel's case all that has happened up to this period is signified by the one word, Canaan. At 5: 22 Moses has asked "O Lord, why hast thou done evil to this people?" Now comes the answer, "*I* have established my covenant. . ." '. The Covenant is clearly meant to subsume within it all the pain and suffering of Egypt before ever Canaan is reached. The Sam. Pent. has recognized this in its translation: 'I have heard the groaning of the people of Israel . . . *so that* I might remember my covenant'.

Accordingly, after hearing how God has remembered his covenant we are not surprised to meet the word 'therefore': 'Say therefore to the people of Israel, I am Yahweh'. For here we have God's own definition of what his salvation entails – (1) it is saving *from* slavery; (2) it is saving *into* fellowship with himself in the Covenant; (3) it is an event that takes place on earth, in space and time, an experience that Israel goes through in the here and now. For this world is the arena in which God's saving action becomes known, not some heavenly sphere, as most pagan religions imagine of their gods. His action is of a person-to-person nature, and it includes the recalling of himself in terms of process. The first element may be sudden and catastrophic – he is about to set Israel free. But his subsequent action is thereafter expressed in terms of the revelation given at the Bush – 'I will become with you', even as you discover me step by step, 'and you shall come to know that I am your God'. Thus Israel would come to 'know' God (cf. Hosea 1–2, esp. 2: 10, 20–23) as God acted to create a new climate, one in which relationships could grow to the point of fullness of fellowship.

'I will redeem you'. This verb is used with both man and God as subject. The action which it describes was originally that performed by the nearest kinsman of one who had lost his property and who was ready to fall into slavery, Lev. 25: 25, 47 ff; 27: 13; Deut. 19: 6. The kinsman then bought him out of this impending slavery and restored him to freedom. We find the verb used in the book of Ruth about Boaz, who chose to marry his kinswoman Ruth and then paid good money to 'redeem' her property as well as her self (Ruth 3: 12–13; 4: 1–12). When applied to God, therefore, the emphasis is upon the graciousness and compassion of the act; 'Fear not, for I have redeemed you . . . you are mine', Isa. 43: 1. God's act of redemption in this sense is clearly redemption from any situation that crushes man – political oppression, moral sickness, war, slavery, national aggrandisement, selfish greed. The act takes place in history, and is visible to all men, for it is 'with an outstretched arm', that is, through traumatic moments of moral crisis and of psychological insight into what it means to be in the hands of God.

'And I will be your God' has another aspect to it again. It is inconceivable that the living and eternal God should reveal himself in terms of a mere half-truth. God can only mean 'and I will always be your God', so that Israel will always be *there* for God to love. This argument for the deathlessness of God's love is that used by Jesus at Mark 12: 26–27 in answer to the scepticism of the Sadducees. The whole passage therefore amounts to a kind of 'Theology of Hope', which is assured to Israel by an oath on God's part: 'I am the Lord'.

9   Humanly speaking, the only apparent effect of this spoken Word, this Theology of Hope, is tragedy. Israel has been brought too low, Israel's mind is now too numbed, to appreciate these tremendous words of grace. Not even the People of God, far less the heathen nations, have it in their nature to make a proper response to grace. So now we observe how grace itself must make the necessary response on Israel's behalf.

10–11   It is within God's plan that Moses should 'go in', right into the unholy of unholies, to meet the evil at its source. Moses would have preferred to meet it on the circumference, and says so. Going in means a total existential involvement in a threatening situation; it means putting one's hand to the plough and not looking back; for it pictorializes for us the total commitment asked of the man to whom the Word has come. To protest, as Moses does, that he is of uncircumcised lips is merely prevarication. Neat English expressions for this phrase are not sufficient, e.g. 'tongue-tied', Knox, 'halting speaker', NEB. We refer back to 4: 26. It was circumcision that admitted a man into the Covenant. Once in, his speech would exhibit his new relationship to God as much as his body.

The question may well arise today about the validity of the material here for the faith of modern man. A simplistic answer might be: 'But the story carries in it the divine signature, so it must be the Word of God'. But God's signature might be forged even by men who are fully sincere in their story-telling about his grace. Yet the more we learn about the culture and religions of the ancient world, and we have learned a great deal since the beginning of this century, the more we recognize that Israel's ways of thought are unique. Most of the material in both J and P that we have examined thus far is to be paralleled with nothing else in the world's literature, in India, China, Polynesia, Africa or South East Asia. So much of what we read here comes as a surprise. We note that, given the

cultural background of Mesopotamia, Canaan, or Egypt, of
which so much study has now been made, we are left with the
conviction that no man could have invented the ideas we meet
with here. True, one Egyptian Pharaoh, Ikhnaton, broke
through the ancient patterns of thought, and invited his
people to consider worshipping one divine Being. But his
religion was merely a philosophical monism, one to which
thoughtful people in many ages of the world have attained
both in East and West. On the other hand, the ideas which
Moses has here examined in his mind can have come from God
alone, because they were contrary both to his own natural
modes of thought, and to his cultural heritage. What we are
reading here can clearly be classified only in terms of Revelation.

14–25   Now we have an instance of P's love of genealogies; cf. Gen. 46: 9–27. These form a thread throughout the
OT and continue into the NT, cf. Matt. 1. They contain
names of men and women of all kinds. In Jesus' genealogies,
for example, there are listed even notorious sinners. The
biblical writers are thus reminding us that the covenant faith
does not rest upon the goodness of man, but upon the faithfulness of God. Yet P's list shows how God keeps on raising up
'liberators' or 'saviours' from amongst the mass of nonentities.
Thus besides Aaron and Moses, Aaron's grandson, Phinehas,
who climaxes this list, becomes the saviour of Israel when the
latter adopts the worship of the gods of the Midianites, Num.
25. The list even includes the cursed, disowned and outcast
sons of Jacob, viz., Reuben, Simeon and Levi, Gen. 49: 3–7.
The inclusion of Levi in this category thus indicates once
again the gracious nature of *my* Covenant.

The priestly tradition, whose interests we shall discuss at
chaps. 28–29, is concerned to show the special place of Aaron,
the 'high-priest', the 'patron saint' of the priestly function
within the covenant community. The list, beginning at v. 14,
focuses on 'the sons of Levi' in v. 16. Both Moses and Aaron
were of the tribe of Levi, 2: 1, the priestly tribe, cf. 32: 25–29.
It is interesting that we do not hear of any line of descent
from Moses, v. 22. Moses did not found a dynasty of saints,
rulers or generals. Ex wants us to see that the people of Israel
are not to be paralleled with the Egyptians ruled by long kingly

dynasties. It is the *People* of God that matters, not Moses, not the 'ministry'. Actually, Moses' grandson turned out, as tradition has it, to be an idolator, Jud. 18: 30. Looking back, however, the genealogy shows that Moses and Aaron belonged in the People of God because they were descended through Leah from the Patriarch Jacob.

The factuality of the advanced ages of the Patriarchs has been mostly dismissed till now. Several considerations come to mind. (1) the high figures seemed to be impossible and therefore fictitious. (2) They represented ancient modes of counting without the aid of figures – for ancient Israel could use only its consonantal alphabet for counting numbers. (3) The very advanced ages attributed to heroes of old were not meant to be taken literally, but were used to suggest that these heroes possessed great vitality. (4) In some genealogies the line apparently moved from one outstanding personality to another, from A to E, without mention being made of B, C and D in between. Thus the latter were soon forgotten, and later on it appeared as if A had lived through the lifetime of B, C and D. But recently we have been challenged to accept the possibility that the longevity of Moses as recorded here may indeed represent a factual memory. For in our time anthropologists are discovering individuals now alive who are reaching the age of 120–140, some of them in the mountainous areas of Ecuador, others in Kashmir, and some in the Caucasus mountains in the USSR (*National Geographic*, Vol. 143, No. 1, Jan. 1973, pp. 93 ff.)

26–27   Ex reverts to his narrative. Looking back over the centuries with pride, he writes, '*This* is the Aaron and Moses to whom Yahweh said ...' 'It was *they* who (in turn) talked to Pharaoh ... so as to bring out the people of Israel', 6: 10–13. '*That* Moses and Aaron', v. 27. The phrases are not very grammatical; but they were evidently penned as we find them in order to maintain the part that Moses and Aaron play in the divine economy.

28   This unusual mode of writing continues. Our passage seems to be a deliberate copy of and reference to the first words in Genesis. At Gen. 1: 1 we have the unusual grammatical form of a noun in the construct before a verb. It reads literally: 'In the beginning of God's creating ... God said...'.

Here we have a similar usage. 'And it came to pass in the day
of YHWH's speaking to Moses....' By this device Ex is declaring
that that 'day' has now dawned which was to be reckoned as
on a par with the first day of creation. In God's purpose his
kairos (to use this NT word again) had arrived. Up till this
moment we have been shown the setting in which humanity
found itself on the eve of God's new action. Now we are to
witness the beginning of the divine act in which the rescue
operation begins in God's cosmic plan for the redemption of
mankind.

The repetition in v. 29–30 of the content of the passage
already penned in v. 10–13 is the biblical way of underlining
the significance of what is being said. For the first act of
creation had come about through the utterance of the Word.
'And God said, Let there be light, and light happened'. Now
we meet with God's second act, this time, not of creation, but
of *re*-creation. It too comes about through the utterance of the
Word, 'The day when Yahweh spoke...'.

CHAPTER 7

THE GOD OF SCIENCE
AND OF GRACE

1–3   The area of Moses' spiritual responsibility is now enlarged, as we enter the first phase in Act II of God's plan. At 4: 16 Moses had learned to be 'as God' to Aaron. Now he is to be more. He is to *be* God to Pharaoh; and to that end Aaron is to be his spokesman.

The concept is quite staggering. The minister of the Word is to do more than just speak the Word. He is to be so identified with it that God himself addresses man through his minister's facial expressions, gestures, learning, and most of all we would suppose, through his complete sincerity and total commitment. Yet in reality God's minister remains a man of uncircumcised lips, 6: 30.

Next in line Aaron is to *be* Moses' spokesman. In Polynesia such a person is still extant; he is called the 'talking-chief'. He speaks the actual mind of his leader.

We have noted the mystery that a man could be called to *be God* to another man. By Ex's day this God had revealed himself to be he who 'empties himself' by coming down into Israel's life. The God of the OT humbly assigns a human being to interpret this reality, that he is ever ready to come down into the fires of suffering. Then Aaron speaks that word to Pharaoh, the Word that had come down when God *spoke*, and which cannot return to God void. Yet at this juncture the Word does not seem to be effective. Pharaoh does not listen to the Word. But we note this, that the Word does indeed operate, but through the opposition of Pharaoh as easily as if Pharaoh had responded in faith. What we are now watching therefore is the reality that God brings good out of evil, as if it were his normal procedure as he handles sinful man.

4   Theologically speaking, this use of the word 'hosts' to describe Israel is most interesting. For it refers to two things at once. It is used first of 'my people Israel', and it is used of the 'hosts of heaven', the stars in the sky. Most ancients thought of the stars as evidence of the existence of divine beings to the extent, as we find in some OT writings, that they are called 'sons of God'. These beings were never fully de-mythologized. In the NT we find them called 'principalities and powers in the heavenly places', Eph. 6: 12; cf. Rom. 8: 38. Sometimes they were imagined in the form of angels. Yet the belief emerges that the host below is in some sense one with the host above; cf. Josh. 5: 14.

5 God reveals himself to pagans just as to Israel by means of mighty acts. The Egyptians too are to learn that 'I am Yahweh' when they see the otherwise inexplicable event of a slave people simply walking away from the clutches of a highly developed army and disappearing over the eastern horizon.

6 'As the Lord commanded'. Moses and Aaron are under orders. They are only servants of the Word. It is God's plan that is in progress, not theirs.

7 If Moses and Aaron were in fact as old as this then the important issue of the dignity and authority of age in the East would be met. If the figures are taken literally in modern counting then we have to reckon with a great lapse of time since Moses escaped from Egypt. Such a long period, however, would offer Moses the opportunity in long discussions with Jethro and others to reach through to a theology such as we meet in this chapter.

8 'The mighty acts of God' begin on a low key. They end in catastrophic events. To this day Egyptian fakirs can handle cobras in the way described at v. 9. We are told that they can make a snake go rigid by pressing on a nerve at the back of its neck. Aaron evidently knew the trick. Yet this makes him no cleverer than the Egyptian wonder-workers in that the trick was no more stupifying than sawing a lady in half is to us today. Moses and Aaron had to learn that they could not defeat Pharaoh on his own ground. Actually 20: 7 forbids the use of magic in the service of God. In this age when the gods are dead, churchmen have at last recognized that they must get rid of this whole area of human existence, the area of human religion, including fundamentalist literalism and biblicism. For they have learned that the word 'religion' does not occur in the OT.

Since, however, we are reading a theological treatise and not merely an ancient national saga, we must ask the question, Why a snake? We saw in chap. 4 that God has already given him the answer. Ezekiel, before Ex's day, could speak of Pharaoh as the Monster, the Dragon of the Deep, the Great Sea-Serpent, Ezek. 32: 3. In our turn we are interested to note that the mythical Monster of European folk-tales, spitting out fire and brimstone, developed from the serpent of Moses' experience, Num. 21: 9. Since flames are red, so the Dragon was always portrayed as such. In the medieval plays for the unlettered masses King Herod, who massacred the innocents, always wore a red cloak. So did Mephistopheles. The planet Mars too is red, the symbol of the monstrous god of bloody war.

Within this setting, then, Aaron knew that the land of Egypt continued to exist only by grace of the river Nile, which rendered it a long narrow strip of fertile land. Beyond that strip, on either side of the River, was illimitable desert; the desert was chaos, the symbol of 'non-being', made terribly real in the thought of the day by its typical and inimical inhabitant, the serpent.

'But Aaron's rod (the snake now gone stiff) swallowed up their rods'. What may have been originally a legendary 'happy ending' to this story in Israel's saga is for Ex the moment when Pharaoh glimpses that Israel's God has power over the wastes of chaos and non-being. Fortunately for the world, Ex did not have at his command philosophical or theological terms to express this profound reality; for human thought is always changing. But humanity is always able to grasp a picture, whether it be a parable, a legend or a myth. Here then, in a theological picture, we 'see' the reality, that while evil is free to do its damndest, yet in the end it always overreaches itself and fails; cf. John 1: 5.

14-16   Moses' rod is a physical object. It is the shepherd's crook he had used in Midian. 'Things' can undoubtedly convey the purpose of their owner. Things matter, because they are part of God's creation. 'And God saw' that matter was *good for* his plan, Gen. 1: 25. We discuss this issue at 33: 19.

Moses' rod is a necessary element in God's saving activity, and appears regularly in the sequence of events. The rod acts effectively in God's purpose only because Moses himself is 'under God'. The pagan magician can do tricks by forcing his god to do them for him. That is the meaning of being a pagan. Many people today still pray to God for some object or for the fulfilment of their plans, and expect the right answer, for their mind is already made up. The pagan is the 'religious' man. But Moses does not make Yahweh work tricks for him. He obeys Yahweh's leading and acts only because he is subject to the Word. When a man submits to God in this way he is in fact no longer 'religious'; he is now as non-religious and as sober as any modern scientist in his field. Moses, under God, here handles scientific phenomena as objectively and as surely as does the trained entomologist, botanist, meteorologist, or any other master of a scientific discipline. The 'rod of Moses' becomes a God-given device that is relevant for thought not only in ancient times but quite as surely for 'post-Christian' man in this technological age. It is a device given us by God to get rid of religion in our thinking – for all the gods of men are dead – and to discover, as we remythologize the rod in the thought-forms of today, that the living God is working in and through both history and science, though wholly other than both, even as he employs both to accomplish the End of his Plan.

'Let my people go, that they may serve me', v. 16; cf. 4: 23. Election is for service. Yahweh had long since chosen Israel and so now looked for Israel's willing faith and obedience. Pharaoh had chosen his own gods, and expected them to serve and uphold his royal rule. Here then we meet with an ultimate clash between the two contrasting views of reality.

17 *The Ten Plagues.* The word 'plague', *maggephah*, 'a smiting', occurs only once, at 9: 14, but it is paralleled once by *nega'*, a word of similar meaning, 11: 1. The last of the ten, anyway, the 'smiting' of the first-born, can scarcely be regarded as a plague. The events to follow, however, are also called 'signs', 7: 3, etc., and 'portents', words we examined at 4: 21. Yet these ten events are to be understood as 'great acts of judgment', 7: 4. They are not (a) mere scientific tricks performed by Moses, as we have seen. Nor are they (b) mere scientifically understandable natural phenomena. They are

(c) evidences of the purposeful, creative judgment of the living God. God is not mere coercive power. He is 'the power that makes for righteousness'. To that end the 'plagues' are expressed in terms of mystery, just as are the mighty acts of God in Christ in the Gospel narratives. It would be foolish, in seeking to *explain* the ten events, merely to explain them away. Demythologizing the biblical message, in the interests of scientific exegesis, has done much harm to the faith of men. This is not because demythologizing is wrong. In fact it is very necessary, for it is the only honest thing to do in our scientific age. But if it is done by those who have not grasped that they are handling not merely scientifically explainable phenomena, but actually the mighty acts of God, then, in their exegesis of the events in question they only too easily 'empty out the baby with the bathwater', and leave us with nothing at all to believe in. But biblical exegesis, whether of the NT or of the OT, must consistently undertake to *re*mythologize in terms of today's thought what has first and necessarily been *de*mythologized – or 'debunked', as the ordinary man might be excused for supposing. In this way the reality of the 'baby' is preserved, and the latter is now understood in terms of fresh, clean bath-water. In the case of OT thought, as we have seen, since there is a oneness of being between the natural phenomena and their *meaning* (the two sides of the coin), it is the meaning of the event that we need to preserve even when our understanding of the phenomenon must undergo a change. As one scholar has put it: 'The stories in Exodus are a case of "reporting with excitement" '. For they display the delight a man feels in his heart as he discovers how the obstacles nature places before human endeavour become allies when they are grappled with under God's orders. Already we feel here a sense of some strange correspondence between the two sides of the coin, between event and its meaning and purpose.

A good case can be made for a factual basis for the order of the plagues, for these can be fitted into the natural cycle of climatic change that the Nile Delta undergoes. Flinders Petrie the archaeologist was the first to show how the 'plagues' could follow one another within a calendar year (*Egypt and Israel*, 1911, pp. 25–36). Several of the 'plagues' can and do occur in any one year and are expected as natural occurrences.

Yet if all ten were to occur in any one year, this would be strange. That they *could* occur in sequence is scientifically possible. That they *should* is most unlikely. That they *did* is the confluent memory of all three traditions. Thus the plagues marked, not just natural incidents, but the turning point in the history of the universe, 6: 28; 11: 7. We are not to look for a total meaning of events connected with each individual plague. It is the cumulative effect of all ten that here becomes the revelatory factor. The whole sequence, even as Ex has strung them together out of the three traditions, reads for us now like the count-down before the rocket goes off. Tension mounts higher and higher; for we the readers know that despite every form of sabotage that human self-will can think up, something quite extraordinary is going to happen at the end of the series, and that there will be an 'explosion' whose outcome will be nothing less than cosmic in its effects.

We must number and name the plagues with the RSV before classifying them.

1. The Nile becoming blood, 7: 14–21
2. The frogs, 8: 1–15
3. The gnats, 8: 16–19
4. The flies, 8: 20–32
5. The plague on domestic animals, 9: 1–7
6. The boils, 9: 8–12
7. The hail, 9: 13–35
8. The locusts, 10: 3–20
9. The darkness, 10: 21–23
10. The first-born, 11: 1–9

We are to recall our ignorance of the extent of the material that lay before Ex in the sixth century. Surely Ex produced his final narrative by selecting from various sources, and then by *rewriting* the material that he had inherited in the form we have it in now. Thus he may well have discarded overlapping traditional material; cf. Num. 21: 14; Josh. 10: 13; 2 Sam. 1: 18; 2 Kings 10: 34; 1 Chron. 29: 29; 2 Chron. 12: 15; 20: 34; 24: 27; 33: 19, etc. It is not necessary to suppose that the various traditions disagreed about the number of the plagues. Thus, even though Nos. 4 and 5, as many point out, read like duplicates of Nos. 3 and 6, their effect on the Egyptians in each case is not identical.

17-22   *The Nile becoming Blood.* There is a natural explanation of this phenomenon; yet of course it does not cover
all the implications that Ex recounts. Each year since the
dawn of their civilization, the Egyptians have waited anxiously
for the flooding of the Nile. Unless this occurs the flat lands
along both banks and the whole of the rich Delta area remain
dry and useless for agricultural purposes. The annual rising of
the Nile is the veritable life-blood of Egypt's economy. The
Nile has several sources. The White Nile originates in the lake
country of Uganda, and then its flow is arrested in the huge
swampy area of the Sudan. This swamp releases its contents at
a fairly even rate so that the White Nile contributes to the
great river all the year round. The Blue Nile, again, with its
tributary, the Atbara, has its source in the mountains of
Ethiopia, which receive their rain only in certain months of
the year.

When the White Nile is low, the swamp fills up with masses
of green organisms composed of decaying algae that then die
in the hot sun. This material then comes down the main
stream as putrid water. When the Blue Nile in its turn crosses
the plains of Ethiopia it picks up vast quantities of sediment, a
red, almost carmine coloured soil. The 'Red' Nile then contributes its tons of red earth to the main stream. Once in
perhaps scores of years this red water happens to join with the
rare stinking water. The flow that reaches Lower Egypt in
such an event then shows itself as viscous, blood-red water,
quite unfit to drink. When it happens, it takes place in the
height of summer.

There is even another phenomenon whose nature was not
apparent in biblical times. Strong volcanic activity was then
taking place along the Great Rift Valley, and volcanoes in
Ethiopia (now extinct) must on occasions have spewed
poisonous, sulphuric lava and ash into the headwaters of the
Nile. Such sulphur kills all fish. This third rare event could
possibly have happened *simultaneously* with the other two.

Moses has to wait for Pharaoh as he goes to the bank of the
Nile in the early morning to worship it; he has to take in his
hand the shepherd's crook which Pharaoh has already seen as
the 'extension' of the Word of the living God, and which had
already invalidated the word of Egypt's wise men. Moses has

to declare his credentials as the mouthpiece of the God of the oppressed peoples whose demands Pharaoh has already haughtily rejected. Then in Pharaoh's presence he has to threaten to smack the waters of the Nile with his 'potent' crook. The waters would then turn into blood before the royal eyes. The Nile would be undrinkable, give off a bad smell, and the fish would float to the top, bellies up, dead. A second tradition records that it was Aaron who acted in this way, to the extent that all subsidiary waters in the distributaries, the man-made irrigation channels, the water troughs for domestic animals and the cisterns round men's homes became contaminated. Ex unites the two stories (the second is at 7: 19–22) so that our record reads smoothly.

Egypt was the most polytheistic nation of the ancient world. In Moses' day its people worshipped some 80 gods. Hapi, however, the divinity of the Nile, was worshipped for providing the people's main source of protein, fish. The first 'plague' is therefore a manifestation of the mighty hand of the living God who is clearly stronger than Hapi, the god of the Nile.

Moses now speaks as if at last he knew that he was the mouth of God, v. 17. In other words, God is now *in* Moses' staff. At v. 25 we read that it was the Lord who struck the Nile, not Moses! At the moment that Moses does the striking, he explains, on God's behalf, 'I am the Lord'.

To call the dirty red water of the Nile 'blood', when it was not blood but water, is an instance of the power of the dramatic speech of the Semite. No one questions Jesus' dramatic pedagogical method when he says: 'If your right eye offend you, pluck it out'. Thus through the dramatic power of Moses' 'prophetic symbolism' Pharaoh 'saw' the blood of his god now slain by the living God of Israel.

We can be distressed that innocent fish have to die. Fish belong in the inarticulate, if not the inanimate area of nature. All the forces of nature are of course subject to decay. Now, if the decay of man, for example the hardening of Pharaoh's heart, contributes to the divine plan as we shall presently see, then it must be so too with the decay of nature. Nothing in heaven or earth is as important as God's creative plan. A whole herd of pigs has to perish that one man's sanity might be restored, Matt. 8: 28–34; and cf. Matt. 8: 34. Clearly the purposes of God embrace the whole of creation.

What the Egyptian magicians did thereupon we do not know. But we do know that the great temptation in the heart of natural man is to be as 'god' himself, Gen. 3: 5. In his heart of hearts man hates the living God, and wants to be completely independent of anything labelled 'supernatural'. By his scientific sorcery man can indeed parallel the workings of God. The Egyptian sorcerers were able to do what Moses did. But, as Professor Toynbee has so brilliantly shown, the history of mankind is strewn with the wreckage of man-centred civilizations, and that includes Pharaoh's. On the other hand, we have with us still that People on whose behalf Moses spoke forth at that transforming moment in the history of the universe.

23–25 Pharaoh now turns his back on God, NEB, contemptuous it would seem of all religion as he understands it. Probably he dismissed what he had seen as 'a mere accident of nature', in that nature can work without any interference from an outside God. And so he relaxes on his couch. But it must have been a frightening week for all concerned.

CHAPTER 8

GOD AND THE GODS

In this chapter we keep to the English numbering of the verses. Hebrew v. 1 begins at the English 8: 5.

1–14 *The Plague of Frogs.* Egyptian society was constituted in the shape of a triangle. At the top was Pharaoh, sitting like a lonely pinnacle upon all the lower strata of the community. At the bottom was the broad base composed of the working people. The triangle, however, was a unity. When Pharaoh decided to reject the Word then all must reject it too. The reality of this situation can be expressed in reverse also. Historically, many tribes and peoples became Christian because the figure-head at their apex made a personal profession of faith. Here we read that 'the frogs shall come up upon you *and your people, and on all your servants*', v. 4; 'that the frogs be destroyed from you *and your houses*'. Sin is always a corporate act.

5 Aaron's 'hand' is in fact the hand (or finger) of God, cf. 31: 18; God uses the hand (or rod) of Aaron, through the command that emerges from the mouth of Moses, which in turn is actually the Word of God. Such choice of language pictorializes for us the means of revelation.

9 Pharaoh clearly has his tongue in his cheek when he begs Moses to 'entreat the Lord to take away the frogs'. After all, this event was no real 'wonder'. Frogs were often a nuisance in Egypt. That they had multiplied as they had done was just bad luck for all concerned. Usually they stayed on the banks of the Nile, and did not stray over the fields.

It is interesting that Pharaoh now asks Moses to name the date for his act. Moses is forcing Pharaoh to enter into responsible action, without his knowing it, for the king is responsible for the fate of the whole 'social triangle'. It is possible that Pharaoh is so sure that the plague of frogs arises from merely natural causes that he believes he can wait for another twenty four hours before having to bow to Moses, hoping the problem will just go away. For the red matter in the water of the Nile would now be drifting north. But the problem did not go away.

For centuries Egypt had experienced annually its 'frog-season', when along the banks of the Nile people groaned nightly at their cacophanous, ear-splitting noise. One particular deity had the responsibility of regulating this annual pest. Her name was Hekht. She protected the crocodiles in the river; these were the enemy of the frogs. On the other hand a plague of frogs means a promising rise in the level of the Nile. So Hekht was also regarded as the symbol of fertility. But now Yahweh was clearly greater than Hekht, just as he was greater than the magicians. They could make the frogs multiply – but they could not rid the land of them. Moses therefore declares to Pharaoh: 'That you may know that there is no one like the Lord our God', v. 10. That, of course, is what Ex wants us in our turn to know, that God is all in all, and that every act that Moses performs before the eyes of Pharaoh is only *ad maiorem dei gloriam*.

The lordship of Israel's God is now further expressed. First, all present see that it is Yahweh who has power of life and death, for he can control the frogs. Second, when the people gathered the stinking, maggot-ridden corpses of the frogs, dragging them into heaps, they were inevitably polluting the sacred soil of Egypt. And the *land* of Egypt was a god itself! But third, the Egyptians had always experienced a mystical regard for the animal world. They had always ruminated on the mysterious fact that man shares this world with cats, dogs, birds, crocodiles, and even frogs. Each of these was therefore deified and worshipped to some degree or another by this extremely religious people. Yet now this act of Yahweh had destroyed for the Egyptians this their basic mystical sense of being one with the animal creation. Ex knew, on the other hand, that the animal creation is not divine, for from the tradition behind Gen. 2: 18–20 he knew that God had put all creatures into man's responsible care.

16–19   *The Plague of Gnats.* The frogs soon died of dehydration, under the heat of the cloudless sky. The Hebrews were not entomologists. Naturally they had no idea that there are hundreds of thousands of varieties of insects. They had names for only a few, so far as we know from the limited vocabulary extant in the Hebrew Bible. Even two hundred years ago the naturalist Goldsmith could say 'There are three or four kinds of dragonflies in England'; and John Josselyn of New England could speak of merely 'the wasp'. We cannot say precisely, then, what insect is suggested here. But we note two things.

Firstly, these insects rose up out of the ground, from the sacred soil of Egypt; Aaron had had the temerity to smite that soil before the eyes of Pharaoh himself. Secondly, the insects evidently became a pest to man, crawling under his clothes and biting or stinging his body. Probably their maggots had waxed fat in the bodies of the dead frogs. Swarms of such insects might well blow about with the wind; the Hebrews in Goshen might well have been free of their unwanted attention.

The magicians were not able to copy nature's act. They confessed themselves beaten. 'This is the finger of God', they said. J. Coert Rylaarsdam (*The Interpreter's Bible*, I, p. 877) notes that this theme is paralleled in the NT by Christ's defeat of the powers of darkness. One wonders what the magicians meant in this case by 'god'. To them any supreme divinity would be as ill-defined as it is today in the mind of those who speak blandly of 'The Good Lord', or of 'Providence', or such like.

20–24 *The Plague of Flies*. If the insect in question was in fact a beetle, then this victory of Yahweh was indeed a great blow to Egypt's pride. There is a variety of beetle that occasionally settles by the million on Egypt, which then gnaws both man and beast, destroys clothes, furniture and plants. Babies and invalids are not able to defend themselves from its attack. These beetles arrive, when they do appear, once in so many years, in the month of November.

Again, the archaeologist has revealed to us how highly the Egyptians regarded the scarab beetle. They saw it as an emblem of royalty and everywhere adored it as a god. 'It adorns the head of Ptah-Osiris, and Khepera was a scarab-headed god'. More than that. 'From the time of the XIIth dynasty, or even earlier, the place of the material heart in all mummies had been taken by an amulet through the influence of which, it was supposed, the dead man would be secured against all the dangers and inconveniences attending the loss of his heart until the day of resurrection. This amulet was in the form of a beetle, the emblem of 'becoming' or of transformation. This beetle had now become a curse.' (G. A. Frank Knight, *Nile and Jordan*, 1921, p. 159.) The significance of this curse was magnified when the heathen onlookers noted that the land of Goshen, where the Hebrews lived, was immune from the localized plague. Goshen lay on slightly higher ground than the pestiferous Nile Delta region.

22   God 'sets apart' this land of Goshen. This action is meant to reveal to the Egyptians that these current events are of eschatological significance. This is emphasized again in v. 23, where God declares he will put an ultimately significant (or 'marvellous') distinction, 4: 21, 'between my people and your people'. 'Tomorrow this "sign" will come to pass', God declares. And of course it happened. And ever since this incident the People of God have remained distinct from all the peoples of the earth, not by blood and race, but because of their very raison d'être; they are the one people that is specially important for the ends of God's eschatological purposes.

Coupled with this divine statement Moses is to say something to Pharaoh that is quite unique: 'I am YHWH in the midst of the world'. This sentence is a development from the words of divine self-revelation in chaps. 3 and 6. Yahweh's nature as he 'becomes with' Israel is now becoming reality in Israel's experience.

Yet we cannot dismiss the actual text of v. 23 too easily. Why did Ex (or some scribe) *add* to the concept of God's 'marvellous' actions the idea of redemption? It would seem that he is inviting us to pay great attention to the story he is about to unfold. Israel is both the eschatologically significant people and the ransomed people, ransomed in order to *be* God's instrument of revelation to all the other nations of the earth. Israel itself is the 'sign' that is spoken of here.

So then the land was 'threatened with ruin', NEB, by 'oppressive swarms', the verbal imperfect form showing continuing action. So the sacred land of Egypt is now perverted by an act of God! God can do to Mother Earth by natural processes what man, in his freedom, can do by atomic fall-out, napalm bombs, or other forms of corruption.

25 Pharaoh is now prepared to allow Moses to offer worship to his chosen divinity (or perhaps the word is plural), but he is to stay in Egypt to do so. To which Moses replies: 'It would not be legitimate to do so'. The point is that to the Egyptians the bull was sacred. They were, in reality, 'sacred cows'. The common people might well have risen in a riot if the Hebrews had killed and then sacrificed what were in a sense the Egyptians' very gods. Moses suggests therefore that he and his people go a 'three days journey' into the wilderness, 'as God keeps on commanding us'. As we have seen, this phrase does not speak of a period of 72 hours, but of a 'clean break' with what precedes. 'Overnight' is not enough to represent such a break, as we know from our own experience. It is only by the third day that, psychologically speaking, the break is complete; see 19: 16; 2 Kings 20: 5; Hos. 6: 2; Matt. 16: 21; Acts 10: 40.

28 At last Pharaoh declares 'I will let you go'. 'It won't be by Yahweh's command' (he means to say) 'but by my grace alone! However, please pray for me'. We wonder to what divinity Moses was to pray on his behalf.

29 Moses accepts this compromise with a compromise of his own. The passage reads like a diplomatic encounter; for example, note the polite circumlocution of 'Pharaoh' for 'you'. It was as if Moses left the conference room to telephone back to his superiors for instructions on the next step in the diplomatic game. But even when the Superior, upholding the terms that his minister, Moses, had already laid down, removed the current plague, Pharaoh remained as bitter as ever. Before this we have heard that Pharaoh's heart 'grew hard' in a passive sense, 7: 13. Now we hear that Pharaoh actively steeled his heart against the compromise that Yahweh had permitted Moses to offer. Feeding the tiger is not always a profitable exercise. It may indeed be necessary at times. But here we see that God knows more about the depths of the human heart than does optimistic man. Moses has to learn what the optimistic philosophies of men are slow to realize, that 'the wickedness of man is great in the earth, and that every imagination of the thoughts of his heart is only evil continually',

Gen. 6: 5; or, with Jeremiah, that 'the heart is deceitful above all things, and desperately corrupt; who can understand it?' Yet paradoxically Jeremiah can look to the day when all the pagan nations shall 'no more stubbornly follow their own evil heart', Jer. 3: 17.

CHAPTER 9

PROPHETIC SYMBOLISM

1–7   *The Plague on Domestic Animals.* The Egyptians abhorred shepherds, regarding them as unclean. So the Hebrew shepherds must have been segregated from the makers of bricks. They remained on the 'common' ('field', RSV) with their charges, where there was at any rate more grass than in the cultivated areas. But it was Egypt's domestic animals that were out on the plains, not the Hebrews'.

Moses is to tell Pharaoh that he is there in the name of 'YHWH, the God of the Hebrews', not, the God of all the earth. The God of the Bible works for the salvation of all the earth by limiting himself to use one people to that end. He is to say, 'The hand of the Lord', that is, an action of God comprehensible by man in a material sense, is about to 'fall' as a 'very severe plague'. This plague may have been any one of a number of diseases, such as anthrax or foot-and-mouth disease.

At v. 4 the same verb is used as at 8: 22. God's act in 'making a distinction' between the cattle of Israel and the cattle of Egypt is one of eschatological significance. God is now about to bring those particular cows into his cosmic plan by means of a particular disease. By this choice of verb Ex is showing us that *all* things, even the most trivial, may be used by God for his purposes. There is no such thing as chance. Nature is not *mere* nature. The evolutionary process within the animal kingdom is not an autonomous movement. Time, too, is in his hands. '*Tomorrow* God will do this thing'.

This plague is a blow at a number of gods. The calf of Ur-Mer, or Mnevis, was adored at Heliopolis as an incarnation of Ra. At Erment or Hermonthis, near Thebes, Mentu, the god of the local nome (county) was worshipped in the form of the bull Bakis. 'At the Serapeum of Memphis one can still see the catacombs where the sarcophagi of the numerous Apis bulls, the embodiment of Ptah, exhibit the lengths to which an aberrant fanaticism will carry an intelligent people' (G. A. Frank Knight, op. cit., p. 160).

6   We read that 'all the cattle of the Egyptians died'. Yet later on we meet with Egyptian cattle. The story is obviously told in dramatic form. The Semitic writer does not expect his reader to be a literalist. His phrase is as legitimate as ours, when we say that 'Everybody went to the concert'. But Pharaoh's heart continued to get 'heavy'. He hated Yahweh because of the destruction of his domestic animals. And so he shook his fist at the sky.

8–12   *The Plague of Boils.* It is clear here that Moses is not acting as a magician. We note that the true magicians of Egypt were not able to copy what he did – anyway they were feeling too sick to try. We today label Moses' performance Prophetic Symbolism. It was N. Wheeler Robinson who gave Moses' act this name; (see his *Old Testament Essays*, 1927, pp. 2 ff; and his *Two Hebrew Prophets*, 1948, p. 85.) By an act of magic a man impels the powers of the unseen to do his will. Moses' act represents the opposite of this. He acts in *obedience* to the Word of God, v. 8; he is merely the agent of the action that God does himself. In this way Moses 'triggers off' God's plan by his action. So actually, by God's grace, it is Moses who initiates the saving purpose of God in Israel. Humanly speaking, at this moment God can do no mighty work unless Moses is obedient to the Word. But once initiated, the Word becomes 'flesh', action, in the realm of space and time.

There is an element of humour in the narrative. At the cry 'Physicians, heal yourselves', the physicians are helpless; cf. Deut. 28: 27–29. This is the kind of humour that appealed to ancient Israel, as when Joseph turned the tables on his persecutors. Mighty Pharaoh is now an object of mirth.

There is however one reality in this world that can actually withstand the power of the divine Word, and that is the free-will of man. Paradoxically, God has himself created this human free-will by the power of his Word. God has done so only because it is his nature to love freedom; evidently God is willing to run the risks that freedom offers. So we watch Pharaoh becoming the willing enemy of God himself. 'Pharaoh did not listen to them in terms of what Yahweh had *said*', v. 12, omitting the word 'to Moses' with the LXX. In other words, Pharaoh's heart had now begun to grow hard *at the Word of the Lord*.

12 *The Hardening of the Heart.* We have left discussion of this profound issue until this point, for it is only now that we are distinctly told that 'YHWH hardened the heart of Pharaoh'. Before that we had learned either that Pharaoh's heart *grew hard*, or that Pharaoh *hardened his own heart*. Modernizing the term does not help us to resolve the problem. If we say that Pharaoh was stubborn we merely evade the theological issue. We merely approach the Scriptures from the level of western and modern individualism, with its emphasis upon personal salvation, and on a man-centred (or, rather *me*-centred) view of the significance of the mighty acts of God.

The three Hebrew verbs employed are not identical in meaning, although in these chapters they are evidently used alike. That Yahweh hardens Pharaoh's heart is declared by all three traditions, J at 10: 1; E at 4: 21; 10: 20; 10: 27; P at 7: 3; 9: 12; 11: 10; 14: 4; 14: 8; 14: 17. That this issue is important, moreover, is stressed by the fact that we are told about Pharaoh's heart 19 times in the book of Exodus alone. Again, it is superficial to dismiss the whole issue as an example of 'ancient ways of thinking', when 'people did not distinguish between primary and secondary causes'. Of course it is ancient, but then so is everything else in the book of Exodus. Paul's thought also is ancient thinking, yet we deem it worth the pondering when he raises the identical question in Romans 11: 7–12. Moreover, long before Paul's day Isaiah had been commanded to make the hardening of the heart the central issue in his preaching, Isa. 6: 9–13. The latter is the only passage in the OT quoted in all four Gospels and in Acts. To dismiss the issue, raised so seriously here, as 'theologically objectionable', as one recent commentary on Exodus does, is itself a commentary on the emptiness of some present-day biblical scholarship.

We understand how Pharaoh could let his heart grow hard, how he could be merely plain stubborn. We understand further how he could indeed ruminate in anger on Moses' insolence, nursing his wrath to keep it warm. Evidently he rationalized upon the conversations he had had with Moses, excusing himself at every turn, justifying his every reaction to the coming of the Word into his experience. This then became a continuous process of hardening of the heart. He would reach a stage when he would consider that Moses did not have a point of view even worth considering. Thus Pharaoh shut the door to dialogue, for now he was completely sure that he alone was right.

There are several important theological issues to examine here, however, and not just the obvious psychological ones. First, Pharaoh did not look far into the depths of reality when he supposed that every man, including himself, was an island independent of his neighbour and independent of God. By now he has received several lessons from Moses (or rather has been given several acts of revelation from God) to show him that Yahweh the God of the Hebrews was in fact Lord of all. The man who continues to drink, knowing that he is on the point of becoming an alcoholic, deliberately hardens his heart against the advice of his friends.

Second, no suggestion is made that God is involved in the hardening process on the ground that Pharaoh was already damned, or had damned his own soul. Rather Ex shows us that God is confirming a situation that not God, but Pharaoh, has created. God is thereby passing judgment on human sin. God plunges Pharaoh deeper into the sin which he has already elected to enjoy when he was offered grace but refused it. On the other hand grace will not be denied. In fact we watch God making use of Pharaoh's elected sin in a completely new and creative manner. God now turns Pharaoh into what we must call God's 'non-elect'. Pharaoh is now elect to be non-elect. The fate of Pharaoh as the non-elect of God is now in opposition to that of Israel, the 'elect' of God. Yet, paradoxically, Pharaoh is God's elect in a manner parallel with God's election of Israel. No one in the Bible is ever elect to damnation.

The Hebrew language expresses this in its own peculiar way: 'I have loved Jacob, but I have hated Esau', Mal. 1 : 2–3. Jacob was the ancestor of the elect people. Esau rejected his election. Esau was the 'non-elect' of God in a positive sense, and so were all his alleged descendants, the people of Edom. Esau was the necessary foil without which the concept of election could not have come alive. There is no moral judgment implied in the word 'hate'. For it means merely what we have noted above, to be elect in a secondary sense, to be rejected from first place, but still to be used in second place in the all-embracing Plan of God for the redemption of all. This *all* includes even Pharaoh and his magicians. All men are needed for God's purpose and plan, even those whom God does not choose in a primary manner. Rabbi Levi once said: 'God's Word comes to a heathen king. God's action in this is like a king who planted useful fruit trees and useless fruit trees. Why the latter? How else could he construct baths and furnaces?'

Cyrus, the mighty pagan king of the Persians, was the chosen of God, even named as God's 'messiah', Isa. 41: 5. Israel, the people of God, when in exile, was also the chosen of God, called to be the servant of God. Yet Yahweh certainly hardened Cyrus' heart, by encouraging him and leading him on to smash his way through the bars across the many city gates which he met, Isa. 45: 2, killing, destroying, looting. It is enlightening to compare the use of terms in Isa. chaps. 42 and 45. In chap. 42 Yahweh delights in his elect servant people Israel, taking him by the hand, leading him, and giving to him his glory. In chap. 45 Yahweh delights in his 'hated' elect servant Cyrus, taking him by the hand, leading him, and giving to him his glory. What is obviously all-important is not the instrument of God's election, but the *end-purpose* of God's elective act. In Deutero-Isaiah this end-purpose is not that Cyrus should conquer Babylon to 'let my people go'. It is that 'by myself I have sworn, from my mouth has gone forth in righteousness a word that shall not return: "To me every knee shall bow, every tongue shall swear" ', Isa. 45: 23. The end-purpose of God lay a long way ahead of the events that were taking shape in 540 B.C.

Third, therefore, the hardening of Pharaoh's heart was done in order to bring about the fulfilment of this cosmic Plan. If the hardening had not taken place, then Israel would not have come out of Egypt 'with mighty signs and wonders'. We must never forget that these signs were of missionary value, as is everything else that God does when he acts in revelation. They demonstrated to the eyes of men then, and still do today, the reality that God is he who has a mighty purpose of redemption for all mankind, nay more, for the whole cosmos of heaven and earth, and all that is therein.

Like all men, Pharaoh had still to learn that he existed only for the glory of God. God could therefore 'hate' Pharaoh in the sense we have examined. Along with all mankind Pharaoh is still invited into the coming 'Kingdom of God', through Israel. As Abraham Heschel points out, the opposite of freedom is not determinism, but hardness of heart. Freedom presupposes, he says, openness of heart, mind, eye, and ear. Freedom is not a natural state; it is a gift from God. The haughty, he says, forfeit it; that then is why callousness is the root of all sin. Israel, he continues, dare not in consequence boast of its freedom, when Pharaoh is still unfree. Israel must leave that issue to God. For when God hardens a man's heart, he assumes the responsibility himself of the question of how and when that heart may be restored to sensitivity (*The Prophets*, 1962, p. 90.)

13-17   Moses is now to re-enact to Pharaoh the grace with which the Word encounters man's self-will. By getting in quickly (that is the basic meaning of rising early in the morning), for it is already February in the second year of encounter, he gives Pharaoh that rare commodity, time to change his mind. So God continues to reveal his patience and love, and to wait quietly even for hardhearted Pharaoh to stop and think.

The LXX interprets what follows by declaring that God's 'sending' his 'encounters' (as it translates the Hebrew) is a very special *kairos* or moment in the Plan. For God's next act is to be in the area, not of objective phenomena, but of subjective experience. It is to be in the *mind* of Pharaoh and of all his people. The conscience of Egypt is now to be smitten, as an act of grace. Egypt is to experience yet more intimate and revelatory 'encounters' than what the human eye has already witnessed. It is true that man's intelligence and conscience are not normally moved to find faith in God by a contemplation of the mysterious facts of the universe. An appreciation of these mysteries certainly bolsters man's faith, but only after he has first found God in his heart and mind. Apparently this is because man does not 'believe' in God by an act of the will motivated by reason; rather, believing man 'breathes' God – he lives, moves and has his being in him.

So Egypt is now called upon to contemplate the very meaning of her existence. 'Till now you have made yourself bigger
than my people', v. 17, cf. Isa. 14: 4–20; 47: 1–13. 'I could
have struck you with pestilence'. This noun bears the secondary
meaning of 'word of destruction'. 'Why did I not? I have
waited patiently because I want you to think things through,
to examine the very raison d'être of human existence. I
desire that you, Pharaoh, should make the discovery that *I
set you up* ("let you live", RSV) in the position you now hold,
and that I did so for two purposes. First, "to let you see my
might", v. 16 (cf. Rom. 9: 17); and second, to "make you into
a missionary", that is, "to have you talk about my Name in all
the land" '. (My translation here is a possible one, yet not
necessarily the only one. It disagrees with the RSV, NEB,
and in part with *Tor*.) Note that at 10: 2 it is the Israelites who
are to be the missionaries. 'You shall exalt the force of your
own ego against my people with the object of not letting them
go; but by uttering my Name you are explaining the essence
of reality, you are witnessing to the power that comes from
the God behind all gods'.

This time, then, God is about to send his plagues upon the
heart, mind, thinking and reasoning of Pharaoh, in the form
of divine encounters within the 'soul'. As Monsignor Knox
translates here: 'Whilst I am about it, I mean to send all my
plagues. . .'. The Word will thus strike a blow at Pharaoh's
assured philosophy in which he rests in a false sense of peace,
and in this way will wreck his faith. Thus we can picture the
Pharaoh who later pursued the Israelites into the Sea becoming
furiously angry, a raging devil; for now he has lost all faith
in the meaning of life. He has lost even what sense of security
he once possessed. To compensate for the emptiness he now
experiences, and in order to 'show them', as he says to himself,
he lashes out in a wild and vicious act of destruction; for the
only aim that a tyrant has left once he has lost his inner
security is to destroy those who he supposes have contributed
to the nihilism that now resides in his soul.

18–21 *The Plague of the Electrical Storm.* Then God fixes a
time. 'Tomorrow at this time'. The event will be an outstanding display of divine fireworks, such as only the tropics
can produce, but which in rare moments occurs also in the dry

climate of Egypt. Such an electrical storm can produce hail
stones the size of hen's eggs. These are of course exceedingly
destructive to wattle houses, and can decimate crops and lay low
whole fields and herds of domestic animals. God thus employs
the natural elements with effortless ease as weapons in the war.
Yet his act is only by way of warning, and so is an act of grace.
The fact that some Egyptians listened to Moses' warning, and
had their servants and animals remain in the shelter of strongly
built stone houses and sheds, suggests that the Word which
Moses mediated has at last begun to reach home to their mind
and conscience. These non-Israelites, Gentiles, pagans, now
'feared the Word of Yahweh'. 'To fear' is not primarily 'to be
afraid of'. Yet that emphasis is included in the word. The verb
means to experience in awe the mystery of the divine encounter within the human soul. Thus it is not the hail, which is
just another natural phenomenon added to those the Egyptians
have already seen, that brings this group of Egyptian officials
to reconsider the meaning of life. For the hail has not yet fallen.
It is, as Moses has been told to say, the realization that all
concerned were now confronted with a basically important
'moment' in the history of revelation. For there and now, for
the first time in the whole history of the Word's 'becoming
with' man, pagan man hears, listens, and obeys.

This eschatologically significant moment in the history of
man occurs at a 'time' that God himself, in his wisdom, sets
within the long period of duologue between Moses and
Pharaoh. The power of the Word is now being *seen* to be
effective. But these individual Egyptians would not have believed as they do had not God first hardened Pharaoh's heart.
Pharaoh, it is now clear, has been elected by God to be the
secondary instrument of the redemption of his own people. As
the LXX puts it of Pharaoh: 'For this purpose you are preserved'. God might have wiped Pharaoh away, as a man
wipes a dish, 'wiping it and turning it upside down', 2 Kings
21: 13. But he did not. For in the wholeness and compre-
hensiveness of his Plan he used the *un*belief of Pharaoh to do
what, humanly speaking, he could not have done if Pharaoh
had believed. In other words, Almighty God makes the wrath
of man to praise him by first inciting certain men to bring
about that wrath, 1 Thess. 2: 16.

The believing element amongst the Egyptians with their shepherds secured their cattle under strong roofing. All the other cattle that were left outside perished. We suppose that human beings would dash for cover from the hail and not wait to round the cattle up slowly. Yet we read at 11 : 5 that the first-born of Egypt's cattle died. That is to say, it was not the cattle of the unbelievers that died later on along with the first-born of man; it was the cattle of the believers who had wisely preserved their life under protection from the hail.

That this kind of thing should happen has been noted all down the centuries. The man of little faith cries, 'Why should God do this to me when I am a better man than my neighbour?' Both Job and a number of Psalmists were tempted to say just such a thing. But faith in God is not an insurance policy against fate; otherwise the reality of faith would be destroyed. This decisive experience in the history of mankind, then, when pagans first learned in their *mind* what the grace and judgment of God really entail, happened at that decisive *moment* which God had chosen within the unfolding and development of his Plan.

22–26   This section may be a doublet from another source. But Ex has successfully woven it into place so that it becomes *theologically* relevant. We note that the *instrument* of the prophetic symbolism here is variously Moses' hand, v. 22, and Moses' rod, v. 23. Moses' rod was charged with his personal mana in a manner that most eastern peoples fully understood. That is why it acted like a lightning conductor and so brought this magnificent electrical storm to earth.

'Since Egypt became a nation'. The idea of 'nation' here could have been expressed by one of several words. By his choice of term, *goi*, Ex emphasizes that the Egyptians are in fact 'Gentiles' over against God's *'am*, v. 26, as Israel is usually called.

All this took place at what Ex would regard as the dawn of civilization. 'Hail, such as never has been in Egypt from the day on which it was founded until now', repeating v. 18 – and it had been founded by the gods! And now that same sacred soil of Egypt was being pounded from the very sky to which Moses had lifted up his arms! Hail-storms, of course, can be oddly local. We read that the land of Goshen, where the

Hebrews lived, was exempt from this terrible storm. But it meant the ruin of the first portion of the Egyptians' grain harvest.

27–35 *The Electrical Storm Ceases.* We must not read a moral confession into Pharaoh's words. He is merely saying, 'I have made a big mistake. Yahweh is obviously the winner, and my people and I are the losers'. The language is that of the law-court. God's purpose in making the hail-storm an issue that should have affected the heart, mind and conscience of Pharaoh, v. 14, although it had affected some leading citizens, had now failed in Pharaoh's case. So when Pharaoh begs Moses with the words 'Entreat Yahweh' there is no suggestion of any faith involvement. His own comfort and peace of mind weigh more heavily with him than any interest in Yahweh's cosmic plan. In reply, therefore, Moses emphasizes the greatness of the living God by calling him the 'Lord God'. This is the only occurrence in the Pentateuch of the juxtaposition of Yahweh with Elohim, except Gen. 2 f.

The note at v. 31 helps us to place the 'plagues' in the cycle of the agricultural year. All grain was sown in December. The flax (used for wrapping mummies) and the barley would be growing strongly throughout January. The wheat and spelt (a poor quality cereal) mature more slowly. These crops would still be too immature, perhaps just coming through the soil, to be much affected by the hailstorm.

CHAPTER 10

LIGHT AND DARKNESS

1–2   The ancient J tradition here clearly expresses why the Lord hardened Pharaoh's heart; it was in order that, literally, 'I might put these signs of mine inside him'. In the OT even Satan is not God's enemy but his instrument (cf. 1 Chron. 21: 1). In the J memory God is very much the God of the poor, the despised and the depressed. Consequently he is all the more the God of that poor Pharaoh whose heart he himself has hardened for his own ends. For Pharaoh is now as pitiable a creature as the least of the Hebrew slaves. Like the alcoholic, he can no longer 'return' to God of his own volition. As W. Eichrodt expresses it (*Theology of the Old Testament*, II, p. 178) 'This is not a case of God's "permissive will", but of a real act of God in whose hands men, who retain their free-will, are clay in the hands of the Potter'. Any other interpretation of this passage would be a reading into the Bible of modern sociological and moral ideas. Actually there is nothing left for Pharaoh to hope for, or for Pharaoh's friends to hope for him, than divine grace. The book of Exodus is thus a story of grace. God must necessarily be the enemy and the saviour of sinners at the same time, Isa. 63: 1–11. In the person of Pharaoh, therefore, we see how God expressed both his enmity and his saving love at the same time for the ends of his cosmic plan. It is for this ultimate reason that Arnold Toynbee can say: (*A Study of History*, 1972, pp. 100–104) 'It does not matter if men suffer; the new world is born'. So then, no power on earth can now stop the exodus, cf. Acts 2: 23–24.

3   To humble oneself before God is the first and primary act required of sinful man. This is because self-satisfaction is man's natural sin. God's forbearance at man's insolence is profound. God may withhold his arm for century after century, but in his own good time that nation that refuses to humble itself before him crumbles in the dust.

4–11   *The Plague of Locusts.* Locusts may appear in Egypt at various periods of the year, but March is the month when great swarms migrate from the Sudan north-eastwards over Egypt and into Palestine. Even westerners who have never seen a locust need no description of their 'total warfare' upon everything that is green. No wonder his courtiers can say to Pharaoh, 'With the threat of this locust swarm don't you realize that Egypt is as good as ruined?' For following upon the previous series of plagues, the locusts, coming as we read in incredible numbers, would wipe out everything that was left growing.

6   'Then he turned and went out'. In his extreme anger Moses must have insulted Pharaoh mightily. A subject would be expected to walk backwards out of the presence of a king until he reached the door. Here there is a memory of what must have struck the onlookers as a shocking incident. The man of God is the enemy of the ambitious, the ruthless, the egotist. We have seen this confrontation take place again and again in history when a minority group is oppressed by vested interests and only the few whose faith equals the disturbance of their conscience 'turn and walk out from Pharaoh'.

Moses' act of lèse majesté on top of the succession of plagues at last forces Pharaoh to act. But he does so only because he is threatened by the big stick. For now he recognizes that Yahweh is stronger than he. The concession forced from him does not include the Hebrew children, for he means to hold them as hostages. Yet the people of God are one family, *all* must be present at the feast, even the domestic animals. God is not planning to 'save individual souls out of Egypt', His concern is with *all Israel* as one 'person', the son of God, 4: 22, or, as we shall see at chap. 19, the bride of God. Again, no personality can express itself without its possessions; even these need to be 'saved'. That is why the promise of the land takes a central place in God's words of love. This feast, which Moses probably adapted and adopted from the Kenites and which was held in the spring time, is later enshrined in the Covenant Code, and becomes basic in the development of Israel's cult.

Pharaoh wavers. 'The Lord be with you', he says. Then adds quickly, 'You'll never leave here with your little ones; I know your tricks'. Finally he admits that 'The men (a word meaning the young men of military age) can go; but you must leave the children as hostages'. The interview thereupon ends in such appalling tension that we realize something must break, and quickly.

12–20   When the locusts arrive they reveal themselves as the sign of God's 'time'. Although Moses has raised his rod, it is Yahweh who *leads* the locusts in as a shepherd leads his sheep, or a general his army. This is a good instance of the identification of first and second causes. The nature of the plague is unique in that never before and never since has such an event taken place. The verb used even hints at humour: 'The locusts had a rest in all the land of Egypt'. Yet here we have an apocalyptic 'moment', one that Joel understood when he regarded the arrival of a foreign army in Judah in its light. This 'moment' even leads to that understood, in Rev. 9: 1–11, as having meaning in the eternal realities.

Egypt is now left to starve. At 9: 32 we learned that in January all the first growth had been destroyed; now, in February, everything left over has been eaten out. We are now in March. This is a picture of 'total war', of the 'scorched earth policy'. Nothing so clearly as this catastrophe can show us the absolute and immutable decision of God to bring in his kingdom, no matter what the opposition may be; cf. Amos 4: 6–12. No wonder then that Pharaoh refers to the event as 'this death'. We learn that obedience to God is no less than life, and refusal to do so is nothing less than death; Gen. 2: 17; Prov. 7: 27; Amos 5: 6.

'Forgive my sin', says Pharaoh; or better, 'I confess my deviation', as he might express himself in a Marxist society, 'against your God, not mine'. But God again takes Pharaoh patiently at his word, and ends the plague by *driving* (a strong expression) the locusts into the Red Sea. Yet he continues to harden the king's heart, for he has not given up his plan to use him for his redemptive purpose; Ps. 95: 8–11.

21–29   *The Plague of Darkness*. This plague reveals the final battle against Amen-Ra, the Sun-god, the source of all life, whom even Pharaoh worshipped as his divine father. In his royal cartouche the Pharaoh styled himself 'Son of the Sun'.

Throughout her history Israel took full account of the mystery of darkness. Darkness is the outward symbol of chaos, that state from which God brought forth light, Gen. 1: 2–3; see chap. 4. Within the darkness, according to eastern thinking, there swarmed demons of sickness and death. Here we have two words for darkness (the LXX even makes them three) standing hyphenated together, clearly an attempt to emphasize the degree of blackness. In fact, the darkness was even 'to be felt'.

The common hot wind of Egypt, the Khamsin, which arrives in March, brings intolerable conditions. It bears with it vast quantities of sand which enters every crevice and cranny in men's homes, lies on their food and penetrates their clothing. The light of the sun can be obscured for days on end. But what we read of here is rather the deep sense of horror that both Israelites and Egyptians experienced when it came. It meant the eclipse of the sun, and thus the eclipse of Pharaoh the Son of the Sun; and yet to the thoughtful it would mean also a reminder of the horror of the human situation should there be no grace. The point is that this story too becomes a medium of revelation.

Once they had left Egypt the second step was to be an act of worship, a sacrifice. 'We do not know with what we must serve the Lord until we arrive there', v. 26; cf. Matt. 6: 34. Moses has still much to learn. We should note that 'to worship' and 'to serve' translate the same Hebrew verb; for worship means *sacrificial* worship.

28   Pharaoh dismisses Moses with the threat that if they should ever meet again Moses shall die. If God had not continued to harden his heart then this threat might have been effective. But it so eventuated that the hardening process led to the opposite result, to the death, not of Moses, but of the first-born of the king! J. Coert Rylaarsdam (op. cit. p. 910) says of this decisive moment, 'Moses' reply, "I will not see your face again", is not just the close of a conference; it is the foundation of monotheism and of freedom'.

It is interesting that as part of the total act of God in 'coming down', in calling Moses, in setting Israel free, and so on, the requirement that Israel should sacrifice to him in the desert *after three days* is continually stressed. By the third day Israel will enter a new world of freedom and joy. Israel will then want to make a spontaneous expression of thanks, an act of gratitude to God for breaking her chains. It is J and E which make this important emphasis, not P. Ex, however, sees fit to weave it into his Priestly source. This is the more remarkable in that the feast was not really spontaneous at all. Israel was to hold it under pain of divine judgment that would fall in the form of pestilence or sword.

This feast, then, was to take place, not on any particular calendar date, but merely three days after Israel was free, whenever that should be. What we discover later, however, is that the feast which they did in point of fact hold was the Passover, and not the Kenite spring festival, and that they even held it on Egyptian soil!

That Israel ought to want to give thanks for her great redemption is obvious; for it was the *pre-ordained will of God* that she should desire to do so, *of her own free will.* In the event, Israel fails to express her gratitude. But God can overrule even man's endemic ingratitude of heart and use even it for his purposes. For the Passover Festival that is the real festival Israel holds becomes basic to the faith of all subsequent centuries of Jews and Christians alike.

CHAPTER 11

THE LORD MAKES A
DISTINCTION

2–3 *Compensation.* It is only too easy to scoff at this passage, as some commentators have done. The incident has even been labelled as 'Spoiling the Egyptians' to the extent that the phrase has become an English proverb. But we are to understand it within its context, and see it in the light of our understanding of the hardening of the heart.

An eisegesis, a reading into the text, would lead to the following: Israel is human. Israel is frustrated, oppressed, bullied, enslaved. Israel's natural reaction to her condition is to hit back at her oppressors. At last she is presented with a magnificent opportunity to 'get her own back', at least in part.

But this is not what we find in the text. Rather we read of two acts of God. First, *God* puts the idea of compensation into Moses' head. He has even to beg Moses to explain the idea to the Hebrew people. Second, *God* moves the Egyptian people to pity and concern for their servant guests, and even induces them to admire Moses. We note, by the way, that the phrase 'the man Moses' is not an idiomatic Hebrew expression. It is a translation of the Egyptian idiom, obviously long remembered in Israel's traditions.

Since the initiative in every succeeding event proceeds from God, and not from Moses, Ex etches for us the outline of a divinely selected mediator between God and man. The portrait develops as the story proceeds. We note these immediately following actions of God:

First, Yahweh *accepts* Israel as he is, a greedy, grasping people, as we all are, possibly moved by a fierce desire for vengeance. Yet God *uses* this human self-will for his own glory. He takes it, and regulates it, and controls it to the ends of his Plan. Second, God sheds his grace (lit. 'the grace *of* the

people') upon the hearts of heathen men and women who do
not participate in the Covenant. What might have been a
greedy scrambling for revenge now becomes an ordered dis-
tribution of compensation. The God of justice moves the
Egyptians to repay the Hebrew people for the years of toil
they have given to building the public works that the Egyptians
now rejoice in, in part-payment, even if it is just 'conscience-
money', for the years they have worked without pay; see 3: 21
and 12: 35–36. These gifts Israel will use later to decorate the
Tabernacle to the glory of God, 25: 2.

4–10   *The Death of the First-born.* Perhaps this section
followed originally in sequence at 10: 24. Thus 'And Moses
said' (to Pharaoh?) needs no new introduction. Or are we
now at the night of the Passover, 12: 1? God has already informed Moses that he had 'come down' into the appalling
situation of human distress, 3: 7–8. Now he proclaims with
majestic emphasis, '*I* will go forth amongst the Egyptians' this
time, rather than amongst the enslaved Hebrews. The 'plagues'
had already revealed that God is Lord of Nature. Now God is to
'go forth' as Judge of the human race.

Before this event God had claimed Israel as his first-born
son, 4: 22. This claim implied that the Egyptians and all
others were God's sons also. But the special election of the
first-born did not exempt Israel from responsibility even as the
secondary election of the other sons also demanded obedience.
In fact, to whom more is given from him more is expected,
Amos 3: 2. At 4: 22 the son Israel had been contrasted with the
first-born son of Pharaoh. This is because Egypt as a whole
was one 'personality', just as all Americans can be summed up
under the name of Uncle Sam. The king extended his 'soul'
throughout the whole people. So when Pharaoh's first-born
died, then so did the first-born of each commoner family,
including even the first-born of the flocks and herds. This
conception, found amongst most ancient peoples, is a powerful
recognition of what Israel knew to be true, that a nation can
exist as a community of sin; so the nation as a whole must
expect a communal judgment.

So terrible, so intense is this judgment, that in a special way
the cry of human anguish that now goes up becomes the first
moment actuating the ultimate and eschatological judgment of

all men. The events reveal that God 'makes a distinction' between Israel and Egypt, as if the Word of God were the sword of judgment, dividing this from that (cf. Matt. 10: 34). But the sword here does *not* separate the evil from the good, as modern moralists tend to suppose. For Israel is no 'better' than Egypt. If this were the meaning of the divine judgment, then God would be a monster of partiality. The judgment we meet with is God's decision between the elect and the non-elect, administered within a world where suffering and sorrow are the woof and web of existence for man and animals alike. For the aim and purpose of the judgment described here is not to 'punish' evildoers out of all proportion to their 'crime', but to advance the Plan that God has in mind, as it works out within space and time, within the framework of a universe that is 'subject to futility', and which is 'groaning to be set free from its bondage to decay', Rom. 8: 20–21.

At v. 8–9 we witness the righteous wrath of Moses, representing the very wrath of the living God. There is here no kowtowing before the absolute power of a human dictator. What we see rather is the birth of the free human spirit, where just one man, secure in the integrity of his faith, can stand before a despotic monster, in whose hands rests the power of life and death, and who can declare with the courage of complete conviction, 'Pharaoh, thus saith the Lord' (cf. Matt. 10: 14, 18).

Finally, at v. 9 we are informed of the ground of Moses' confidence. He discovers that Pharaoh does not listen to him 'in order that my wonders may be multiplied'. Moses finds repose in the awareness that he is caught up in a purpose far transcending that which is obvious to the participants at the moment, a purpose in which he is proud to play his own little insignificant part in faith and joy.

God's action is now at its climax. He is now 'becoming with' Israel in a transformingly near sense, 13: 10: 'God will now take possession of Israel' (Rylaarsdam, op. cit., p. 913.) His sovereign use of Israel for the sake of the world now begins. But at once there follows, as it were, an awesome pause, as if 'There was silence in heaven for about half an hour. *Then* I saw . . .', Rev. 8: 1.

It is no argument against the basic authenticity of the

plagues, especially of this final one, the death of the first-born, to declare that there is no record of the plagues in the monuments of Egypt. There are three points to make:

(1) Each of the plagues could be regarded by an onlooker as a natural disaster. Each one of them had occurred at intervals already throughout Egypt's history. It is only the eyes of faith that see their unnaturally heightened quality, and recognize that they follow unnaturally close upon each other over a single period of eight months.

(2) The Egyptians did not record their defeats on their monuments. They simply ignored them.

(3) There is certainly a degree of legendary accretion to the tales. Naturally they made good telling down the ages until eventually they found written form. What is important, however, is that Ex made use of his sources, not as an historian might do seeking 'mere' facts alone, but as a theologian who had the insight to see the hand of God in those far-off events, and so to interpret the plagues accordingly.

11   Pharaoh knows his own mind, and acts upon it. In OT thought there are no good intentions. 'The action of the will is identical with the *nephesh* (the 'personality') that in its totality desires it' (Joh. Pedersen, *Israel*, I–II, p. 132). This is why the judgment of God rests, not upon the sin, as many today take for granted, but upon the sinner.

CHAPTER 12

THE PASSOVER

1–10   Ex is a theologian rather than an historian. Here he takes historical material from both J and P and weaves their contributions into a single narrative. This then becomes both theological interpretation of the far past and revelation of the mind of God.

Curiously enough, the first words of *Torah* ('the Law') to be given to man occur here. This emphasises that God's Word was not expressed first in the wholesome free air of Sinai, but in the unclean atmosphere of Egypt. The Word, though given *to* Israel, is not *for* Israel, but for the *world*. And since a new era has begun in the history of man, to mark it a radical change in the calendar takes place.

Men wait the autumn rains eagerly in the Near East after the hot, dry summer, for only if they come can nature be reborn. That is why New Year was celebrated in September. Now however it is to be held in the period March–April, at which we have now arrived in the cycle of the plagues. The result is that the Passover, celebrated in the spring ever since, has, on the one hand, negated the nature-worship of the Canaanites, and on the other hand has given the world the date of the Last-Supper-Cross-Resurrection sequence. And so this 'beginning of months' has become for the Christian world, as well as for the Jews, the beginning of the new creation. We read of it here, as if the feast were celebrated within a closed room, and with the horrors of Egypt shut out of sight. However, we observe a balance held between the individual home and the 'congregation'; this balance is maintained when each head of a family slays his lamb simultaneously with his neighbours. In 515 B.C. Ex witnessed a *public* act (Ezra 6: 16–22). On that occasion the *priests* killed the Passover lamb. But this family festival reveals an emphasis that was recovered by the first century A.D. Its centre is the *home*.

The lamb (the word can also mean 'kid') reminded Israel that God cared about their daily food, and was of course concerned for their health and well-being. For all were, could we say, 'the lost sheep of the house of Israel', cf. Ps. 119: 176. The lamb itself was a gift from God; Israel did not create it. It was to be one-year old, that is, 'kept' carefully, v. 6, till sufficiently grown to feed a normal family. And it was to be without blemish, that is, without disease.

The 'fourteenth day' represented, of course, a double seven-day week, a period of time Israel had learned from the Babylonians. The Passover itself covered a week of seven days. The use of the term 'congregation' on certain solemn occasions, as in Deut. at the giving of the Law, in 1 Kings 8: 14 ff, at the dedication of the Temple, and at the republishing of the Law by Ezra, emphasizes the truth that the people of Israel are constituted by the Word of YHWH as the bearers of the divine covenant and promise.

The blood of the lamb was evidently regarded as a protection for the family. The idea was clearly taken over from a nomadic practice in the desert, not from Egypt. Nomads could hardly hold a 'harvest festival' as settled agriculturalists could. Instead they sacrificed the first of their flock to the god; and they did so in the night of the full moon at the spring equinox. Israel is now to do this 'in the evening', lit. 'between the evenings'. Rabbinical commentators are not unanimous on the meaning of the phrase. There are four suggestions: (1) It is the time between the sun touching the horizon and disappearing over it. (2) It is the time between sunset and the appearance of the first evening star. (3) It marks the time when it starts to get cool till sunset. (4) From 3 p.m. to 6 p.m. or sunset. The phrase occurs in P only.

The lamb's blood is to be sprinkled on the beam that lay horizontally above the door, and on the two upright posts that formed the sides of the entrance to the house; so, as the family went in and out, they saw the red blood, the sign of being under divine protection; cf. Ps. 121: 8.

Roasting the carcase whole on a spit would allow all the blood to drain out (for the blood was already associated with God's positive care) and also allow all the fat to drip to the floor. If the carcase were eaten raw or boiled the conditions of this acted parable would not be fulfilled. The unleavened bread exhibited the reality that the family was living through a moment of urgency when there was no time for unnecessary baking. Yet they were to regard the bread as 'bread of affliction', Deut. 16: 3, reminding them of the pain they had known in Egypt. Leaven in Hebrew thought stood also for corruption. We note that the eating of bitter herbs was likewise to represent that bitterness. We note again that since the God of Abraham, Isaac and Jacob was here 'with' each family, so too must Abraham, Isaac and Jacob be with them. This awareness of one's ancestors has largely been lost in the West, but not so in most other lands. It is a realization of the 'communion of saints', and not a form of ancestor worship. Finally we note the emphasis laid upon the participation of the children in the preparations for the feast, and that non-Israelites are welcome guests at the table of the Hebrew family.

10   There is a 'onceness' about the great moments in human life. This evening meal is to remain just such a memory once and for all. Yet family meals in later times may incorporate this onceness into them. But this special evening can never be grasped again. That is why the remains of the carcase were to be burnt. Then, in order to exhibit the fact that life flows on like a river, the families are to wear such clothes as men would wear who are starting off hurriedly on a great adventure into the unknown future. In fact Israel here is being told to 'take no thought for the morrow', for sufficient unto the day is the food for today.

11c   Unexpectedly we meet a detached sentence: 'It is the Lord's passover'; and with it there ends the description of the feast, and there opens the description of God's 'passing over'.

12–13   At 6: 6 J and at 7: 4 P God had promised to bring Israel out 'with an outstretched arm and great acts of judgment'. We have now witnessed nine mighty acts. This tenth one, the destruction of the first-born of both man and beast, and presumably of the gods as well, is in a sense a total act, and not merely a local act. To say that God would strike the gods is an example of the Hebraic way of expressing the unity of heaven and earth. It will be Israel only that will be passed over in judgments (in the plural), that is, when God expresses his moral judgments. Israel is excepted by grace, in that when God 'came down' he 'became with' Israel, and elected her for his own ends.

The *moral* judgments are explicable from 4: 23. Since Pharaoh had not spared Yahweh's first-born (after nine chances to do so) Yahweh would now no longer spare Pharaoh's first-born, the crown prince, and all the little princes in the hopes of the common man. Infantile diarrhoea? can spread quickly. Our information that *only* the first-born, and not the fourth or sixth-born, consistently caught the disease, may well be attributed to pious story-telling.

We must not read into this incident the idea of 'punishment', far less of 'vengeance', as the LXX does. Punishment is a dangerous English word to use. It is too often inserted into the English text where it does not occur in the Hebrew; cf. in the AV the six reiterations of Amos from Amos 1: 3b onwards. Sinful man puts a degree of glee and satisfaction into the word 'punish'. This is impossible of God. Rather, God 'chastises', 'corrects', 'judges' (executes moral judgments), always with compassion and creative concern. To that end we note the emphatic use here of 'I am YHWH'. From it therefore we learn the necessary content of the verb 'visit', as at 3: 16; 4: 31; 13: 19; 20: 5; 32: 34; 34: 7. The AV therefore incorrectly translates this word by 'punish'. The verb really conveys the idea of the living, personal God entering into a human situation in a personal manner, that is to say, as 'I AM with you', his holy presence thus itself becoming a judgment upon the sinfulness of what is taking place. The principle of justice must stand, however, else there would be moral chaos in human life. Isaiah, Jeremiah and Ezekiel in later centuries all regarded Egypt as the 'broken reed', upon whom Israel could never depend. Israel had asked Pharaoh to let them go to sacrifice to God. Pharaoh had refused. So now Egypt herself must provide the sacrifice; cf. 2 Sam. 21: 1–9. That then is the judgment of which 'the blood shall be the sign', v. 13; cf. 4: 21.

14–15 Despite the implications of the blood, this festival is to be a time of joy. This command to make it so expresses a paradox, viz., that it is possible, and evidently the will of God that it should be so, for a believing man to thrill in his heart to the joy of fellowship with God even when he is walking through a battle-field, a mental hospital, or a hurricane devastated area. God commands the joy. Thus it must come from his eternal being, and so be 'an ordinance for ever'. The festival is to last for seven days, the time that God took to create heaven and earth. Passover begins on a Sabbath and ends on one. This issue is raised again at 16: 23. Passover denotes that at the end of the seven day period a new aeon in the life of the cosmos will begin. The feast will thus 'turn into' a memorial. This is an active and not a static term. Israel is not merely to have happy memories of a long-past event. To 'remember' here is to throw a bridge back over the centuries, and so join up the past with the present. Traffic can then pass in both directions. Again, no one is to break away from the common body of the people. *Extra ecclesiam nulla salus* (outside of the Church there is no salvation) is as true today as then, even though today we do not dogmatize on the bounds of the Church. In this verse, then, 'Israel' is clearly used in a theological sense.

16–20   We are now trafficking on the bridge. The holding of a 'holy assembly' and the application of the Fourth Commandment belong to a later period in Israel's history. But the genius of Ex is to record them as if these practices were instituted in Moses' day. By so doing he builds a bridge over the centuries, and his contemporaries share in the first Passover with that ancient generation. For it was 'on this very day I brought your hosts out of the land of Egypt: *therefore* you shall observe this day, throughout your generations, as an ordinance for ever'.

Over the bridge the figure of Moses never passed. The present day liturgy of the Passover never even mentions his name. For, as Ex wants us to realize, he is writing the story, not of Moses, but of God.

21–23   *The Passover Again.* Ex puts the two sets of instructions together (see at v. 1 above) in a continuous narrative. The families, after obeying all instructions, are to shut themselves into their houses. They are not to see Yahweh in action, for the question is, is it really Yahweh who is passing by? Ex here raises a profound theological issue, and as he does so how meaningful the word *pesaḥ* becomes! 'Yahweh (?) will now "pass over" (or "limp over", or perhaps "skip over") the Israelite homes and enter into the homes of the Egyptians to destroy *their* first-born babies; cf. 1 Cor. 10: 9–10; Heb. 11: 28. At Psalm 78: 49, where this incident is referred to, we read that God let loose on the Egyptians his anger (using four different words for anger); thereupon this wrath is interpreted as 'a company of destroying angels'. The AV is clearly wrong in translating this by 'evil angels'.

We are to remember that God does not possess attributes. God does not possess wrath. Rather, God acts in wrath and in judgment. Because God is personal, the living God, the Father, 4: 22, the human mind can 'see' the meaning of his actions. Thus at Ps. 78: 49 God, *in his wrath,* that is to say, acting wrathfully, is pictoralized by the term 'angels', angels that incorporate (*not* convey) the wrath of God. God's wrath is not evil. The angels are '*de*stroying angels' only as they bring about corruption and even annihilation in accordance with the will of God. Peace, *shalom,* on the other hand, basically means *con*struction, wholeness, integration. The opposite of *shalom* is *ra',* 'evil', not as mere moral lapsing, but as that which is destructive, disintegrative, atomizing. Isa. 45: 7 puts this reality in succinct language. 'I am YHWH' (as at Ex. 6: 2); 'I form light and create darkness' (the contrast declared in Gen. 1: 2–3); 'I make weal, *shalom,* and create woe, *ra':* I am YHWH, who do all these things', RSV.

At Gen. 1: 2 we note that darkness is not 'of God'; but in the next verse we read that light is 'of God'. So at Isa. 45: 7 God only needs to 'fashion' light, for it is there already to hand; but he must 'create' evil, for evil is not 'of himself'; and this word 'create' is the verb found at Gen. 1: 1. This passage therefore declares that God is Lord of all, of both that which is of himself and of that which he must create in order to further his ends of redemptive love. Just as the hardening of Pharaoh's heart is a window into this basic reality in the nature of God, so too is this description of God as both destroyer and saviour at the same time; cf. Deut. 32: 39. Egypt has now overstepped the mark of her calling as God's secondary instrument, as Isaiah before Ex's day had already interpreted the actions of Assyria. In her cruelty she had 'gone too far'; cf. Isa. 5: 26; 8: 5–8; 10: 5–11. In such a situation innocent babies must necessarily

suffer along with the rest of the corporate body of the nation,
in fact they may even be the first to suffer (cf. Matt. 2: 16).

24   The price of Israel's freedom is a terrible one. Despite that, God even adds a bonus. Israel is to be saved, not
only *from* slavery, as he has *said* (not 'promised' as the English
versions say – for God's 'Word' alone is enough), but also *into*
a new land and into a new life, one which God will *give* them.
Once arrived there Israel's response to God's act of terrible
grace is to be that of *service*. The Passover rite is therefore
meant to sum up for Israel what service in general means;
service is to be Israel's *work* at all times (the Hebrew word
means both), performed in joyous gratitude for what God had
done for her before she was able to help herself. At the moment,
though, Israel is to do nothing at all to save herself. She is just
to be obedient, bow her head, worship, and wait for God.

29–32   That night, as the outcome of the Word spoken
at 11: 6, 'there was a great cry in Egypt'. Goethe has called it
'St. Bartholomew's Eve in reverse'. For here we see the first
movement in the long 'count down' leading to the 'explosion'
that must occur at the end of the second aeon when what the
NT calls the Last Judgment will take place. Even those in the
pit (or 'dungeon', RSV) God smote, we read. This pit thereafter becomes the symbol of the bottom of Sheol, the land of
the dead.

Pharaoh suddenly discovers that he is no longer a god; he is
but a man, a father who has lost his little boy, Num. 33: 4. At
last then we hear the answer to God's command 'Let my people
go' in Pharaoh's words, 'Rise up, go forth. . .'. So this midnight
sees the death of the old, the birth of the new. Pharaoh's
logic, however, is in order: 'Go and worship', he says to
Moses; for he is aware that absolute commitment in awe and
obedience to the living God is the only response that miserable
man can make when the gates of Sheol are opened; 'and
bless me also', he adds, poor creature that he is. For he too is a
first-born, and like all mortal men, he is afraid to die, even
though he has no compunction about ordering the death of
others. Surely God heard the prayer of this lost human soul,
mediated as it was through the lips of Moses.

The question remains – does God kill babies? God sends his
agent, his 'missionary', the angel whose task is to 'destroy'.

We cannot therefore take the blame off God and put it on the angel, or Satan, or on any other creature. Yet it is obvious that we must demythologize the story, and then remythologize it in language that describes reality as our minds conceive it today. When we do this we face the natural processes of disease keeping to their own laws, laws which God has created. These laws, just like all other laws, such as those that govern earthquakes, whirlwinds, and the rest, are created to work in the complete freedom with which God has endowed nature. This freedom is made visible here even as the babies die. God does not avert the disaster, for then he would obstruct the freedom of the germs to move from man to man. But these free laws are *his* laws. They are 'of him'; he made them. And so God himself, as the book of Exodus reveals, suffers with the babies who die through the freedom given to nature.

Yet God uses the freedom he has given to nature for a greater good. God does not rule his creation; rather, he sustains it. Evil produces situations in history from which there is no way out – except by suffering love. So even the deaths of babies are caught up into the great Plan that God is working out in human history.

33-36 Here we have a variant on the issue some have called 'The Spoiling of the Egyptians'. The Egyptians are now so eager to 'throw out' the Hebrews, as the LXX puts it, that they give them what they want just to get rid of them. This is now the third time we learn of this incident. There must be a compelling theological reason for this. First, Israel now shares in God's judgment on Egypt. Second, since it was only the well-to-do amongst the Egyptians who brought to light all those precious objects, we see God imposing his fine only upon those who can afford to pay. So the Gentiles unwittingly bring their gifts for the glory of God (cf. Isa. 60) in that, as we have noted, God will later on use them for building the Tabernacle, 35: 10 ff. But third, Israel planned otherwise. Israel used them to create the golden calf, chap. 32. This then is that ridiculous people to whom both Jews and Christians belong; Rom. 9-11.

37-42 The exodus from Egypt begins quietly, on a low key. Israel simply walks away on that unique Sabbath day when God himself kept the watch. No wonder Jesus said: 'The

Sabbath was made for man' – for man to enjoy in freedom. The people go out with the flesh of the lamb in their mouth, and with their dough and kneading bowls on their shoulder. But they do not go alone. Israel is not God's people merely by blood or race. It is a people of all kinds and colours; they are 'a big swarm' composed possibly of groups of other depressed Semitic tribes called collectively 'Hebrews', as we have seen. Some from the south would certainly have black skins. We recall that Moses' second wife was probably black, while his first one would be brown like an Arab today. 600,000 warriors came out, an incredible number as it stands.

This number of young men of military age implies a total exodus of some two million people. See also at 38: 26; Num. 1: 46; 11: 21. Before medical science succeeded in keeping alive new babies, populations were small. There were only two million people in England in Shakespeare's day. Queen Anne lost all 17 of her children and had no heir. Two million people could not have gathered round one rock in the wilderness for a drink. Clearly we are not meant to think in modern, scientific terms. In Egypt a god is pictured just like a man, but depicted as a giant. Thus if God was *in* Israel, then the promise made to Abraham must be expressed in giant terms.

G. Mendenhall (JBL, LXXVI, Part 1, March, 1958, p. 61) offers however a satisfying explanation of the huge figure. He shows that the unit which we might call a 'clan', as in Jud. 6: 15, was known then as an *eleph*, a subsection of a tribal group. Using census lists in Num. 1: 26 he arrives at a total of 598 such military units, thus producing 5,500 fighting men in all. Later on the meaning of *eleph* was fixed at one thousand. This change caused huge numbers to be calculated in later times by those who did not know the original meaning of the word. Here then we meet with 600 *elephs* or military units that would produce a fighting force of some 2,500 warriors. The total number of Hebrews leaving Egypt would then amount to some 10,000 persons.

Ex likens this great moment to a 'day' in the life of God, in the same manner as the word is used in Gen. 1. However, it is rather a 'night' in which *God himself* keeps vigil. The word in the original occurs only here. This is a unique event. It is also an extraordinary idea. 'On that very day', then, the new day in the life of God (!) is when the exodus takes place.

43–50 *The Development of the Passover Ritual.* With the words 'The Lord said to Moses and Aaron' we once more meet the reality of the living nature of the Word. The descendants of those who came out at the exodus had by Ex's day discovered that God had long since incorporated them into his ongoing Plan. Clearly God regards all Israel as one body, especially from the point of view of the passage of time, v. 47. But Torah, God's revealed Word, is meant for Israelites and Gentiles alike, v. 48, for (1) it was first revealed, as Ex believed, not in Sinai, but while Israel was still in the land of Egypt, and (2) it was offered to a 'mixed multitude' from out of all the peoples of the earth – for a man could become an Israelite by choice (cf. Rom. 9: 7). Thus Passover is God's gift, through Israel, to all men, male and female, Jew and Gentile, bond and free alike.

Who may, and who may not, eat the Passover?

(1) 'Foreigner', *ben nēkher*. Israel was the 'son' of Yahweh, 4: 22. This phrase here means 'son of a strange god'. The 'foreigner' is thus not an alien, politically speaking, rather he is a pagan polytheist.

(2) 'Slave' *'ebhedh*; he is the necessary machine without which society would collapse in a pre-industrial age. He becomes an adopted Israelite once he is circumcised. There are two kinds of slave. One was bought. He was usually a foreigner, but was often accounted one of the family. Through circumcision a male slave entered the mystical and spiritual unity of Israel, and became part of the psychic, national, religious whole. The other kind was the child born to a slave who was already part of the household.

(3) 'Sojourner', *toshabh*. A non-Israelite, one who was not a member of the covenant people, but who, possibly for business reasons, was living temporarily in the land of Israel, and accepting the care of Israel's rule of law.

(4) 'Hired servant', *sakhir*. He was an employee, usually a foreigner, like a Southern Italian today who is temporarily employed in Switzerland or Germany.

(5) 'Stranger', *ger*. He was an aborigine, the descendant of one of the groups known as 'Canaanites, Hittites, Amorites,

Perizzites, Hivites and Jebusites', 3: 8, the traditional names of the peoples conquered in Joshua's day. Most of them remained where they were. Solomon enslaved them for a time, 1 Kings 9: 15–21. Circumcision represented the willing entrance of even an aborigine into the People of God. Of course, if he were still the 'son of a strange god', naturally he could not partake in the Passover. 'Come near', v. 48, is the technical term used for coming to worship at the later period when the Passover had become institutionalized.

CHAPTER 13

ISRAEL'S BIRTH DAY

1–10   This section, possibly originating with the D tradition, demonstrates a particular biblical genius. Ex takes from it an ancient tabu and reinterprets it theologically. He does so on the basis of that other biblical emphasis, that 'In the middle of the garden stood the tree of life'; that is to say, life is God's first and basic gift, presupposing all else. The first-born of man or beast is thus specially sacred; the later-born win their sanctity from the pioneer.

We are meant to see that this Passover day, including the whole movement to freedom culminating in the crossing of the Sea, was Israel's birth day. Egypt was the womb from which Israel emerged as a child of God. Israel is to mark his birthday therefore by a 'birthday party' and a date on the calendar. It was to be in the month of Abib.

8   The high moment of the 'party' is the recalling of what *God* has done. Though Israel is one corporate personality, yet each individual father is to tell his individual son the meaning of God's action in the singular: 'It is because of what the Lord did for *me* when *I* came out of Egypt'. What we meet here is the advocacy of 'faith by recall', of obeying the word 'remember', the realization that 'by strength of hand *the Lord* brought you out', *not*, by eating bread which your own hand has baked, v. 3, since man is not the author of his own salvation. Man cannot introduce his culture and civilization into the land of milk and honey by his own abilities; man must learn in all ages that he cannot build the perfect society.

So once again we hear the command, this time from a completely separate tradition, to use the exodus as a 'sign' that God alone is Saviour. Israel is to 'remember' the event, by instituting two-way traffic on that bridge from the past to the present. In this way, 'I', an individual, make 'God's history' *my* history. Literally we read, 'It was because of *this*, that is, what God did for *me*, in bringing *me* out of Egypt'. The individual must not keep quiet about the grace of God. He is called upon to pass on the knowledge of it to each new generation.

11–16   Ex has skillfully re-joined the narrative that ended at 13: 2 by continuing to use the singular, even when he quotes from a different source. It is the individual still to whom the new instructions are now given. We read of a theological reason for the practice of consecrating the first-born, an ancient custom in the desert, but a meaningful sacral act once Israel is settled in Canaan. Just as God 'passed over' the slain lamb, 12: 12, and saved all Israel, so each Israelite is now to 'set apart' or 'make a passover' of each first-born child and animal. Of rights the first-born should die. But God decrees for Israel a means whereby its life can be 'ransomed' by another life. We are not told, *at this point*, what the ransom price of a baby is. This is made clear later. But we are told that the price of an ass is a lamb. Unless a ransom is paid for the ass, the ass must die.

'Redeem', RSV, is not correct, as often in the RSV. *Ga'al* is to 'redeem'. *Padhah,* the word used here, is the correct word for 'ransom', as in buying a slave in the market-place. But since it may describe an action of God, the word was early 'demythologized'. Even then it carried the idea of the costliness to God of his act of rescue: cf. 34: 20. In this case the father's act is costly. In later years the price was reckoned at five silver shekels, Num. 18: 16; cf. Luke 2: 23–24.

17–22   *The March Begun.* 'Man proposes, God disposes'. And God is wise. The road to paradise does not run in a straight line. God knows how completely unprepared Israel would have been to enter the land of milk and honey if they had reached it in two week's time along a well-built highway only 120 miles in length. Moreover, on this coastal road Israel would have run into detachments of Egyptian infantry, well able to make havoc of a civilian army. Breasted believes that in those days there was even a kind of Maginot Line across the 'royal highway'. But on the southern route down to Sinai the garrisons that had guarded the copper mines on the western slopes of the mountains had by now been withdrawn. But at the moment 'the way of (i.e. leading to) the wilderness' that

Israel took lies between the land of Goshen and where the Suez Canal is now to be found.

There is a pun expressed in v. 17, 'God did not *lead* them'. *Naḥam* looks and sounds like the verb 'he changed his mind', or as the EVV put it, 'he repented'. Man left to himself normally takes the wrong road. God however both leads man and at the same time helps him to change his mind. Here God leads Israel towards the 'Red Sea'. This is really the 'Papyrus Sea', or the 'Sea of Reeds'. Actually Ex uses anachronistic language, in that the Philistines, v. 17, began to arrive and settle along the coast, coming from the Island of Crete, only from about this time onwards. But such language is permissible in the same sense as we can say that Columbus discovered 'America'.

18   The idea of being 'equipped for battle' is followed up throughout the whole long history of the People of God, except that the nature of the equipment varies. The word is unusual. Some think it is a mis-spelling of 'fifty'. The MT may thus mean 'in platoons of fifty at a time', that is, in war formation; cf. Josh. 1: 14; 4: 12; Jud. 7: 11. A recent commentator suggests 'in five companies, sc. (1) vanguard, (2) rearguard, (3) camp followers, (4) and (5) flanking escorts. Others believe that this is an Egyptian word, meaning 'armed with a lance'.

An important piece of equipment was the mummy of Joseph. (His bones were finally buried at Shechem, Josh. 24: 32). These bones were a sacramental sign for Israel of the continuity of God's Plan, and evidence of the fulfilment so far of the promise that God had given to Abraham; see Gen. 50: 25. Israel was clearly being taught that the little moment through which they were then living was in reality a link in the 'salvation history' whose past they knew something about, but at whose future they could only guess.

19   We have seen that 'visit' means, as the LXX suggests, a kind of 'episcopal visitation', with God coming into the midst in person. At Gen. 50: 25–26 the presence of Joseph's bones seems to suggest the localization or particularization of this divine visitation.

Each day then they pulled up their tent-pegs (the literal meaning of 'they moved on', RSV). So vivid is this verb that we almost hear the hurry and scurry, the children romping, the mothers packing, the fathers heaving and shouting, the animals neighing and mooing – all excited by the new knowledge that 'this is not your home'. That home always lies ahead.

The Lord now *led* them, 'going before them', first, south east, and then back up north-east to the Egyptian frontier. Such manoeuvering would create confusion in the minds of the Egyptians. Israel even moved at night. For God, by the use of a pillar of cloud by day and by a pillar of fire by night, led the way himself. This almost lyrical note occurs at v. 21. 'The Lord is my light and my salvation' Israel learns to sing. What better way is there to *picture* this reality than by the story we have in this saga? For God himself is Light, and God himself is the Way.

Two suggestions are made today: (1) The pillar of cloud and the pillar of fire were produced when a caravan or marching army held to the custom of sending a burning brazier on ahead. (2) The saga may reflect a memory of a volcanic eruption over on the east coast of the Gulf of Aqaba. We shall discuss this hypothesis later.

With insight the Midrash (second century A.D. Jewish Commentary) says here: 'Among mortals it is the pupil who carries the lantern for his teacher; but of God we read, "And the Lord went before them. . .". Among mortals slaves carry their master. But God carried Israel on eagles' wings, 19: 4.'

CHAPTER 14

CROSSING THE SEA

1-4   Having to double back on their tracks must have been a severe test of faith for the Israelites. The emphasis of the story, however, is always upon Yahweh, not upon Israel's state of mind. All that happens, we note, does so in order to redound to the glory of God, not man.

5-9   Ex still regards Pharaoh's heart condition as a serious issue. In the final analysis it was when Pharaoh *broke* his promise to Moses that the glory of God was revealed! cf. John 13: 31. Israel now 'went forth defiantly', literally, 'with a hand raised high' – almost 'with clenched fist'. The defiance that Israel expressed against Pharaoh was rooted in her confidence that Yahweh himself had promised to bring Israel out 'with a strong hand', even, as we might say again, 'with a clenched fist', 6: 1; 7: 4; 9: 3; 9: 15; 13: 9.

6-7   The RSV here improves upon the AV by adding 'other' to 'chariots'. 'Officers' derives from the noun for 'three'; it means 'the third man' in each of the royal chariots; the driver drove, the warrior fought, the third man gave the orders. The war-chariot had reached Egypt long ago at the time when the Hyksos kings had introduced the horse. Writing centuries later, however, Ex unifies the Egyptian and the Israelite modes of fighting. Assyrian and Hittite pictures show three persons in a chariot, the driver, the warrior and the shieldbearer. In Moses' day however the Egyptians put only a driver and one warrior in each chariot.

10-14   All the frailties inherent in human nature are now portrayed realistically in Israel's reactions to events; and these are seen in contrast with the loyalty and steadfastness of Yahweh. Ex is careful to show, however, that even at this traumatic moment Israel does not turn for help to other gods, far less does she curse the living God. Instead she weeps like a helpless child in the arms of her mother – for she knows that there is nowhere else to weep. Israel saw the Egyptians 'marching after them', or rather 'bursting out upon them'; having in their turn 'pulled up their tent pegs' the Egyptians were thrusting eagerly forward.

Israel is now standing, literally, between the devil and the deep blue sea. She is facing a total confrontation with the powers of evil along with the real possibility of total destruction. Would it not be better for Israel never to have known the taste of freedom? Would it not be better to put back the clock and reject the pressures of history? What happens now therefore becomes the Word spoken to men at all times who find themselves in such a situation.

Even though the people have now put the blame on Moses, there comes from the lips of the latter one of the great statements of history: It issues in three clauses: (1) 'Don't be afraid'. (2) 'Plant your feet firmly on the ground'. And (3) 'Just watch'. Israel is now to *see*, not investigate or understand intellectually, the 'salvation of Yahweh', which *he* will do *now*, today. 'Yahweh will fight *for* you'; 'You must just remain quiet'. The redemptive love of the living God is here expressed in simple, pictorial terms, using history as the medium of revelation. In fact Moses' three clauses appear throughout the whole biblical revelation. For (1) see Gen. 15: 1; 21: 17; 26: 24; Josh. 8: 1; Jud. 6: 23; 2 Kings 2: 16; 1 Chron. 28: 20; Matt. 1: 20; 28: 5; Luke 1: 13, 30; 2: 10; 12: 32; Rev. 1: 17. For (2) see Isa. 7: 9; 26: 3; Pirke Aboth 2: 8. For (3) see Neh. 4: 20; Isa. 30: 32; 53: 3–5; Ps. 35: 1.

In the NT we read that Paul believed that the Church, the People of God, was born at this moment in history, and that it was 'baptized' in 'infancy' into the new life of forgiveness, freedom and joy, and that this all took place through the prevenient grace of God, 1 Cor. 10: 1–4. The salvation that God had wrought in Israel at the time of the Exodus however was now confirmed, declared Paul, enfleshed, reactivated, universalized and personalized in Jesus Christ.

We note six points about this salvation of Yahweh. (1) Yahweh brings salvation, not man. He alone can do so, for 'There is no Saviour but me, says Yahweh', Isa. 43: 11. The NT is quite clear about this; we read at Matt. 1: 21: '. . . You shall call his name Jesus (i.e. Joshua or Jehoshua)' for the name means 'Yahweh will save his people from their sins', not Jesus. And Paul's summary expression in 2 Cor. 5: 19, that 'God was *in* Christ, reconciling . . .' preserves the only possible emphasis. It is only when Christian theology is firmly rooted in the Torah that the uniqueness of Yahweh as Saviour is guarded and maintained.

(2) This salvation is for *you*, plural. The Israelites were not expected to find salvation one by one, as Paul recognized in 1 Cor. 10: 1–4. There he shows that all were 'baptized' before they could make any profession of faith; it is only later that the Decalogue (chap. 20) is addressed to *individuals* in Israel.

(3) Yahweh's salvation covers all aspects of life; he brings Israel into a totally new situation, economic, political, social as well as personal; and Yahweh's act wipes out with the waters of the sea the past sinfulness of Israel as 'my people' seen in their whole former way of life.

(4) His salvation is costly to himself, for he effects it from *within* the situation, 3: 2, 8.

(5) His salvation is free, to Israel and to all who have joined her in her exodus flight; cf. Acts. 2: 47.

(6) His salvation is 'for ever', v. 13, that is, it has an eschatological orientation. Or equally, the eschatological becomes historical, political and social.

15 Now follows God's second great proclamation. We say glibly that the command 'Tell the people of Israel to go forward' came from God. But the intuition that the idea had indeed come from God had first to formulate itself in Moses' mind before he could venture to utter such words. Moses has to be fully convinced that God is revealing himself in two capacities at once, that is, both as Saviour and as Lord; cf. Ps. 103: 7.

16 The unity of will between God and that of an obedient man is expressed again. For it is not clear who divided the sea, whether it was God, or Moses with his crook – surely a picture of the condescension of divine grace. Pharaoh's chariots could now have easily caught up with the lumbering refugees; but this possible discrepancy is of small account when we are dealing with theology in pictures. We hear now that Pharaoh's people have become infected with their king's 'disease'. For hardness of heart has now smitten the Egyptian warriors, just as millions of Germans hardened their hearts against the Jews merely from reading Hitler's *Mein Kampf* or from hearing him speak on the radio; cf. Luke 13: 1–3.

10–20   'The angel of God went behind the host'. God, *in* this special manifestation of himself, is thus both prevenient grace and retrospective grace at the same time. For here God both goes ahead of Israel *in history*, and comes behind Israel *in history*, yet at the same time *shares in* the particular historical moment *with* Israel. 'If God is spoken about, in all the J references to angels, apart from the human beings concerned in the story, then the story-teller uses YHWH or *elohim*. But if God is spoken about as perceptible to the persons in the narrative, the story-teller uses the phrase "the angel of YHWH"' (G. von Rad, *Old Testament Theology*, I, ET, p. 287, ftn. 13). This passage therefore witnesses to the fact that the work of the incarnate Word does not begin with Jesus of Nazareth; but as Jesus himself said, the Word has always been present in the Church of God; cf. John 8: 58.

We now watch what happened to the 'prototype generation' of the People of God. They had to learn at first hand, so to speak, what later generations could experience at second hand. This is that God's people are not meant just to 'put their trust in God'. For *my* decision to do so requires an act of *my* will; and so my decision becomes a human 'work'. Israel learns here that what she has to do is simply to *remember* that *God* is faithful, and that consequently he is able to save.

It is only in recent years that we have learned how unstable the areas of Suez and the Aegean Sea were in Moses' day. It has long been known that there is a deep fault or crack in the earth's surface that runs from the mountains of Lebanon down under the Sea of Galilee, along the deep Jordan Valley, the Dead Sea, the Arabah, the Gulf of Aqaba, the Red Sea, across into Africa, and down the chain of Central African lakes. But it is only recently that a consensus of scholarly opinion has been reached that the two continents of Asia and Africa were in strong friction in early Old Testament times. (For the 'plate tectonic' or 'sliding plates' theory of the cause of the phenomena experienced at the crossing of the Sea, see *National Geographic*, Vol. 143, No. 1, Jan. 1973, especially the maps on p. 6 and p. 11. Earthquakes were known as late as NT times, cf. Matt. 25:54; 28:2; Acts 16:26. 'East wind' – LXX has 'south', perhaps a more exact memory. Where the Suez Canal now flows, in Moses' day there was a number of shallow, papyrus-filled lakes).

A severe earthquake may well have heaved the Suez area several feet up, when the bottom of the Gulf of Aqaba would subside to an equal extent. The waters of the shallow *Yam Suph*, the Sea of Reeds, would then drain quickly away. Simultaneously there would be a tremendous wind caused by the quick elevation of the land surface. Then a second earthquake movement, again caused by the 'moving plate', could have swung the Suez area back to its original level or even lower, thus causing the sea from the Gulf of Suez to roar back into the *Yam Suph*. We must not forget that a tidal wave from the ocean, 35 feet high, overwhelmed the city of Tokyo at the great earthquake of 1923.

22–25   Yet we read: '. . . the waters being a wall to them on their right hand and on their left'. Verse 21 is usually attributed to the basic J material that Ex used; it speaks factually about what happened at the moment of this earth movement. But between the time of Moses and the development of the P material the 78th Psalm was penned. The author of this Psalm admits that he is not reporting factually on Israel's history; in fact he tells us that he is writing poetry. He calls his poem a 'parable'. Poetry seeks to express the *meaning* of events, and not provide a mere photograph of 'what actually happened'. The author of Psalm 78 looks back over the history of his people and sees how God has indeed been a 'wall' to them from the days of Egypt. P then copied this fascinating idea into his description of the events.

Deutero-Isaiah then goes beyond the Psalmist here. Isa. 51:9–10, again using the vehicle of poetry, identifies the waters of the *Yam Suph* with the waters of the primal chaos, which all men supposed to lie underneath the earth; cf. Ex. 20:4. These waters were typified by the 'monster', Rahab, the serpent, the dragon, and so on. This myth dealt with the birth of creation. But Isa. 51 demythologizes this ancient semitic explanation of origins, then re-mythologizes it in theological terms, identifying God's *redemptive* activity at the crossing of the Sea with his *creative* activity when he brought the heavens and the earth into being. All God's work is *crisis* and *life-giving*, including even his 'strange work', Isa. 28: 21, that is, his work of bringing life out of destructive flood, of victory out of defeat, even life out of death. That is what Ex is now able to expound by his skilful intertwining of sources.

. 24   In the early hours of the first 'day' of salvation history 'Yahweh *looked down*' on the battle (with the slight note of ennui we hear at Gen. 11: 5, when God still had to 'come down' to man even after man had attempted to climb up to God.) He then 'clogged their chariot wheels', so that Egypt cried out, 'Yahweh fights for them against us'.

  26–29   All is over by 6 a.m. Ra, who was not only the Sun-god in the person of Pharaoh, but was also the apotheosis of Egypt's military might, is now beneath the waves. The Egyptians 'fled (headlong) to meet it' (the returning waters), v. 27, as if they were driven along by fate. 'And the Lord routed the Egyptians', RSV. Yet the verb actually means that he 'flicked them away', shook them off as a man shakes fleas out of his bedclothes. Nowhere in Ex's narrative is praise ever given to Moses. For Moses is only God's 'hand'. All that happens is of Yahweh alone; Deut. 11: 4; Ps. 78: 53; Heb. 11: 20; for *he* is the 'wall' of his chosen people.

Throughout both the OT and the NT we meet the un-ashamed picture of the Lord as a warrior. He is the Lord of hosts, or armies; he leads Joshua into Canaan; his apparel is stained with blood shed in battle, Isa. 63: 1. The key to this is always in the emphasis: 'It is I, who announce that right has won the day, I, who am strong to save', Isa. 63: 2 NEB. Thus there is no discontinuity between the God of the exodus and the God of the NT whom we meet in the bloody figure of Christus Victor; he leads his 'army' to victory, singing 'Onward Christian Soldiers' as they go.

  30–31   'Yahweh saved Israel that day'. 'Justice must not only be done', we say, 'it must also be seen to be done'. 'And Israel *saw* the Egyptians dead . . . and Israel *saw* the mighty hand which Yahweh employed (lit. 'did') against the Egyptians'; that is, God acted visibly in a definite historical situation. We might paraphrase as follows: 'One thing I know, once I was blind, but at the *Yam Suph* I *saw*!' Consequently the people 'feared the Lord'. Israel stood before him in awe and wonder, and, we must remember, in literal fear as well. But that fear led on to faith.

The last sentence of the chapter uses a challenging and disturbing phrase, the like of which is found only once again in the whole OT, at 2 Chron. 20: 20. 'They believed *in* Yahweh', we read, 'and *in* his servant Moses'. Or, more accurately, 'they committed themselves in trust to Yahweh and to his servant Moses'.

What is challenging is that the same grammatical form is used for faith in God and for faith in a man. The Targum feels compelled to demur by paraphrasing with 'And they believed in the Word of Yahweh, and in the prophecy of Moses his servant'. We might expect such a sentence as 'They put their faith in Yahweh, and believed *that* Moses had led them well'. But no. For in the mystery of the incipient incarnational process a man, if he is himself totally committed to the Word, can become an 'extension' of the Word, or, to use the language of this chapter, become the very *hand* of God. The Word *written* is never enough. The Bible is to be found in countless homes, but seldom has any impact on those who dwell therein. It is the word *preached* that is at the heart of God's basic choice for the locus of the Word. In Eph. 1: 12 the saints are to *be* a praise of God's glory, not just to praise his glory. Normally the Word is simply not heard without an interpreter, the name Deutero-Isaiah gave to the prophets, Isa. 43: 27. The preacher therefore becomes as important in the Plan of God as any other aspect of the Word now on its way to becoming flesh. For the preacher is he who says quite simply 'This means that'. Only then does Israel 'see'.

Ex would therefore expect us to agree that the 'ordained ministry' is basic to the very existence of the People of God. Without it the Church would not value the Word of which it is the custodian, just as without 'believing in Moses', Israel would be much less likely to 'believe in the Lord'. Here the ministry does not create the Church. Rather the ministry here is *of* the Church, of the *esse* of the Church, for without it there would be no faith within the Church; without it there would be no People of God, even though, paradoxically, the People of God actually preceded Moses! This then is why the Church can thank God for the apostles *and the prophets* – the greatest of whom, according to Jesus, is Moses; Luke 16: 29; 24: 27; John 3: 14; 5: 45, etc.

CHAPTER 15

THE LORD IS A WARRIOR

This vigorous and highly theological poem has reached Ex in a form which shows that it by-passed the collection of material we call J, E and P. Probably it was *sung* down the centuries, perhaps even with accompanying dramatization. In the original Hebrew it swings along as does the ballad poetry of many lands, such as in 'Half owre, half owre to Aberdour,/ 'Tis fifty fathoms deep./ And there lies gude Sir Patrick Spens,/ Wi' the Scots lords at his feet.'

It was the wisdom of Israel to recognize that the poem contained the basis of her faith. This is because at the historical events of the exodus she had seen that Yahweh was her Warrior-Saviour. Being poetry, however, it does not give an exact description of 'what happened'. Instead we are presented with a picture of a storm at sea. The main emphasis, however, is upon the steadfast love of Yahweh and his guiding care. As we learn here, the exodus, like the cross, has no religious value apart from its interpretation as an act of God.

To insist that 'Moses sang the poem', or that 'all the people sang it', or that 'Miriam sang it', v. 21, is beside the point just as it is to declare that Moses *wrote* the poem. Firstly, it was clearly not written down till after several generations; and secondly, it was God's doing that the poem grew and developed in the minds of any number of people.

1–2   'Yahweh has triumphed', not *I*, not *Israel*; and Yahweh has triumphed over not just the forces of Egypt but also over the forces of Nature (cf. Job 37: 40; Jonah 1: 4). 'For . . .' (this word introduces a credal statement as at 3: 12, and means something like 'I declare that . . .) he is the God of war; he is the Lord of hosts, the hosts of Israel on earth, and of the heavenly hosts above. Israel has been set free in order to set others free, to be the 'freedom-fighters' for mankind. To Hebrew ears the very name 'Israel' sounded as 'Yahweh fights'; so now Yahweh is destining Israel to fight the Holy War. Since this reality is echoed in the Magnificat and the Benedictus, it means that the NT faith rests first of all upon God's primary act at the Reed Sea.

'Yahweh has *become* my salvation', a use of the verb, as we saw at 3: 12, that belongs in the very name of YHWH. But Yahweh is still linked with what has preceded this event, he is still 'my father's God', the God of Abraham, and so the God of the ancient covenants. Later generations were very aware of this sequence of God's saving acts; cf. Josh. 24: 3; Isa. 51: 2; Ps. 47: 9; and see Isa. 43: 27; 58: 14. In the same way Paul makes 40 references to the exodus in his Epistles.

3–10 The directness of the expression 'The Lord is a *man* of war' represents the naiveté of a faith that sees no problems if the Word decides to become known in terms of flesh. This is reflected in v. 6, where God's 'right arm' shatters the enemy, echoing the words found in previous chapters. He is 'glorious in power to save', v. 6; his act is a revelation of his majesty, v. 7. He sends his wrath ('fury', RSV) like sending an angel to be his instrument to burn up the enemy. For Egypt is merely stubble. God is pictured as an almighty Dragon, v. 8, snorting the fire of his wrath through his nose. The word 'fury' derives from the verb 'to burn'. Deuteronomy and Isaiah could both speak of God as Fire, Deut. 4: 24; Isa. 10: 17; 30: 27; 33: 14; cf. Matt. 3: 11. Or we see a fiery wind (coming from a volcano in Arabia?) whipping up the sea into a heap (or 'dyke' or 'dam') and leaving the bottom 'congealed', or 'frozen' or 'curdled', as scholars variously render it.

Yahweh is furiously angry at the powers of evil; cf. Mark 3: 5. In Ps. 78 his wrath is turned even upon Israel for not believing in the reality of his wrath. Here the enemy is shown to be greedy for blood. 'My desire shall have its fill of them', v. 9, the enemy say, using the same phrase as does Sheol when it greedily awaits the descent of the dead, Isa. 5: 14. Egypt's boast is an echo of Lamech's, Gen. 4: 23–24, the prototype of natural man lusting for blood.

11 Yahweh had a heavenly council to refer to: cf. Ps. 77: 13; 82: 1; 86: 8; 89: 7–8 (all of these passages are poetry!) These 'gods' were lesser divine beings, therefore actually non-beings, figments of human imagination. They exist, even as

Satan does, only because man believes in them. This is true
of all human religions. 'Majestic in holiness', or, with the
Versions, 'amongst the holy ones', i.e. the gods, or even, with
the LXX, 'clothed with glory'. By such means as this ('God
amongst the holy ones') Israel brings out the reality that God
is not a mere monad like the Allah of the Qoran. For God
can speak of himself as 'us', as the Head of a divine Holy Body,
Gen. 1: 26; Isa. 6: 8.

12–15   'The earth swallowed them', RSV. Here, as in
Babylonian and Canaanite literature, 'the earth' may refer
to the realm of the dead, viz. Sheol, since there is no definite
article on the noun; cf. Gen. 2: 6; Isa. 29: 4; Jonah 2: 6;
Psa. 148: 7, etc. God's wrath is here directed at Egypt. But
if it had been directed at Israel, the latter too would have been
swallowed up in the Underworld, Num. 26: 10. God is no
respecter of persons.

Yahweh's 'steadfast love', RSV, is his *ḥesedh*, that noun for
which there is no English translation, but which is rendered
variously by 'mercy', 'loving kindness', or one of a dozen other
English nouns; cf. the refrain in Ps. 136. In this love he has *led*
Israel as Israel's Shepherd, cf. 32: 34, in order to reach God's
'holy abode', RSV. In later days this would be the Tabernacle in which God's Presence dwelt, chap. 40. But as used in
the poem the word can mean a 'sheep-fold in the desert', or a
'camping-place for the night'.

We might ask if such an appropriation of God's steadfast love
by 'the people whom thou hast redeemed' is either tenable or a
mark of honest scholarship, when at the present moment
research points to the probability that not all of Israel stemmed
from those who crossed the Reed Sea; it would seem in fact
that only the 'Rachel' tribes came out in Moses' day, i.e.
Ephraim, Manasseh and Benjamin. Many scholars believe
that these three tribes were later joined by others who made
their way independently into Canaan, or who had never left
that land at all. If this theory is correct then we meet with the
manner in which God's Plan may proceed by the method of
adoption. At Josh. 24 there occurs just such a consolidation of
all the known tribes. There the covenant-making mentioned
at 24: 25–27 binds all of the tribes together as one, so that now
all can look back upon the exodus as *their* experience of the

grace of God. In later centuries those who returned from Babylonia are representatives of all twelve tribes, even though they had reached there in different centuries, Ezek. 37: 15–22. One listens to a class-room of second-generation Japanese children sitting amongst white children in a Californian school. All repeat in unison: 'Our fathers came over on the Mayflower'. In the same way all Israel could say: 'A wandering Aramean was my father; and he went down into Egypt and sojourned there, few in number; and there he became a nation . . . and the Lord brought *us* up out of Egypt with a mighty hand. . .'. Deut. 26: 5 ff. Even non-Israelites are able to repeat this credo, since, as we noted at 12: 38, they too were adopted into the People of God. In Rom. 9: 25–26, where Paul quotes Hosea 2: 23, we see that he is aware of the principle enunciated here, and is able to assure all men that through the one Israelite who was born in Bethlehem they too can now join in this great statement of faith; Rom. 11: 17–24; 1 Cor. 10: 1–5.

18   The poem ends with another basic credo, one that is well developed in later centuries; cf. Ps. 99: 1. It is the belief that God is king, the opposite of the notion that a god dies and rises again, as in the contemporary fertility cults, and it is found as early as in the poems preserved in Num. 23 and Deut. 33. The Israelites 'adopted' this idea too in days long before they had a human king, and although they had suffered so terribly under the king of Egypt. Under the latter they had experienced an amoral wielding of power. But in the poem we have the beginning of the triumphal march of Yahweh the King *with* his people till in the end he is crowned at his Holy Mount, the centre of the kingdoms of the world.

Israel thus recognizes that the concept of kingship demands also that of kingdom, cf. 19: 6. The nature of the kingdom too depends entirely on the nature of its king. This is why the later phrase 'The kingdom of God' is quite independent of geography, and defines the rule of a God who cares and who shares his life with his people in their ordinary secular exist- ence. Also it is to stand (with the LXX) 'for ever and to eternity and still more'!

19–21   The exultation of the moment is well marked by observing the women-folk. They might have crooned for their dead warrior-husbands, but here they sing and dance with abandon to Yahweh. They are expressing their gratitude to God for his 'salvation', 14: 13; 15: 2, not just with their mind, but with their whole being. This is not a 'religious' moment. Israel does not have a religion. Religion is that which man thinks about the divine. The Bible, in both Testaments, is interested in 'religion' only so far as to set it in contrast with Revelation. The reality set forth here is something that God has *done*. All that man can do at the moment therefore is to respond to God's act with exuberant joy. In a real sense, then, Miriam is born of this situation. God has now created the faith and co-operation of his people. Israel's faith is thus quite *sui generis*, and the exodus event is an absolute beginning; or, as the *Wisdom of Solomon* puts it plainly, the exodus is a new creation.

22–24   A whole new section of the book of Exodus begins here. We might head it *Wanderings in the Wilderness*. Ex has made a skilful continuous narrative out of the J and E materials at his disposal.

The excitement is over. The break with the past, and the reality of the problems that now go with a new life are once again focused upon by the use of the phrase 'three days'. But God is already in this new situation three days ahead of Israel; cf. 3: 18; 8: 27, and especially Num. 10: 33. Also in this new life Israel must learn to stand upon her own feet; a clutter of slaves who were not allowed even to think for themselves have now to learn to be responsible, decision-making adults – and immediately they fail. Only Moses keeps his head, and keeps his faith.

The first problem is water. Moses, in faith, uses a homoeopathic method of sweetening the waters, one which he had probably learned from his learned father-in-law. What he did, scientifically speaking, is not of first importance to us. The whole story may even be an aetiological legend. What is important is what God was doing in and through the incident. Israel's first free, self-chosen act in the free world of Shur is the act of Adam and Eve. Israel rebels against the God who has given freedom to man. As in Eden, with its four life-giving rivers, so in Shur. That Yahweh should be Israel's 'Fountain of life' now that they are out of Egypt and dependent upon their own resources Israel refuses to believe. This refusal forces Moses to 'shout' to God, shout with his whole being, physical and moral, in furious anger. (The English 'cried' suggests petulance or fear.) And God gives him the answer he needs. For Moses, unlike his people, is completely sure that, if only you have faith, salty water is no more difficult to sweeten than is removing a mountain to another place. Yet it is still more important, Moses recognizes, not to worry about what we are to eat and what we are to drink. For these problems belong to God.

To understand the issue here the use of the unexpected verb 'showed' is central. The basic meaning of the verb is to 'shoot'. But to 'teach' is to shoot ideas from one head into another. In doing so, however, the teacher 'reveals' what is in his own mind. We note that the noun from this verb is *Torah*, the theological name given to the Five Books of Moses, the Pentateuch. If Moses had performed on his own initiative as a mere medicine-man and thrown the bough he had selected into the brackish water, Israel would have just drunk gratefully, and learned nothing. Secular social service, the many good organizations or private agencies that work within the framework of our democratic society all do good work in giving drink to the thirsty. But after having given them drink, they leave them as thirsty as ever. Ex wants us to see, however, that giving a cup of cold water to a thirsty man *in the name of the Lord* is not mere social service; it is an eschatologically important moment in the ongoing Plan of the King.

25–26 The root of the noun 'statute' is 'to carve', 'to cut into', 'to chisel'. The word therefore pictorializes the unshakable reality of the mercy of God.

27 After smiting his people with thirst, Yahweh heals them with pure water, and soothes them with shade from the heat they encounter at the oasis of Elim. This oasis had twelve springs. Ex believes, of course, that all the twelve tribes were present there, so that there was one spring for each tribe, and one date-palm tree for each of the 70 clans that formed the People of God. Ex was thus declaring symbolically that the whole multitude of men, women and children, and strangers too, now encamped at this place were under the care of God's healing love.

CHAPTER 16

TAKE NO THOUGHT FOR THE MORROW

This chapter draws on all three sources, J, E and P. Driver would put the order of J as v. 1-5, 9-12, 6-8. We should compare the story here with Num. 11.

Six weeks after these exciting events just recorded Israel experiences a reaction. Before the exodus they had been a 'non-people'; now they are designated a 'congregation', RSV, a 'community', NEB and *Tor*. The exodus had been God's doing, not theirs; yet they do not yet trust this God who has done so much for them. Israel's unbelief is well expressed in verse in Ps. 78: 19, 'Can God spread a table in the wilderness?' 'This people' even accused Moses of being God's instrument to kill them off the moment they are born into their new freedom of life.

Arnold Toynbee, in *A Study of History*, 1972, p. 87, speaks of the transition of a people from a static condition to a dynamic activity, as one in which the genesis of every civilization consists. The unknown quantity, he says, is the reaction of the actors to the ordeal when it actually comes. 'Physical causes only operate through the hidden principles which play a part in forming our spirit and our character'.

4-5 God answers Israel's unbelief with words of love. He will not only provide bread for his people, he will *rain it down* upon them. So that its appearance will not be regarded as merely another natural phenomenon, like the plagues in Egypt, it is called 'bread from heaven', or, as Ps. 78: 25 calls it, 'The bread of angels'. In return they are to 'walk' in God's revelation, a word which later Judaism employs as a technical term.

Both at 15: 27 and here we note how close we are to the tone of the Sermon on the Mount. Even the clauses in the Lord's Prayer grow naturally out of this *historical* activity of Yahweh in the days of Moses.

(1) Our Father. We find this at 4: 22, where God is known as the Father of Israel.

(2) Which art in heaven. It is from there that he sends bread, 16: 4.

(3) Hallowed be thy name. 'Do not come near the spot where I am revealing my Name, for it is holy', 3: 5.

(4) Thy kingdom come. See at 15: 18.

(5) Thy will be done on earth. This has been happening historically.

(6) As it is in heaven. See 16: 4.

(7) Give us this day our daily bread. NT scholarship discusses the unusual word *epiousios*, 'daily', which occurs at Matt. 6: 11. Its origin and meaning are both in doubt. Does it mean 'necessary for existence', or 'for the current day', or is it 'the bread that belongs to today', as the Peshitta suggests, 'for our need'? The simplest explanation of the word is that it represents what is *pictured* at Ex. 16: 4, 'the thing of the day on its day', as the Hebrew says, with a double portion to cover the period when a man was not to do any gathering. In other words, 'our daily bread' comes to us from God by grace alone, with enough for holidays as well. This *daily* care now continues over the period of a whole generation. God does not give Israel a lump sum, so to speak, enough for 40 years. His kindness is to give enough for each day at a time. Paul regards such a divine action as sacramental, 1 Cor. 10: 1–11.

(8) And forgive us our trespasses. As Yahweh has just done, and which Israel has *seen* to be done.

(9) As we forgive them that trespass against us. The incident before us *created* in Israel the willingness and the ability to forgive Moses and Aaron.

(10) And lead us not into temptation. Do not bring us to the test. This is what Israel, hopefully, had learned about God in 15: 22–27.

(11) But deliver us from evil. What God had now done for Israel.

(12) For thine is the kingdom. See 15: 18.

(13) And the power. See 15: 2, 6.

(14) And the glory. God's glory has been made manifest as forgiveness and compassion, 16: 7.

(15) For ever and ever. This phrase depends upon the fact

of God's being I AM, the God of Abraham in the past, and the God who will be, 3: 12, in all days to come, 15: 18.

Since the book of Exodus presents us with a revelation of God expressed in historical pictures made visible in the life of Israel, the biblical theologian can be bold to assert that the one and only proof of God which we possess is the fact of Israel. Only those theologies that *begin* their thinking at this point can stand the test of time.

Moses now invites Israel to see this food as a mark of the compassion and forgiveness of the God who had already liberated them. This mark he calls God's 'glory'. Glory is frequently pictured in the OT as a kind of envelope around the person of God, aglow with light and fire. Man cannot see God, but man may see his glory, that is to say, man may discover God's presence-in-love and know the joy of being forgiven; cf. 33: 22.

In the evening, Moses said, quails would arrive. Israel was thus to live entirely by grace through faith, and must not expect to live by sight, by proof, or by an inner experience. After the quails would follow darkness, as at Creation, a kind of cosmic pause in God's act of grace. Then on the following day, the manna would arrive. With the coming of the light men would see God's act of renewal.

7–12   The minister of God is aware that of himself he is nothing. All that is happening so wonderfully and so graciously is of God alone. Yet, as God's spokesman, Moses, through Aaron, must summon all Israel to 'come near before the Lord'. Thus Moses creates a situation consonant with that of a law court. God is Judge; Israel is the accused; Moses is Israel's advocate; the court sits beneath the open sky; the sun, moon and stars are the witnesses. And so there is born a type, a Gattung, of prophetic utterance known to scholars by the Hebrew word *ribh*, one that continues down the centuries and ends only at Pilate's court in Jerusalem; cf. Isa. 1: 2 ff; 40: 1–2; Micah 1: 2 ff, etc. In judgment also God is all grace. They turned and 'looked towards the wilderness', and saw the emptiness of desolation, the area which their semitic neighbours peopled with the powers of evil. But Israel saw, not waste, but glory, in terms of what we have suggested above at v. 6; cf. Psa. 104: 1–4.

Moses now demythologizes this ancient picture thinking and uses it promptly to interpret theologically the nature of God. Yahweh is indeed unknowable; he dwells within the thick darkness of the storm-cloud from the desert. But particularly he reveals himself by means of his 'robe' as he makes himself known to Israel by being *with* them in their need of him. '*Then* you shall know that I am Yahweh your God', when my glory is made visible as compassion *experienced*.

13–21 The two natural events are therefore seen in a new light. The people had sighed for the 'fleshpots' of Egypt. There they had been depressed and impoverished slaves, had seldom eaten meat, or even bread 'to the full'. Now God showers fresh meat upon them, and so much 'bread' that they have to leave aside what they cannot eat. Here then is grace answering unfaith.

People brought up in Egypt would not have known what quails looked like. Every year great numbers of these birds migrate from Europe to Africa over Sinai; they avoid Egypt's deserts. After crossing the Mediterranean Sea they rest in Sinai. In days before modern man ruined the ecology of the area they appeared in far vaster numbers than they do today. Sinai was then not nearly so dry as it is now. It was only in the Middle Ages that goats destroyed the vegetation that Moses met – brushwood, including the tamarisk and the acacia trees mentioned later.

That there is theological significance in the manna is suggested by the question asked in wonder – '*Man-hu*, what is it?' This of course is only the popular etymology of the word. Manna was probably a juicy exudent of certain plant-lice which fed on the sap of the tamarisk tree. This turns hard overnight, and melts again when the sun grows hot, when the ants plunder it. We might translate as: 'A fine, scale-like thing, fine as hoar frost'. Yet the LXX has 'like white coriander seed', cf. John 6: 31. What we are interested to notice, however, is that God *each day* set a table before *each one* of his people, and *each day each man's* cup ran over.

22–30 This is the first time that the word Sabbath occurs in the Bible as a noun in its own right, though it is implied in 12: 14–19, 42, and in Gen. 2: 1–3. It is preceded here by another new and very emphatic noun built from it, viz.

shabbathon. In later centuries this longer word was used for special rest days, such as the Day of Atonement, the Feast of Trumpets, the first and the eighth days of the Feast of Tabernacles, and so on; cf. 35: 2; Lev. 25: 5.

Using the developed theological insights of P, Ex herewith declares that this special day of rest points to something so basic to Israel's election that it even precedes the Decalogue. It belongs with the rescuing of Israel and the saving of her life. In this sense then this Sabbath was made for man. Throughout six days God had created the heavens and the earth, and then God rested on the seventh day. Throughout the six weeks that followed the crossing of the Sea, v. 1, God had *worked* in the heart and mind of Israel, and had *created* the new relationship to himself by eliciting from them an obedience that Moses was helping to maintain. To mark this new creation Israel was being given the chance to join with Yahweh in resting upon this new seventh day. In joy and peace and quiet they might discover through worship and through *remembering* what God had done and how God was both Creator and Saviour. God was thus using this Sabbath day to create in their consciousness the *meaning* of their election, even although some in Israel persisted in putting greed before faith, v. 27. Yet Yahweh persists with grace. 'See!' says Moses, v. 29; 'Apply your mind to this and *see* its significance' (NEB misses this emphasis). Three times over this special Sabbath is called 'today'. The emphasis made here thus lifts it into the sphere of the eternal 'today', through its eschatological and sacramental significance. Israel needed this 'sacrament'. Israel could not believe in grace alone. So they were to go back to where they had already met with grace, each man to his 'place', RSV, v. 29. (This is a pregnant word in Hebrew. Literally it means 'the space a man needs to stand on'. So it pictorializes the dignity of the individual person; compare the Scottish paraphrase 54: 4, 'Then will he own his servant's name before his Father's face, and in the New Jerusalem appoint my soul a place'.)

This passage does not deal with Ex's idea of the origin of the weekly Sabbath referred to in the 'Fourth Commandment'. Israel had adopted the weekly rest-day from the Babylonians long before. We find the seven-day cycle already in Gen. 29:

27; Jud. 14: 12; 2 Kings 4: 23; 11: 5 ff; Amos 8: 5; Hos. 2:
13; Isa. 1: 13. In Gen. 1 of course we meet with the seven-day
week, that is to say, a quarter of the moon's phase. In Babylonia
the word spoke of a tabu, for on the 1, 7, 15, 21 and 28th days
of the month one dared not offend the gods. Israel, however,
demythologized, even denaturalized the Babylonian Sabbath,
and made it independent of the moon's quarters, and finally
put the celebration of it 'under God'. There is no moon-
worship connected with the Sabbath in the OT. In fact, Israel
secularized the day, using it for the refreshment of man and
beast, for joy and not for fear; the soil even was to benefit
from its celebration.

31–36   We now have a new name for the People of God,
viz. 'House of Israel'. Israel has already been called 'The sons
of Israel', 16: 9, as well as God's 'son' in the singular, 4: 22.
We are witnessing an ever-deepening meaning to the words
'congregation' and 'community'.

Moses now localizes, 'incarnates' God's gracious goodness
by bidding Aaron undertake the cultic act recorded at v. 33.
By Ex' day, Aaron was regarded as the 'high priest', literally,
of all Israel's cultic development. We have no knowledge of
the fate of this particular manna, preserved in a sealed jar,
nor do we know when it met its end. (The LXX piously
embellishes the word 'jar' to 'a golden pot'.) Probably it did
not survive the capture of the Ark by the Philistines, 1 Sam. 4:
11. Hebrews 9: 4 reminds us that when the pot of manna was
placed at that one spot on earth where God had made himself
known in a special way, 40: 34, worshipping Israel could
recognize the union of the mystery of the 'holy' with the
mystery of divine compassion and grace. We note in passing
that Ex presupposes the existence here of the Tabernacle that
is built only later on, chaps. 35–40. But since he believes that
the manna continued to be available throughout the whole
forty years, what seems to us to be a discrepancy is not such to
him.

The bestowal of the manna ends, according to Josh. 5: 12,
once the people reach the 'land flowing with milk and honey',
for there they find all the natural food that they need.

CHAPTER 17

ROCK OF AGES

1–3   Now follows a rapid decline of faith in which even Moses himself acquiesces. It happens in the context of the second 'water-story'; the first was at 15: 22–25; there is a third at Num. 20: 2–13; and it happens while Israel is travelling 'by stages' (see Num. 33: 1–49), that is, by a day's march at a time, 'according to the commandment of the Lord'.

The mean element in Israel's indictment of Moses is that, like some hard-bitten and disloyal strikers today, they are 'merely claiming their rights'. 'All we claim is what is due to us; it is not our concern where you are to find the water, that is your worry, not ours. But we won't stand by and see our children thirsty'. They 'stoned the prophets' indeed, says Luke 13: 34. Yet selfishness and disloyalty between man and man are ipso facto disloyalty to God.

4–5   Once again Moses 'shouts' to God, all the pain and the fear and the loneliness of the situation in his cry. The answer comes quietly and soothingly. Moses is to do the daring thing; he is to show that he is not afraid of his people's threat to lynch him, but is to demonstrate that he is wholly committed to Yahweh. He is to select a few leaders who believe as he believes and he is to walk right along in front of the threatening crowd, holding in his hand his old shepherd's crook, the rod he had used to strike the Nile. On that occasion the rod made the Nile undrinkable. Would the people notice it now in his hand and remember? What would he use it for on this occasion? Could it now give them drinking water, the 'water of life', in the dead wilderness around them?

6   Complete security of faith could not be better pictured than by the words of God, 'Behold, I will stand before you there'. The verbal active participle can mean anything in the way of movement except standing still! Even as Moses moves around, looking for the right spot to act, God is *with* him in all

that he does. God is the God of prevenient grace. Wherever
Moses turns, God is there first. In the darkness of the moment
Moses stretches out his rod, in faith. Is he acting simply as a
'dowser'? Ex would be shocked at the very suggestion. This is
because he believed that God had reached and was standing
at the rock before Moses did. So God was there when Moses
struck it. The water that issued from it was therefore God's
gracious gift to Israel once again; it was a sign of creative
life in this wilderness of selfishness and insolent unfaith.

A legend about this rock circulated towards the end of the
OT period. It told how it broke off from its base and rolled
along after Israel as the people travelled, stopping when they
stopped, but always opposite Moses' tent. The water then
issued in twelve streams according to the number of the tribes
of Israel. Targ. Onk. on Num. 21: 7 also suggests by way of
interpretation that the Rock that followed Moses continued
with Israel on their journey. Yet when St. Paul, in 1 Cor. 10:
3-4 declares: 'All ate the same supernatural food, and all
drank the same supernatural drink. For they drank from the
same supernatural Rock which followed them, and the Rock
was Christ', RSV, some commentators dismiss his exegesis
lightly as 'mere rabbinical allegorizing'. Such is a superficial
judgment. For the Rabbis retained into the early Christian
period the genius of the OT for expressing theology in picture
language. Paul knew that the manna and the water were
mere physical elements; yet he called them both *pneumatikos*.
But so had the Psalms before him, when, in picture language,
they had spoken of 'the bread of angels'. Paul is merely being
true to the Priestly theological interpretation of this event.
He is saying that 'the Word addressed Moses; the Word
"kept moving" ahead of Moses till the Word was present at
the Rock'. And so he ends his argument by saying, 'and that
Rock was the eternal Word'; cf. also Deut. 32: 4, 15, 18; Isa.
17: 10; 26: 4 – all of which are in poetic language.

7   The whole incident shows us that the great sin is to
ask the question, 'Is the Lord among us or not?' Israel, in con-
tention, *meribah*, looks for proof, *massah*, not noticing how God,
by his very nature, gives food to the hungry and water to the
thirsty; cf. Ps. 95: 8–9; Matt. 11: 2–6.

8–13   It is Amalek that takes the initiative in this battle.

Israel does not provoke it. The Amalekites are the people named from their ancestor Amalek. They were probably not a tribe, but a loosely federated desert people. Amalek is Esau's grandson, according to tradition. His descendants are therefore identified with Edom, and Edom is the 'non-people' of God that had scorned their election, selling it for a pot of soup.

Israel is now refreshed after drinking the water that God has provided. The story that follows is no doubt founded on a factual incident; but it is told in the manner of 'The Pilgrim's Progress'. The latter narrates the truth, but in parabolic pictures.

We note that for once we do not have the phrase, 'The Lord said unto Moses'. Instead we watch Moses reacting to the situation by using his own common sense as a leader of those men, women and children for whom he is responsible under God. We watch Moses, the man, becoming Israel's 'guardian angel', 2 Kings 2: 12; Dan. 12: 1, on the ground that, as we noted in chap. 3, the OT draws no line between God's agents on earth or 'in heaven'. This passage shows no divine objection to the defence of the innocent, especially when they are attacked by lawless evil. Yet this attack represents still another divine test; so we learn that it becomes part of Yahweh's total plan and will for his people. For Amalek represents the basic wickedness of mankind, Gen. 6: 5: 'Amalek was the first of the nations, but in the end he shall come to destruction', Num. 24: 20 – part of Balaam's oracle.

They fight at Rephidim. But this name itself is symbolic. The word means 'props', 'supports'. The choice of name is therefore a midrash on the action of Moses' two friends in propping up his arms when they grew tired. Moses himself does not lead the fight; Moses is the intermediary between God and man, sitting high up on a hill, part-way 'up' to the divine. He himself must not fail in intensity of purpose or in strength of body. When his arms drop, the enemy prevails. But when his arms are (literally) 'faithful', v. 12, that is 'steady', the God who is faithful honours Moses' faithfulness. Yet God continues to do so even when Moses, through sheer weakness of the flesh, cannot hold his own arms up any longer.

By calling Moses' crook 'the staff of *elohim*' (the Hebrew word for God) Ex declares that God is involved in Moses' symbolic action. The E tradition, through which it comes down to Ex, is more prone to midrash, parabolic writing, than the others. But we are to remember that Hebrew man believed in the creative power of both word and action. In like manner the Maoris of New Zealand once sought to conquer the spirit of their enemy by symbolic acts of defiance before they met them hand to hand in close combat. In the same spirit, the name Joshua occurs here, and most properly. For the name means 'Yahweh saves', 14: 13. The presence of Joshua is thus in part an interpretation of the event in which he shares.

14   We are not to regard this divine command as emanating from 'that savage god of the OT, Jehovah'. To suggest this is to approach the book of Exodus from a humanistic angle, and to set ourselves up as its judge. The biblical view is that there is no such thing as love, no such thing as goodness, no such thing as evil, per se. These nouns describe only concepts, not realities. If there is no man, then there is no love. What is real is 'a person loving', 'a person hating', 'a person *doing evil*', or '*doing good*'. 'Goodness' is thus the act of a person as he gives a cup of cold water to a thirsty man. As the non-people of God, Amalek is jealous of Israel's election. Writing almost contemporaneously with Malachi, Ex can agree with that prophet that God *hates* Amalek (or Edom), Mal. 1: 2-3. It is only the sentimental humanist who is aghast at such biblical language. God hates, God rends like a lion, Hos. 5: 14, 13: 7 ff. God even destroys his own people, and not just Edom, like a forest fire that turns and laps up even the few trees that the flames have missed, Isa. 6: 13. The biblical God would not be righteous himself unless he hated evil. God would not be love unless he were willing to destroy all that seeks to destroy love. Yet even such language is not biblical. This is because hate does not exist apart from men who harbour hatred in their hearts; who make war on the innocent; who 'love' to destroy all that is creative and wholesome in the activities of other men. That is to say, God's hatred of evil can be turned only upon *people* when they act hatefully. The love of God for his world must of course be effective in the end, since it is the love of *God*. That is why his love must necessarily destroy, not perverted wicked-*ness*, but perverted wicked *Amalek*. God's war must be perpetual war, till he wins in the end, when he 'wipes out the remembrance of Amalek from under heaven'. Thus, so far from being the word of a fierce war-god of old, this passage is in full conformity with Christ's ruthless condemnation of wicked *people* (cf. 'Woe unto you . . .') and with the terrible symbolism that we find about the wicked in the book of Revelation.

15–16   No wonder Moses regards the Word of God that is addressed to him as unspeakably good news, news that must be told to all generations down the centuries. It is that 'God is victorious over all the powers of evil'. In God's good time he will not only destroy all the Amaleks of history, he will see that they are even '*forgotten*'.

Awareness of this divine promise motivates Moses to set up an altar, that is, express an exultant 'thanks' to God. He calls this altar, 'Yahweh is my banner'. Moses would probably erect an object like a signal pole. Was it formed from 'the staff of God' that he had carried? Did it have a cross-bar, so that on the top of the hill there stood a cross with out-stretched arms, as many scholars believe? The phrase, 'A hand upon Yahweh's banner', RSV, is obscure. NEB interprets by translating, 'My oath upon it'. *Tor* has 'Hand upon the throne of the Lord'. But whatever action took place, it was clearly meant to be a solemn dedication of the pole. Its erection celebrated the immediate past victory of Yahweh over Amalek; but it also promised Yahweh's final triumph over all evil in whatever form it would seek to incarnate itself in human history. Moses could act thus in faith because he had heard Yahweh promise Israel that he would become *with* his people, 3: 12, always.

CHAPTER 18

THE HEATHEN BLESS THE
LORD

This story probably emerged from the E tradition, conflated
with an element of J. It displays what appears to be real
historical verisimilitude; cf. also Num. 10: 29–36; 11: 11–17;
27–30. Some scholars believe this chapter hides the making of a
treaty between the Midianites and the Israelites and that v. 12
speaks of a covenant-meal between them.

Even Jethro now knows, living some distance away, how
everything that has so far happened to Israel is what 'God had
done ... how Yahweh had brought Israel out of Egypt'.
Israel, he recognizes, is indeed 'God's People'. God addresses
her, not as 'you slaves', but as 'my people'. Zipporah, Moses'
wife, was one of them. She had borne her part in the tension of
God's visitation of his people. Moses seems to have spurned
her for her daring and obviously unwomanly act recorded at
4: 24–26. She had had to stay with her father when Moses
returned to Egypt. This vouches for the basic historicity of the
tale, showing that husband and wife had long been separated.
One of their two boys is called 'A resident-alien there', and
the other is called 'God is my help'. The meeting between the
two strong men, Moses and Jethro, is well described in terms
of the polite formalities of desert peoples. Ex, for theological
reasons, places this meeting at Mount Sinai, 'where he was
camped' (or, 'kept on encamping').

6   'One told Moses'. We are glad to note that, in telling
his story, Moses makes no reference to himself, but gives all
the glory to Yahweh; for the way to win men into the biblical
faith is to forget the pronoun 'I' and merely tell what great
things the Lord has done. Jethro is so overcome at hearing the
whole story of the mighty acts of God that he thereupon 're-
joices', RSV, but more probably 'identifies himself' with

Moses and with the purpose of God that is being revealed in
Israel. He then goes on to bless Yahweh in such a manner
that he shows he has commited himself to the Lord entirely
in response to what he has heard. He is the first pagan outside
of Egypt to be won by the recital of *what God has done in history
and through his people, Israel.* Jethro then seals his new-found
faith with an act of sacrifice (what its nature is we do not
know), followed by a religious feast. To this 'all the elders
of Israel' are invited; they go, of course, representing the whole
people of God.

Once we let ourselves think as Ex thinks we see how extraordinary it is that a foreigner like Jethro could come straight
into the fold of Israel's knowledge of God by faith alone, yes,
and that merely by *hearing.* How extraordinary it is also that
the new convert should at once *bless Yahweh*; for in early days
the verb actually meant to put the hands upon the head of the
one to be blessed. How humble is the God of Israel!

The so-called Kenite hypothesis of the origin of the name
Yahweh stems from here. It is that Jethro had from the beginning worshipped the divine Being under the name YHWH
(or something like it); and that Moses learned this name
when he lived with Jethro. Then he gave it to the divinity
whom he met at the Bush. On the other hand, the fact that
Jethro identified himself with *Moses'* understanding of the name
Yahweh only when he heard what Yahweh had *done*, serves
rather to reverse the order of thought.

13–27   Now that Jethro has identified himself with Israel
he possesses the necessary qualifications to offer revolutionary
advice. 'To inquire of God', v. 15, incidentally, implies that
Moses 'gave Torah' in reply, 'decisions', RSV, 'laws', NEB,
'teachings', *Tor*, as the priests did in later centuries. But of
course God gave the Torah to Israel only later on in the story.
On the other hand, in the deeply creative experiences through
which Moses was living we cannot doubt that elements of the
Torah, later formulated at Sinai, were already forming in his
mind.

'The way in which they must walk' shows the 'pedestrian'
nature of Moses' faith, as something to be lived and worked
out in the secular sphere. 'Choose able men' (or, 'physically
strong', or 'morally acceptable'); the verb implies 'insight'

on Moses' part into the character of men. The parallel narrative in Num. 11 calls these men 'elders', old men, and puts their number at 70; cf. 1: 5, where this number has already been attached to all Israel. Yet 'elders' have already been mentioned at 18: 12 *before* the selection of 'judges'.

22 'To judge' means more than to settle disputes. Any trained counsellor today, for example, can help husband and wife reconcile their differences. But it requires a knowledge of the mind of God to teach the couple in question what the mind of God is for them. The minister has a much more profound task to do than the marriage counsellor. Thus we find that Jethro advises Moses, the minister of God, to do all the preaching and teaching, for he represents the people before God, v. 19, leaving the wise advice and legal guidance to the 'unordained'. We see no line drawn between 'religion' and 'law' at this point, however, in that Moses undertakes to adjudicate the hard cases himself, v. 26. Yet the distinction between the two reflects the two types of law we shall meet later on, viz., the apodictic, as in the Decalogue, and the casuistic or case-law, which occurs in the Book of the Covenant, 20: 22–23: 33.

Ex notes that the saving act of God at the Sea preceded the ability to place law and order in their proper setting in the nation's life, that is to say, grace precedes law. Then, after the four-fold qualifications of the 'judge' we meet with a series of military terms, corresponding to our colonel, captain, sergeant and corporal. In other words, despite this new vision of law and order, Moses cannot escape from regarding Israel as still 'the army of the Lord'.

CHAPTER 19

THE COVENANT

Chapters 19–24 are recognized as one coherent whole. Ex fits this unit into his total narrative.

Three months to a day after leaving Egypt Israel reaches Mount Sinai. They are now to spend almost a year at its base. Ex expects us to realize that a divinity dwelt in this two-mile long, three-peaked granite ridge. The ridge is composed of Jebel Musa (7519 ft.), Jebel Katerina (8551 ft.) and Jebel Serbal (6759 ft.) as they are known today. Jebel Musa (i.e. Mount Moses) is the only one of the three with any level ground below it suitable for setting up a camp. One of these peaks was known to Moses as Horeb. Moses now 'goes up to the divinity'; but it was not the god of the mountain but Yahweh who 'called (down) to him out of the mountain'. The reply came from him who is 'I will become with you' whom Moses had met before; cf. 3: 12 'You shall serve God upon *this* mountain'. Yahweh's 'withness' is both historical and particularistic.

3-4   No matter how high Moses climbs Yahweh is still beyond his reach. Yet Moses can always *hear the Word*. The people do not hear. The Word comes in rhythmical prose and in poetic language: '... shall say to the house of Jacob, and tell to the people of Israel; ... how I bore you on eagles' wings'; cf. Deut. 32: 11.

The eagle was known for its unusual devotion to its young. It too lived on mountain tops. In teaching its young to fly it carried them upon its back to those great heights that overlook the plains of Sinai, then it dropped them down into the depths. If the baby was still too young and too bewildered to fly, father-eagle would swoop down beneath it, catch it on his back, and fly up again with it to the eyrie on the crags above. And that, says the divine voice, is 'how I brought you out of Egypt to myself'!

5-6   The words that Moses 'hears' and formulates in these two verses crystallize as one of the basic events in the story of man. For here Yahweh (and it is always Yahweh, never Elohim) now promises to be 'with' all Israel in an intimate and unconditional manner within the framework of a covenant. In response Israel is to do two things – (1) obey, and (2) guard the covenant; both responses, however, being dependent upon the initial act of Yahweh.

(1) Israel is not asked to believe in God. That notion is pagan, in that believing requires an act of the human will. The Psalmist put it well when he said, 'Relax, and know that I am God', Ps. 46: 10. Ex too insists that what Israel has to do is just to 'remember' what *God* has done, 13: 3; cf. 1 Cor. 11: 24. Thereafter follows obedience. It is in obedience that a man finds fullness of faith, not in philosophizing about life.

(2) Israel is not required to 'be good'. Israel is given the task of guarding the Covenant, that is, of being faithful to *it*, and so to proceed through the wilderness of life knowing that the Plan which God has in mind is to come to fruition through the special relationship he has elected to maintain with his people. Thus there is no suggestion of merit on Israel's part, nor is there any suggestion of reward.

Within only the last twenty years it has been discovered that in those days a clan or even an individual might choose a special god and enter into a type of covenant with him. There is an extensive literature on this issue. But of course Israel did the reverse. In this passage it is not Israel that chooses a god; it is Yahweh that chooses Israel.

This special relationship is described pictorially. Near Eastern kings were masters of all their lands and peoples. The king owned everything. He owned even the possessions of his subjects. Such owning, however, would give him little personal satisfaction. In his palace, therefore, he kept a box in which lay his own very special jewels. At times he would lift them out, handle them, and say to himself, 'These are my very own'. In the same way, though Yahweh was Lord of all the earth, 'for all the earth is mine', Israel was to be that box of jewels whom God could enjoy in a special way. Yet Israel's special relationship is not one of favouritism. Israel is to be a 'kingdom of priests'. A priest is not concerned with his own salvation;

his concern is for the salvation of his flock. He is the intermediary between God and man, and custodian of the Revelation. In this way Israel is to be God's corporate priest to all
mankind, Isa. 49: 6; 61: 6; and to that end must remain
closely bound to God within the bonds of a covenant. She
must be a *holy* nation, i.e. set apart, since she is now bound to
the *holy* God; cf. Deut. 7: 6; 14: 2; 26: 18; and 1 Peter 2: 9.
Israel now has a job to do; this is a blessed thing for her; it
will give her a sense of joy and meaning and purpose in life.
L. Köhler puts it: 'There is scarcely a word which is so central
to the OT as the word joy. It is Israel's task to serve God with
joy and with a glad heart'. Prof. James Hastings wrote at the
beginning of this century: 'Covenant theology expressed the
difference between a God whose purpose was known and whose
character could be trusted, and a God whose nature was
mysterious and whose actions were unpredictable'.

The word used here for 'nation' is that which described any
unhallowed Gentile people. Israel's holiness is to come through
obedience to the divine will. In fine, since all the earth belongs
to Yahweh, and Israel now belongs to him in a special way,
Yahweh has given all the earth to Israel – not to possess, but
to serve and to care for under God. Israel, free of any world
dominion, is now free to be the servant of the world.

World community through human organizations, such as
the United Nations, is therefore not an ultimate, but only a
proximate goal. Judaism has before it the ultimate goal of the
Messianic Age, Marxism of the perfect society, Christianity of
the Kingdom of God. Ex shows here that only God can bring
about the ultimate kingdom of love and justice. Ex would look
back to the Return from Exile in 538 B.C. and see its incom-
plete nature as the attainment of only a proximate goal. Over
the door-way of the United Nations building in New York
is engraved Isaiah's passage, 2: 4, about beating swords into
ploughshares; but in this inscription the preceding verse is
ignored; it declares that nations shall one day live in peace
together *when they have listened to the Word of God that has reached*
them through the covenant people.

The concept of covenant is basic to the biblical revelation. God
loves covenants. He has already made covenant with all mankind, Gen. 9: 8, and with each of the Patriarchs in turn. Yet

each new covenant is essentially a development of the one preceding it, and expresses ever more clearly the basic biblical reality of the sovereignty of God. In other words, there is only *one* covenant between God and man. Yet Ex would know the passage that speaks of a new covenant still to come, Jer. 31: 31–34. The word for 'new' in it that Jeremiah uses is a form of the word for 'new moon'. The new moon, really the full moon in OT times, is not a different moon each month. Jeremiah does not speak of a 'second covenant' apart from the first. It is always the same old moon, but each time renewed and fulfilled in its beauty. Jeremiah looks to the day when the imposed covenant of Exodus 19 will be individualized and internalized, that is, when Israel's *personal*, living God will enter into a new depth of *personal* relationships with 'each' *living* Israelite, Jer. 31: 34, all of whom belong together within the whole covenant people of God, Ezek. 11: 20. Thus if the NT writers declare that this Jeremianic hope became history when Christ called the one and only Covenant *his* Covenant (note that the word 'new' at Matt. 26: 28 is missing in the best texts – cf. RSV) this new covenant cannot in any sense supersede the old; rather it is the flowering and confirmation of the ancient covenant made at Sinai. The phrase 'new covenant', we should note, occurs only once in the NT, at 2 Cor. 3: 6, and there it is clearly a reference to the words used by Jeremiah. So Ezekiel can express the ultimate potentiality of the Covenant, bearing as it does the explosive power of the Word within it, as a 'total', 'comprehensive', covenant, Ezek. 37: 26. For such adjectives convey best the meaning of the Hebrew *shalom*. In his *Theology*, (I, p. 38) Eichrodt is now able to say that history began *on that day* (19: 1), with the utterance of the Word, v. 3, because, he goes on, 'on that day Church History began'.

7–8 The tragedy is that Israel did not keep her word. The reality of Israel's infidelity was especially clear to Hosea. He likened this covenant between God and Israel made at Sinai to the covenant of marriage with Moses acting as the minister, and Israel, the Bride, replying with the promise 'I do'. Hosea thus gave the Covenant a whole new dimension. He used the word *ḥesedh*, 'loyalty-in-love' to express what should ideally be the cement binding the two parties to the covenant as one.

The Covenant is therefore not to be taken lightly. It is a deep mystery of grace. As Abraham Heschel put it: 'The Covenant means history as God experiences it'. It is eschatological in its significance, belonging to both time and eternity. It leads us back to the heartening assurance, as we have noted, that the fact of Israel in covenant is the one proof of God that God has thought necessary for us to have. Paradoxically, then, the revelation of the Covenant is made from out of a 'thick cloud'. For God continues to remain the Hidden God even as he lets himself be the Revealed God; that is why the 'people could hear' only because of the dedication and obedience of Moses to the call of God to be the interpreter.

10–25   It was John Wesley who invented the saying 'Cleanliness is next to godliness'. Perhaps he was thinking of a passage such as this. Basically we find here the ancient concept of *taboo*, and meet with primitive rites of cleanliness common to all desert peoples. If today we imagine that ancient man lived a 'natural life' to the extent that he was uninhibited about sex, then we have only to note here that the worship of God took precedence over sexual customs. Man's awareness of this is symbolized by his putting on clean clothes; cf. Matt. 22: 11–13. And once again the suggestion that Israel held the right precedence and that her customs did not just develop from natural life in the desert is expressed by using the phrase that God continued to remain three days ahead of her, v. 11.

Now it is as if the great mountain shook from a high voltage electric discharge, so that only those wearing rubber boots, such as Moses wore, could venture upon it. So great and awesome is the divine Presence that mere man dare not approach the Majesty; cf. 2 Sam. 6: 7; Acts 5: 1 ff. Even the domestic animals share in man's culpability, for of course they are part of the communal *nephesh*, personality, of the whole people. Israel can exist in the marvel of the Real Presence by grace alone. The idea of an electric discharge is underlined by the description that follows of a tropical storm, with great flashes of lightning and peals of thunder, trumpeting and echoing from peak to peak. The sounding of a ram's horn, v. 19, marked from early days the opening of a sacred festival heralding the entry of the god into the sanctuary. The very ground now shakes from the thunder-claps, the peaks are lost in the black rain clouds columning up to heaven in tall pillars that in turn are lit up from within by the lightning flashes that look like fire.

The symbolism of the whole passage is that at this eschatological moment we have a union of earth and heaven (the sky). What we have here therefore is a theological picture of 'the first day of the last day', because of the reality that 'our God is a consuming fire'. Isaiah 33: 14 can ask the question, 'Who can dwell with the devouring fire?'

The narrative does not fall into the error therefore of regarding the divinity of the mountain-tops as actually *being* the storm itself, as we find in contemporary Canaanite literature. The distance between Yahweh and his world of Nature is altogether preserved by the words, 'Yahweh came *down* upon Mount Sinai, to the top of the mountain', v. 20, so that Moses has still to go up if he is to hear the Word at all. When there, Moses has to repeat his instructions about the awesome holiness and otherness of God in order to emphasize that the people are not to 'break through' under any circumstances. For the whole mountain is now an offering of fire to Yahweh. According to a secondary tradition, however, Aaron is to go up and enter the awesome holiness, as a symbol of the priestly intermediary between the living God and sinful Israel.

This whole long and moving build-up is meant to preface the absolute eschatological significance of the divine utterance that is to follow in chap. 20. It points to this, that we dare not take the Ten Commandments as the mere summation of the conscience of humanity, but see them as the Word of God issuing from out of the mystery of the Godhead. The Ten Commandments are not even addressed to all humanity. They are addressed solely to the Covenant People of the living God.

CHAPTER 20

THE DECALOGUE

The word 'Decalogue' means 'Ten Words'. The word 'commandments' does not occur here. We have ten statements, ten fiats, from out of the mystery and awe of the storm on the mountain. We approach the 'Ten Commandments' wrongly if we separate them from this context, regard them as timeless utterances, and seek to apply them to the life of all mankind.

Let us note the following:

(1) The 'Ten Words' are not all commands. The first is a pronouncement of grace.

(2) Coming from the thunderous divine voice, 19: 19, these 'Words' are alive since God is alive. Therefore they can grow and develop and adapt themselves as the centuries proceed. They do not represent a Kantian categorical imperative, but the will of the God who has said he would continue to become 'with' Israel.

(3) They are addressed, not to all mankind, but to the Covenant People alone, 19: 3–6. As an element in Israel's election to service the people are to obey these Words, enflesh them, so to speak, and thus to witness to them in the eyes of the world. In this way Israel will fulfil the promise that God had made to Abraham, Gen. 12: 3, 'By you all the families of the earth shall be blessed'.

(4) They are addressed to a nation that has just been rescued from slavery. Thus they are to be seen as constituent elements in the life of a free people whom God has willed into being. We are to remember that the *dabhar*, the 'word', is both Word and Power-to-make-the-word-effective at the same time.

(5) They are not directed at the whole world. The living of the moral life can be expected only of a people that has first been saved. Morals follow upon grace.

(6) The word 'thou' is to be retained, for each Word is addressed, not only to the people as a whole, but to each

individual as a unique personality. This new thing in the world's history is to be emphasized; cf. 'Son of man, stand upon thy feet, and I will speak with thee', Ezek. 2: 1.

(7) The Decalogue is propositional revelation. Since it is the Word of the *living* God it too is 'alive'. This Word renders human words eternally significant. The Word is the 'backside' of the word. It alters, translates, meets new cultures, becomes flesh in ever new situations; it is the Word in it which gives the word the germinating power it needs to fulfil itself. The Word is *not* Law. It is the Revelation of 'I AM with you', by the very nature of his being with us. Thus the Word is no longer 'in heaven', but 'in Israel's heart and mouth', Deut. 30: 11–14, so that Israel can now *do* it.

In the original the Words are, of course, not numbered. There are at least three possible ways of numbering them. These are:

(1) The Jewish way, to which we adhere here.

(2) The Greek Orthodox and Reformed way. That is to call v. 3 Commandment number 1.

(3) The Roman Catholic and Lutheran way. That is to make vv. 3–6 the First Commandment, and then to cut v. 17 into two commands.

The Jewish way alone, I would submit, (1) sees the words in their context, (2) is aware that living words grow with the passage of time, (3) recognizes the relationship between God's saving act and the moral life, and (4) provides a neat 5–5 set of words to fit upon two tables of stone in the big consonants that appear in the Sinai script we now possess.

Here is the possible original short form of the Decalogue:

Plate I

I	I, YHWH, am thy God	3 words
II	Thou shalt have no other gods in my Presence	5 words
III	Thou shalt not use YHWH's Name perversely	5 words
IV	Remember to keep the Sabbath day holy	4 words
V	Respect thy father and mother	3 words

Plate II

VI	Thou shalt not kill	2 words
VII	Thou shalt not commit adultery	2 words
VIII	Thou shalt not steal	2 words
IX	Thou shalt not give false evidence	3 words
X	Thou shalt not covet	2 words

The First Word, v. 2, may well have been just ANI YHWH, as at 6: 2, a matter of two words. This might then have become 'I am the Lord your God'; and then later generations, teaching it to their children, would get them to sum up the basic credo of Israel by adding, 'who brought you out of the land of Egypt, out of the house of bondage'. We note that YHWH does *not* say 'I am the Creator'. The whole emphasis is upon redemption. But then redemption is re-creation. In this way the later Jewish heritage wisely kept the moral law in perspective as the *outcome* of what God had done first. Here then is the residuum of a preamble such as was used in ancient secular codes; cf. Lev. 26: 13.

The Second Word, v. 3–6, emphasizes the uniqueness of YHWH, and thus the uniqueness of Israel's election. It does not make an explicit statement on monotheism, for it presupposes the existence of other gods. But that makes it highly relevant today, in that the People of God are still tempted to put Self, Success, Fellowship, Social Justice, before or in place of YHWH, the God of redemption. In the cold light of the Exile in Babylon Deutero-Isaiah could rate all other gods as 'no-things', Isa. 44: 9; 45: 5, 18; 46: 9, in the sense that shadows are indeed *there*, but are not original; they are the non-being, the chaos, spoken of in Gen. 1: 2, over against the Light that God has 'said'.

5   God is a jealous God. He wills to be the only God of Israel. The Jewish translation, *Tor*, renders rightly by 'impassioned'. Yahweh has the zeal and passionate love for his Bride, Israel, that a good husband ought to have for his wife. No third party, no 'eternal triangle' is permissible in the new relationship. Yahweh's anger is the just indignation of the husband who is cuckolded. Yahweh passionately expects Israel to be totally loyal to him, even as he will always be totally loyal to Israel. If Israel should be disloyal to her election, then the Passion of God will become event, and will 'visit' in the experience of the whole extended family; cf. 3: 16. In Moses' day, as in ours throughout the Third World, all four generations of one family lived together in the one village, even under one roof. Thus it is inevitable that if the headman 'commits adultery' with a foreign god and in this way disrupts the passionate love of the true and happy marriage, his

grandchildren and even his great-grandchildren living with him are bound to experience the penalty of his disloyalty. 'A drunken captain creates an undisciplined crew'. There is therefore no question of God's punishing children as yet un-born, as some people read into this 'Word'. However, while God's judgment on apostasy remains *within the family group*, his love for all men *uses* the right relationship between himself and the bride as the vehicle whereby thousands may see what love means and entails. This passage is echoed in many places as a kind of 'Old Testament Creed'; e.g. 34: 6; Joel 2: 13; Jonah 4: 2; Neh. 9: 17; Ps. 86: 15; 103: 8–10; 145: 8 f.

One danger of teaching this Commandment outside the Covenant is to suggest that the 'god of the OT is cruel and vengeful'; or again, the idea of loving one's god in ancient Greece would have been quite fantastic. As Aristotle said: 'It sounds odd for a man to say, "I love a god" '.

The Third Word, v. 7. 'In vain' refers in Israelite tradition to perjury rather than to profanity. We saw at 3: 13 that God's 'Name' is his very essence, and that that essence is his self-giving to be 'with' Israel for ever. Thus there is power in the Name. How demonic it would be then to use that power for selfish ends. Thus this Word speaks of a perverted attitude to man's relationship with God, of a denying of God's 'with-ness', of a despising of his act of redemption and of his saving purpose for the world within and through the Covenant. It is akin to the NT's phrase, 'sinning against the Holy Spirit', Luke 12: 10. The man who perjures himself in a law suit exhibits that he is so disposed by nature; for he calls good evil, and evil good; he sees the work of God as *shau*, 'vanity', non-being, Isa. 59: 4, or as the work of Beelzebul, Luke 11: 15, whose essence is to destroy and not to create. He separates the Name of God from its meaning, thereby denying its sacramental substance; cf. Deut. 23: 21–23. On the other hand, Yahweh is always faithful to his Name, Ps. 89: 35. He acts 'for his Name's sake'.

The Fourth Word, v. 8–11. 'Once you were slaves. Now you are free. I give you this one day in seven in which to rejoice. Even if you must sweat as a wage-slave on the other six days, on the Sabbath you can rejoice and say, "Today at least I can call my soul my own. No one dare order me about today. On this day I bring to mind that God has freed me from slavery." '

It is not only the whole village, including its hired workers and pagan itinerant labourers, who are to remember the Sabbath day, even the animals are to share in its joy. Deut. 5: 15 adds: 'Remember, you were once a slave'.

Seen within its context, as Ex planned we should do, keeping the Sabbath day holy has a positive intent. One stops work *in order to rest and rejoice*. Too often men have found only a negative intent in it, and have supposed that God forbids work, and even play, on the Sabbath day, so that to work on the Sabbath is an offence against God. But its holiness comes from man's being able to share in God's holy joy. For God too rested after he had created all things, and rejoiced in them. 'He saw that they were good'.

The Sabbath rest has become God's good gift to all mankind. Even China and Japan keep one day in seven as a rest day. At the French Revolution a ten-day week was tried, but soon abandoned. The seven-day rhythm that began at Sinai is now seen to be a necessary element in the structure of the human frame. Thus loyalty to God's will has been found able to withstand the totalitarian pressures of dictators and the narrow views of those secularist sociologists who wish to do away with the biblical festivals and to make 'all days the same'.

Before the Fall work was a good thing; Adam joyously tended the Garden. After the Fall, work shared in the curse. The Sabbath rest given here is therefore an aspect of God's grace to sinful man; honest work, real labour, can now be confined to six days, Luke 13: 14; for work is not the whole of life. Work is not made for man. It is the Sabbath that is made for man. This is because God himself both works and then sees his work in perspective on the Sabbath day, Gen. 1: 31; 2: 1–3; Prov. 8: 22–31; Mark 16: 20; John 5: 17; Heb. 4: 9–10. Thus the command to cease work virtually means: 'Get your toil finished by the sixth day, for on the seventh day you are to join God in his joy'; cf. Mark 16: 20.

But the Rest known to God, v. 11, to which the OT looks forward is not to be a ghostly experience. Deut. 1: 34–36; 12: 9; Num. 14: 21–23; 32: 10–12 all see it as the outcome of the occupation of Canaan. Later generations looked for a Sabbath rest to be lived out at and around the historical Jerusalem. The heavens would then co-operate and produce the ideal climate, Zech. 8: 12. The city of Jerusalem would be in fact the 'City of Peace', Isa. 65: 19 ff, with no weeping, no distress, no sickness, no hunger, no thirst, but with Israel *enjoying* physical work that was no longer a curse; and even the cosmic rules of Nature would be turned upside down. All this was clearly to take place in the realm of the 'flesh'. The Sabbath Rest known to God is therefore not to be experienced by incorporeal souls after death in a world of pure spirit. This Fourth Word, therefore, leads straight to the 'shocking' NT affirmation, not of the immortality or transmigration of souls, but of the resurrection of the 'body'. It leads to the prayer 'Thy kingdom come on earth' (in the flesh) 'as it already exists in the experience of God'. The Sabbath Rest therefore has to do with the 'universal restoration', Acts 3: 21, NEB, the great hope to which the NT points.

The Fifth Word, v. 12. This holy joy is to be incorporated within family life. For the Sabbath spirit is what creates the spirit of the holy family within the Covenant, providing the scaffolding for a life of mutual love and concern, 13: 14; 33: 8; Amos 3: 1.

The First Tablet clearly displays a unity of revelation. It begins with the self-revelation of God as he who is *with* his people in covenant, and who must therefore be zealous for the continuation of his Plan for them and through them. They are to remember who they are and that they are to live by grace alone; consequently that grace is to be displayed in their own family life. Children will not respect their parents unless the parents respect their children. The 'covenantal family' becomes the witness in miniature to the meaning of the universal covenant.

The Second Tablet now expresses five direct requirements for the maintenance of the 'holy' life of Israel, and these are expressed apodictically. All of them being negative, they exclude from Israel's life those extremes of behaviour which would destroy the family relationship. Thus they leave vast areas of human behaviour unmentioned. Yet in these areas the People of God is free to live its life. For the positive assertion is made that it is only when family life is held in high regard that a healthy and stable society can continue 'long in the land'.

The Sixth Word, v. 13. In the centre of the Garden stands the tree of life. No individual therefore has the right to take another man's life. Only God may do so, and only after a judicial trial, through the persons of his judges. These men, because they dispense divine justice, are known as *elohim*, 21: 6. Yet we note that elsewhere in the Torah (1) the Holy War is permissible, Deut. 20: 1 ff; 23: 10 ff; (2) animals may be slain for food, Gen. 9: 3; (3) the *elohim* may choose to prescribe capital punishment, 21: 12 ff, something that Jesus does not explicitly forbid, Matt. 5: 21. Infanticide, however, comes under this Word, and by implication, abortion, 21: 22.

The Seventh Word, v. 14. The word adultery in Israel's early days was confined in use to the disruption of the husband-wife relationship by a third party. As time went on, however, the parallel between human marriage and the Covenant made at Sinai came to the fore, so that fornication of any kind came to be included under the Seventh Word. For pre-marital intercourse, homosexual experimentation, sodomy, unnatural lust for an animal, or any activity that today we would label 'porn', because of the Covenant relationship, was eventually included in the word 'adultery'. 'Such a thing is not done in Israel' says Tamar to her half-brother, Amnon, as early as the eleventh century, when he merely sought to lie with her once. Such an act is called a 'descent into Sheol' in Prov. 7: 27; for lust is as much self-destructive as it is destructive of the family experience of Israel. Only those outside of the Covenant are unaware of the seriousness of adultery, which in Israel may lead to the death penalty. For they are unaware that the marriage of two individuals within the Covenant reflects an eschatological revelation. Once a man has heard God address him within the Covenant as 'thou', he can only look reverently upon a woman as a 'thou' also, and not as an object on which he can vent his lust.

The Eighth Word, v. 15. There is a sense in which possessions are holy. For no one owns his possessions, in that he will not take them with him when he dies. Rather they are on loan to him from God to help him develop his personality if he employs them to good purpose in his inter-personal relations within the covenantal fellowship. Things, then, are gifts from God in trust to individuals, and so are inviolate.

The Ninth Word, v. 16. Justice is an absolute. It comes through *elohim*, judges, from *elohim*, God. Therefore the perversion of justice is a form of rebellion against God; it inhibits right relations between man and man within the Covenant; cf. 23: 1–3; Lev. 19: 15–16; 1 Kings 21: 10; Amos 2: 6–7; Isa. 1: 21.

The Tenth Word. v. 17. Coveting is an expression of greedy desire. It leads to oppression, cheating, violence and acts that disrupt the peace of society. At 11: 2 'neighbour' meant a foreigner, an Egyptian. It could well do so here also; cf. Deut. 5: 21; Rom. 7: 7; 13: 9. Unfortunately greed is the basic attitude of life of our western acquisitive society. This Word interiorizes much that has gone before, and warns the People of God to guard even their *thoughts*. Clearly it is of the grace of God that God refuses to be 'with' the individual 'thou' unless that 'thou' is willing to be united *with* his fellowmen. The Decalogue shows that it is impossible to love your neighbour unless at the same time you love and obey God. For how else could Israel be 'holy'? cf. Lev. 19: 17–18.

It is clear that this 'ethical code' is not equivalent to our 'moral teaching'; nor is it set before us as a series of 'moral values'. It is an exposition rather of the ethos required of a people living in covenant relationship with 'I AM with you'. Therefore the cement into which the commandments are set is loyalty. Thus the Decalogue is neither rational nor experimental, neither idealist nor pragmatic. It is a set of guideposts for a community that must now live together in an exalted fellowship where loyalty to one another is understood and expressed as the response to the loyalty of him who first loved his covenant people. This love Israel has now *seen* in an historical situation, that is, it is *revealed* love. That is why Israel now *fears* the Lord, v. 18; for God has come to *prove* his people by means of his Word uttered in the Decalogue. It is clear that obedience is the only possible response Israel can make; cf. Amos 5: 4–6; Ezek. 20: 11.

21–26 *The Book of the Covenant* (so-called from 24: 7, and covering 20: 22 to 23: 33). Our author has set this second Code in his total narrative following the Decalogue in order to spell out in detail what loyalty to Yahweh is in everyday life. H. H. Rowley actually calls this Code a Commentary on the Decalogue. Thus in v. 23 Ex applies the first two 'Commandments' to a society greatly influenced by Canaanite beliefs. Israel, however, is not to make metal gods 'to be *with* me', for Israel's God is already 'I AM with you'. Yahweh had first sacrificed *himself* by entering into the fires of Egypt in order to redeem his people, chap. 3; therefore sacrifice must become an integral part of Israel's response – and it can take place anywhere that Yahweh chooses, v. 24. The altar was the main traffic junction between the gods and men. Israel is not to worship God merely in general; worship is to be in particular places and at particular times. And worship is to be made only by the pure in heart. Thus there is to be no incitement to carnal thoughts, v. 26. We recognize then that if Israel upholds this little Code she does not earn God's love and salvation; for she has already received them. But since the Word is an event, a creative event, it means that all down through history this Code will exert its creative power in binding Israel to the God who, while his people were still slaves, acted first to make them into his instrument for his world.

The Greek ideal in life was *theoria*, pure contemplation, as against practice. The Hellenic philosophers thus made the great refusal, believing that ecstasy and not the return to hard, practical *doing* the will of God was the be-all and end-all of the spiritual odyssey. Because of this, like so many modern cults and philosophies stemming from the East, they missed the one basic and central truth about the Book of the Covenant emphasizes, viz., the requirement of love for people.

CHAPTER 21

FREEDOM UNDER THE LAW

1–6   To love your neighbour is to do for him what God has done for you. As we saw above, the ethics of the Covenant Code are the expression of gratitude of a people redeemed by grace. An instance is that an Israelite might need to sell himself as a slave. In olden days slaves were a necessary element in the economy, until eventually machines could take their place. But our Code is concerned with Israel as the 'family of God', 20: 12. Israel's need, therefore, was to humanize as much as possible this necessary evil. No social system is perfect. The one taken for granted here at least provided a form of 'social security' against unemployment, sickness and old age. The result is that the word 'love' literally creeps into a situation now radically different from the experience of a nation under the lash of a taskmaster; cf. Deut. 15: 13–14.

Ps. 40: 6–8 expresses such love in verse; and Hebrews 10: 5–7 makes it ultimate, even though the author has chosen to use the mistranslation of the LXX. This love reveals itself as willing, total commitment. It subsumes in its sweep the wholeness of man's life, making no distinction between religion, morals and law, for these are inextricably intertwined. This is to be a nation of people *free* to love its neighbour; and since it is a 'kingdom', 19: 6, its King is here expressing *his* rule, as he moves forward with his Plan for all men, in and through the freedom and the love this people is invited to display. For just as an individual Israelite may say, 'I love my (human) master; I will not go out free', so too all Israel will learn to say, 'I love my Master; I will not go out free' of the yoke of the Torah. 'O how I love thy law!', Ps. 119: 95. God rules in his kingdom 'not by might, nor by power, but by my Spirit, says the Lord of hosts', Zech. 4: 6.

7–11   The woman's rights are well preserved here in comparison with conditions to be found even today. For although she is a servant in the sense that she is part of the economic machine, here she is a member of the free people of God. For once the slave enters service 'with his body', v. 3, he must go out 'with his body', i.e. as a personality in his or her own right, like Onesimus in Paul's letter to Philemon. We note that polygamy is acceptable in the early stages of the story. Why should it not be so also if a polygamous people in Africa enters the People of God in its first generation?

12–14　　Violence is part of man's nature. Justice is the essence of love. Without justice the moral basis to life would perish. But the door is open towards him who commits manslaughter inadvertently. Here we meet with the concept of 'Providence', one that is expressed in the theological story found at Gen. 4: 15 ff. So we rightly keep the word Providence in our legal terminology today. For it is not fate, the Greek *moira*, that rules our life, but the living God. Awareness of God's care develops in later legislation to the provision of cities of refuge, Deut. 4: 4 ff; 19: 1 ff; Num. 35: 13 ff; Josh. 20. Yet we note how God's care is first of all for the individual *thee*.

15–22　　These items are not ideas about 'human values'; rather they deal with human rights. Values are abstractions which do not exist. Here is the revelation of the divine mind applied to concrete cases, to persons living within the redeemed community. These 'ordinances', v. 1, do not represent general principles to be applied to all mankind at all times. They leave room for growth and development. Even the accused man has value as a person. The Code does not call for imprisoning him. Rather he must rehabilitate himself by hard work, and so it is he who must pay the doctor's bills.

23–25　　The *Lex Talionis*, the 'principle' of 'An eye for an eye', is also to be seen in this light. For even by Ex's day the 'principle' had long been superseded. Yet we are to acknowledge that the *Lex Talionis* is a milestone in human progress not as yet reached by many today. 'If you touch me, I shall kill all my hostages' is an acceptable procedure in modern politics and gangsterism. Gen. 4: 23–24 expresses in verse this reality about human nature: 'A man (merely) hit me, so I killed him in return. In the case of Cain, vengeance was seven times. I, Lamech, demand it seventy seven times'. The *Lex Talionis* thus regulates unredeemed man's natural lust for inordinate vengeance. Jesus goes the next step. Referring to Lamech's song, he tells Peter to *forgive* seventy seven times, Matt. 18: 21–22.

26–27 Again we meet with the utmost respect for the dignity of the human personality; a slave is honoured as if he were a prince. Love is not to be universal, but particular. We are not to say 'I love mankind'. Ex is not concerned to show how love 'developed' by comparing Code with Code. Our historical critical approach to the Torah leads us to try to do just that. It suggests even more. Some scholars would isolate the earliest legislation within this one Code and suggest that later additions were even 'forgeries'. Others, on the contrary, would insist that Moses is responsible for everything that is written here. Ex, however, goes in neither of these directions. He regards Yahweh as the author of the Code, and not Moses, 19: 9. Yet he also attributes it to Moses on the ground that Moses was the mediator of this Covenant Code out of which the legislation of the subsequent centuries sprang. Thus Ex did not make an historical but a theological judgment on this Code, and since he believed that God's love does not 'grow', he is not concerned to keep distinct the various stages in the development of the Law.

28–32 Domestic animals are to be cherished; but men are worth more than the beasts. This *principle* is here expressed in terms of practical situations. Such situations are not, of course, the only ones that might arise. The decisions made here therefore become guides for all other possible situations in the future. Thus we could well transfer this regulation from 'ox' to 'car' and apply it to the carnage on our roads. This is basically because the regulation does not deal with oxen, but with human greed; so we could apply it equally to man's lust for speed.

33–36 The 'Law' is a Word of the living God intervening to save Israel from self-destruction. It is a gift from God; he gives what he ordains as an expression of his love. And since Israel is a living people, the Law is not a fixed Code valid in the same sense for all time; it must grow as Israel grows and develops. It reveals the total sovereignty of God over every aspect of human life. That is why we see here no separation between what we call the sacred and what we call the secular.

CHAPTER 22

THE HALLOWING OF ALL LIFE

The English numbering of the verses in this chapter is one behind the Hebrew. RSV places v. 3b and v. 4 after v. 1.

18–19   We return to 'apodictic' laws as in the Decalogue. These are couched in the form 'Thou shalt not. . .'. God's will is that a man should have a natural relationship to the natural order, not a perverted one. The practice of sodomy leads to the destruction of the divine-human fellowship. Our loathing of 'porn' comes only from the revelation we receive of God's loathing of it. Lev. 18: 23–25 asserts that the Canaanites pursued bestiality. We know that bestiality was common too amongst the Egyptians, at least at a later period (Herodotus, II, 46). The Egyptian myth of Mendes the sacred ram is quite other than the biblical myth of the relationship between man and the animals in Gen. 2: 24.

Magic is equally a perversion of man's relationship to Nature, and is an insult to the majesty of God. The sorceress, representing man's approach to Nature in terms of magic, sought to manipulate its laws to human ends. The modern scientist rejects the way of sorcery, in that he approaches Nature humbly, and seeks to open up her secrets in a questing spirit of faith and wonder. As he does so he finds himself in the heritage of Israel's ancient law.

20   'Utterly destroyed' is 'put to the ban', that which Joshua did to the cities of Canaan. He 'sent them up in smoke' to Yahweh as a ritual act of worship. We are to remember that in biblical times there are no abstract qualities. Thus love, joy, sin, disloyalty and so on do not exist in themselves. It is people who love and rejoice, who sin and are disloyal. There is nothing in the OT of the superficial preaching we hear today: 'God loves you but hates your sin'. Sin must be the act of a person. Consequently the disloyal *person* brings judgment on *himself*, not on his sin. The ultimate sin is to repudiate

God, and so it requires the ultimate judgment. A valid theology of the Cross of Christ depends upon this basic OT insight.

21–24 The prescriptions of the Code depend upon *what God has done*. We are to love our neighbour *because God has first loved us*. To repudiate God's redemptive love and then to exploit our neighbour is to call down upon ourselves the ultimate judgment. We are to remember that once we were in Egypt ourselves. We should note that this *moral* command is implanted right at the heart of legal enactments! v. 23b is unique to all ancient laws. Most Codes allowed for appeal to be made to the king, but never to a god. Obviously it is the revelation of God's grace that alone brings grace into a legal Code. The Targum actually concludes the verse with 'For I am merciful and gracious, says Yahweh'.

25 Money is part of the natural order. Since it comes from God it is there to help *people*, those with whom we are bound up in the covenantal society. Note: 'If *you* lend money ('in advance', RSV) to any of *my* people *with* you (sc. 'for I AM with you') who is poor, you shall not be to him as a creditor' (sc. 'For I am not a creditor to you'). A man is more important than money. Money is not meant to be a means of commercial gain or of increasing one's wealth. That is done by hard work and through natural productivity. There is no suggestion of the modern idea that the poor are unwitting failures at becoming individual possessors. Yahweh covenants with the whole nation, including the poor, and not with an élite leadership.

26 'Garment' is the all-purpose cloak of the period. It served as a blanket at night and as a coat on a cold, wet day. This very particularized item thus expresses a basic aspect in human relations. A man must pay the fine exacted of him by law, but the law must cease pressing him at the point of his basic needs. Without his cloak he has lost the dignity of being human. And such is not the will of the God of compassion. The prophetic insight later stressed that Israel must be ever mindful of the poor and needy, particularly the widow, the orphan and the aborigine. Amongst the people of God there are no class distinctions.

29–31 This ordinance has special importance in that it has produced many echoes. For example, in Rom. 16: 5 and

1 Cor. 16: 15 Paul uses it to explain that believers are set aside for God and so for eternal life. Paul employs the LXX word *aparchai*, 'first-fruits', thus translating both 'fullness' and 'outflow', RSV, found here, at the same time.

There is a deep theological principle expressed in 29b, cf. 13: 1–2; 34: 20. The principle covers all life, that of both man and beast. The first-born child or beast represents and subsumes all succeeding births. All men and all beasts so consecrated are then *whole* or *holy*. Both however can become unholy or unwholesome. A diseased or torn carcase, now covered in flies, is not *wholesome* for food. So the instance stated here points to the holiness or wholesomeness expected of all life lived under God. Zech. 14: 20–21 looks to the day when all human life will thus be holy. Being a people consecrated wholly to God, Israel must learn to consecrate to him all aspects of human life, even in such details as personal hygiene and home cooking. This understanding of God's will is greatly developed in later years, for example in that other collection of ordinances that we call 'The Holiness Code', Lev. 17–26.

CHAPTER 23

THE ANGEL OF THE COVENANT

———

1-3 This ordinance is dependent upon the basic word *shau* that occurs in the Third Word, 20: 7, where RSV translates it by 'in vain'. The man who despises God's purpose and plan joins with those whom today we call thugs, muggers or unscrupulous promoters. The emphasis of the Hebrew is on ruthlessness. It is morally, not just legally, wrong to subvert justice. Yet it is equally wrong to favour the poor through mere sentiment, v. 3. Interestingly enough, some modern scholars have rejected this ordinance as being far fetched; by the addition of one letter they want to read: 'Do not be partial to a *great* man. . .'.

4-5 The reverse of ruthlessness is compassion. The emphasis is not on kindness to animals, but concern for the men and women whose livelihood depends upon them. These verses are virtually a command to set yourself alongside, incarnate yourself in, the anxiety and pain of heart of simple folk. You are to do so, because that is what God himself does, 3: 7-8. These peasants may be either your national enemies, or warped individual neighbours who hate you personally. In a casuistic inset, then, we have a command to love a *particular* enemy. The effect of this command grows and develops throughout the whole of the biblical period; cf. Job 31: 29; Prov. 25: 21 ff; Rom. 12: 20; Matt. 5: 44 f.

6-8 Until a decade or two ago it was taken as axiomatic that the great prophets, particularly Amos, 'invented morals'. After profound and wide-spread research in the many branches of biblical science, most scholars now agree on the priority of the various Codes in the Pentateuch. The eighth century prophets saw it as their task rather to recall their people to what God had already summoned them to do as brethren within the Covenant.

We note (1) how Yahweh speaks of 'your poor', members of

the Covenant People for whom *you* must be responsible; cf.
Deut. 15: 11; and (2) how Yahweh breaks into this command, personally intervening with the words, 'I will not
acquit. . .'. By this method, 'morals' are shown to rest upon
the revealed will of God. Once again such a divine irruption
is too hard for some scholars to accept, beginning with the
Greek translators; these propose to alter the text to 'Thou
shalt not acquit. . .'.

9   Yahweh had loved a minority racial group in Egypt;
it was when they were there that he *knew* them, 3: 7, and
entered into their pain. That then is how Israel is to *know*
the very soul of the indigene.

10–19   *A Cultic Calendar.* Several themes emerge here.
(1) Man is meant to be a good agriculturalist, using what
scientific expertise is available. (2) Agriculture, like all else in
life, is not an end in itself. It is for the good of man, with
special reference once again to the underprivileged. But since
God created the animals also, and 'saw that they were good',
the conservation of wild life is an element in the proper practice
of agronomy. (3) The festivals which all peoples hold to mark
the cycle of the agricultural year are sacramental signs of the
love of God. Israel is to connect the 'natural' seasonal festivals
with the historical actions of God which reveal his saving purpose. (4) To this end even old taboos and strange customs
learned from pagan neighbours are to be caught up into the
overarching purpose of the God who has now revealed himself in Israel's history. Thus A. Alt can say: 'The cessation of
cultivating the land is "ritually conceived fallowness" '. (5)
'Take heed to all that I have said to you', v. 13, is a reminder
that the Code is in fact revelation. Especially is this true in
the realm of 'other gods', for these are the mere apotheoses
of soil fertility. It will be by loyalty to Yahweh alone that
Israel can become God's 'guinea-pig' community. For Israel
is to let the pagan word see what life lived in fellowship with
and obedience to God can really be like. (6) This calendar was
made meaningful for believers in later history by the insertion
of a command to bring one's first-fruits into the 'house of the
Lord'. Philo the philosopher goes so far as to say that Israel,
the People of God, *is* the 'first-fruits of all mankind'; by so
saying he focuses the content of the Covenant Code on its

end-point in the Plan of God. This faith in the meaning and significance of their election can be maintained only if the representative heads of the people remind themselves thrice yearly what their faith is all about. The Festivals that developed are (a) Unleavened Bread or Barley Harvest; (b) Wheat Harvest or Pentecost; First-fruits; (c) Booths or Tabernacles; Grape and Olive Harvest; (d) New Year; Day of Atonement.

19b In the fourteenth century B.C. boiling a kid in its mother's milk was an accepted ritual act. Probably beginning as an ancient taboo it was later bound up with the acceptance and use of incest as an act of worship. This particular command therefore should be seen as a guide to Israel to reject *all* Canaanite ritual, since it all fell under the ordinance at 22: 20.

Appendix to the Book of the Covenant

20–26 This deeply theological passage sees the revelation at Sinai in the light of God's continuing purpose in and through his people's history. This purpose is now stated in the form of promise, promise of God's continuing presence. Our genius today is to express theological ideas in complicated abstract terminology. Ex's heritage taught him to express ideas as if he were illustrating them pictorially on a blackboard. Thus, instead of discussing 'prevenient grace', the OT theologian painted a picture of an angel going on ahead; cf. Mark 14: 28; John 14: 2. An angel in the OT is always portrayed as a man, and never with wings; for he is a *picture* of the divine Person acting in serving love. The Cherubim and Seraphim, on the other hand, were part animal, part human, part bird, because they represented, not YHWH, but the gods of men. This pictorial method meets the needs of most people. It shows itself in the myth, the fable, the anthromorphism of the OT and the parables of the NT. Thus we dare not pass v. 20 by with the words 'primitive thinking'.

At 3: 2 we saw that the concept of an angel pictured a reality difficult to express in theological jargon. That this angel here was never forgotten is shown by the statement at Mal. 3: 1, written shortly after Ex's day. The angel, the messenger, was an entity independent of the sender, yet he conveyed the will, even the personality of the sender *in his own person*. He was not the postman, who could go home after delivering the message. Rather he was like a flame of fire whose task it was to convey the original fire to an object. Only then could the flame disappear (cf. Ps. 104: 4, also picture language, not, of course, scientific language). That is why in Gen. 31: 13 the Angel can actually say 'I am God'; cf. 14: 19. Our Angel here is directly connected with the Covenant, Mal. 3: 4; 3: 16–4: 4; therefore he represents the 'covenanting love' of God. For God is in essence what he manifests in action, and vice versa. Yahweh's Name is *in* him, 3: 13–14, that is to say, the essence of his Being is present pictorially in the Angel, even though he remains hidden outside of space and time as I AM WHO I AM. For the Angel acts as Yahweh acts, pardoning or not pardoning as he wills. Note that in v. 21 it is the Angel who pardons, but in v. 22 it is Yahweh who does so, if Israel but obeys his voice spoken *in* the Angel.

Later rabbinical speculation made great use of this pictorial thinking, as did the NT. Thus the Angel came to be called variously Metator (measurer), Metatron (from *meta-thronios*? 'sharer of the throne'), *sar-ha-panim* (see 25: 30), the Lesser Yahweh (III Enoch, 12: 15) etc. (See my *From Moses to Paul*, 1949, pp. 104–113, etc.) The relationship between Yahweh and the Angel is naturally confusing to us; for example, we continue to read, 'You shall serve Yahweh your God, and *he* will bless . . . and *I* will take away. . .'. The RSV, following the Versions, alters the reading here, not recognizing the theological nuance implied.

Because of this theological introduction, then, the judgments expressed in the Decalogue and the Code appear as more than mere words. 20: 1 had said, 'And God spoke all these words. . .'. Now we see that the word which issues from the mouth even of man, if spoken with intent, can behave like an arrow that hits its target, Isa. 55: 10–11.

This is one of the first passages in the literature of mankind to conceive of history as events moving forward in a straight line, and so implying a beginning, a middle and an end. The ancient near east regarded history as a circular movement, ending where it began, on the ground that this is what happens in the cycle of the year. And, of course, the gods were really the apotheoses of the cycle in themselves. The Greek historians, with Herodotus as an example, broke through this cyclical view of events, and learnt to report history in terms of cause and event. But still they never conceived of the story of man *as going anywhere*. Thus all they did was to transfer the idea of the annual cycle to the cycle of the various ages of man. The Hebrews alone, on the other hand, saw *meaning* in history. This is because they believed that God is *Lord* of history; he made it; he sits outside of it; he has an end-plan in view; he is I AM. And yet, paradoxically, he may enter into it, and guide it and direct it from within. It is not as I AM that he does so, then, but as 'I AM with you', or, as is pictured here, as the Angel in whom dwells God's Name, the Angel who conveyed in himself the Word that came to Moses out of the Bush. And now this Angel is to lead Israel in a Holy War, v. 22, against all those who incorporate in their own persons the powers of evil against which God has already committed himself to fight, ever since the foundation of the world, Gen. 1: 1–3. That is why Canaan is to become 'your land', the 'Holy Land'. For till now the very soil of it had been the locus of the 'false', 23: 1, gods of the peoples listed by God himself.

The key-note of the passage, however, is 'I will bless . . .', v. 25. For the presence of Yahweh *with* his people in their never-ending war is everything they need; with the result that a Psalmist, writing before Ex's day, can exclaim, 'Yahweh is my light and my salvation: of whom could I be afraid?', Ps. 27: 1. It is tragic that in the early Middle Ages the OT was a closed book. The Crusaders suggested that they were conducting a Holy War against the infidel. Toynbee has called the First Crusade a Christianized Viking Expedition, for it attempted nothing that God could 'bless'.

27–33 God is the God of justice. He takes man's rebellion seriously. 'I will send my terror before you', not, this time, 'my Angel'. So we meet with a very important element in the revelation that remains a constant in the theolgoy of the People of God. 'My terror' is to be paralleled with 'the angel of destruction' mentioned in chap. 12. This 'terror' is pictoralized here as hornets. Obviously the Canaanites were driven from their lands neither by panic nor by a swarm of insects, but by God himself, v. 30. He goes about it in his own way. For the settlement of the land took place historically only sporadically and gradually, as we see from Jud. 1. Many indigenes remained in the villages, cf. 1 Kings 9: 20 ff, etc. The land was never wholly devastated; the cycle of nature was never completely disrupted. Ex has no term to handle our word 'ecology'. Rather he expresses, as here, his belief in the unity of all creation. Heaven and earth, and nature itself, fight for Israel, since it is God's will that is working out in the Holy War.

33   There may be an awesome pun in this verse. The MT runs, 'If thou shouldst serve their gods (I swear) that *he will become, yihyeh,* a snare to thee'. That is to say, not the god(s), but *ehyeh,* I AM, himself will become Israel's snare, 3: 12; cf. Jer. 50: 24.

CHAPTER 24

THE CONFIRMATION OF THE COVENANT

As Ex tells his tale, confirmation is made in two stages. In E's tradition we have the section 24: 3–8, where the people accept the Covenant and Moses then confirms it; and in J's, we have 24: 9–11, where Moses and the elders ratify it at a sacrificial meal; but of course Ex skillfully weaves the two traditions into one episode. He might have chosen to complete his book with chapter 23. But as a contemporary of Haggai and Zechariah he must have been acutely aware of the second exodus which had taken place in stages from 538 B.C. onwards, when his people returned from exile in Babylon. Yet now by 520 B.C. God's second act of redemption was clearly not complete. It has not yet been sealed in a sacramental act. In the eyes of the Chronicler writing 180 years later still, the Exile was not formally over until 515 B.C. That date completed the 70 years of exile that Jeremiah had expected. In that year a great Passover celebration took place. The instigators of this Passover may well have been Ex and his school. At it the newly completed Temple was dedicated, so that at last, after 70 years of 'exile from God' the people were brought back into sacramental communion with Yahweh once again. It may well be that by publishing chapters 24–40 of his book in this period Ex influenced his contemporaries to travel the path they actually followed. For this section of his book deals with two great issues that had to be handled in Moses' day, (1) forgiveness of sin, cf. Zech. 3: 1–5; 5; and (2) sacramental communion with the God of the Covenant, cf. Ezra 6: 19.

1–2   The mysterious words that begin a whole new section, 'And *he* said' reveal, as the Rabbis were aware, the vitality of the Word; cf. 33: 9 (where EVV wrongly add 'The Lord'). The phenomenon of its use occurs also in the NT; cf.

Luke 5: 1, 2, 3, 4, etc.; Eph. 4: 8; 5: 14, etc. The Word comes to Moses with a command to meet a new situation. The figures 70 and 12, representing the whole Israel of God, appear again at v. 1 and v. 4; cf. 1: 5.

3–8   'All the words of the Lord' may equally well be translated by 'all the actions of the Lord', in that there is no distinction between the word and action when God is their author. With man there is, for sin drives a wedge between the two, even though, in Hebrew, the one word *dabhar* covers them both. Jesus interprets this in a parable at Matt. 21: 28–31. Ex would mean that these 'words' which Moses was now reporting were not only the Decalogue along with (as he would suppose) the Covenant Code; for he would expect Moses virtually to preach a sermon at this point. In it Moses would explain how all God's *acts* in bringing Israel out of bondage and then in making a Covenant with his people were bound up with God's *words* spoken at Sinai, the whole together being the *Word* of Yahweh that Yehweh *said* to Israel. The inference is that Moses, as 'minister' of the Covenant, here interprets to Israel the words of the 'Bridegroom', 19: 3–6. The 'Bride', Israel, now responds, as at a wedding, with the answer derived from 19: 8, 'All the words which the Lord has spoken we will do'. As we have seen, this is how Hosea understood the confirmation of the Covenant. The Greek version adds: '. . . and we will do and be obedient', thus forming the background of the word 'obey' of Christian marriage. For although the Covenant was God's great *gift* to Israel, still it takes two to make a covenant. God may supply the food, but Israel has still to eat it.

The act of worship that follows marks the sacramental union between Yahweh and his people. That it is *his* people is shown by the use of the number 12. Moses and Aaron and the elders are all old men. Moses, however, has the wisdom to realize that his ceremony points to the future; so he gives teen-age lads an important part to play in the act of worship. We note that, since these youths here do what was completely forbidden to laymen in Ex's day, the latter cannot have made any changes when he handled the text.

At Gen. 9: 4; Lev. 17: 11 and Deut. 12: 23 we find this phrase repeated: 'The blood is the life'. So then spilled blood means 'life poured out' in a sacrificial act. Moses' act at the altar, therefore, for at it the life of God and man met, symbolically unites the life of God poured out for Israel with that of Israel poured out for God. (The burnt-offering was for the praise of God; the peace-offering was for fellowship with him; cf. Zech. 9: 11). We note the thrice repeated phrase, 'And he took . . .', as in Mark 14: 22–23. 'He took half the blood . . .' for Yahweh. 'He took "the written Word" ', thus setting the reading of it firmly within Heilsgeschichte, the story of God's Plan; cf. 1 Cor. 11: 23. 'He took half the blood . . .' for Israel, saying 'This is the blood of the Covenant which Yahweh has made with you *in accordance with all these words* (or deeds)'; cf. 1 Cor. 11: 26. We realize that since it is Yahweh who makes the Covenant, the action of pouring out his blood must refer to the future as much as to the past.

The sacramental act here is clearly interpreted by the written Word, and the Word by the Act. We note that the Word is not identified with a book. What happens is that the Word becomes event *here*, in that it makes itself known at the level of man's understanding. Thus the NEB's 'on the terms of this book' is misleading. To use very human language, Israel is now not merely God's adopted son, 4: 22, God and Israel are now no less than 'blood-brothers', bound together in a pact that *both* parties have now sworn to keep. Moses 'dashed' the blood over the people, shocking them as the blood ran down their faces, forcing them to realize that along with joy, peace and fellowship, the Covenant requires life from the shedding of blood, life coming out of the depths, from the chaos that was there when the Word was spoken in the beginning, Gen. 1: 2–3.

9–11 This verse picks up from v. 2. It makes a remarkable theological assertion. The 70, *because they are now in covenant*, are granted as pure a vision of the holiness of God as Moses has received. Amongst them, moreover, is Aaron, the prototype of the priest throughout the ages. A literalistic reading of the passage is of course absurd. This is obviated by the 'as it weres' to be found within it, and by the declaration that what they did see was 'under his feet'. The 'pavement of sapphire' would be the deep blue semi-tropical cloudless sky seen from the almost otherworldly viewpoint of a mountain

peak; cf. Ezek. 1: 26. Once again we have the Semitic genius
for representing reality in picture terms. In a lyrical experience
of God's presence the elders remain normal, balanced human
beings, for eating and drinking is a necessary human act to
maintain life. No ecstasy, no mysticism, no glossolalia here.
Soberly they enter into the great mystery that the God whom
they worship is not affronted by their presence, but accepts
them simply as they are, even though they are trespassing on
his glory. The essence of the revelation of the Beyond is thus
that forgiveness is a reality. What began as a mere picnic,
contributed by the food and wine they had carried up the hill
with them, and which they had now eaten with pleasure in
happy fellowship, becomes that 'heavenly banquet' in which
the believer in all ages since then has come to share. The
Targum implies this by rendering the uncertain word 'chief
man', RSV (MT 'corners', 'supports', LXX 'multitudes') by
'elect'. Thus, for even the ordinary believer the clouds that
hide the Mystery, 19: 18; 20: 18, can evaporate, and any
ordinary meal may by grace become an *arrabōn*, a pledge, of
the End; cf. Rev. 19: 9; 21: 15–27.

12   Ex now puts into story form the reality that the Decalogue is 'of God', and that it comprises both commands and
Torah ('law', RSV). The latter is given for Israel's 'instruction'.
This word is a verbal form; from it the noun *torah* derives. The
verb means both to teach and to reveal at the same time. This
is because it describes a relationship between persons as they
communicate with each other. As the teacher teaches, the
student obtains a revelation of what is in his teacher's mind.
Therefore Torah should not be translated by 'law', for this
produces a wrong understanding of the relationship between
God and Israel within the Covenant. God has given commandments indeed, as in the Book of the Covenant; but it and the
Decalogue together do not comprise a Mosaic 'Law'. Rather
they represent the revealed mind and will of God for his elect
people. That the Torah is chiselled on stone tablets suggests the
immutability of the divine will; for God himself is Rock,
Deut. 32: 4; Ps. 18: 2.

The awareness here that the Torah is immutable helps the
Christian to understand Jesus' attitude to it. In the Sermon on
the Mount Jesus neither abolishes the Law nor substitutes

another one for it; rather he recovers the Law's original intention, confirming that intention in his own life and teaching. Jesus confirmed the Torah, however, with the one and only Israel, not with some new body called either 'the Church' or 'the new Israel'. The plural of the word Israel never occurs. 'Church', *ekklesia*, is the LXX rendering of the word 'congregation' of Israel found in the book of Exodus. Or, as Ds. J. H. Grolle puts it: 'The names New Testament and Old Testament should never be used, just "the Bible", for the names are not biblical. For "Old Testament" we should say *Tenach*, a composite word that Jews use to name the Torah, the Prophets and the Writings'. Heinrich Bullinger, Zwingli's successor in Zürich, declared that since the New Testament calls *Tenach* 'The Scriptures' some fifty times, then the New Testament is a supplement to it, even as the Talmud is a supplement to *Tenach*. Jews and Christians thus share the same text; they hold in common the basic text of the one and only Covenant. On the other hand they each seek to do what Deut. 30: 14 asks for, to 'bring near' into 'today's situation' that Torah which God gave to the world that Ex has now recorded. The Talmud and the New Testament are in fact both forms of 'oral tradition'. Both must therefore be scrutinized in the light of 'the Scriptures', the original Torah, part of which God gave to Israel at this moment when Yahweh entered into sacramental union with his people through the shedding of blood.

15–18   The story is now given a cultic and devotional setting. Moses enters into the mystery, just as does the High Priest in later days, when he enters the Holy Place in the Temple. The divine encounter takes place on what is clearly meant to be a Sabbath. This Sabbath is the day after a new six-day creative period in which God plans, not the heavens and the earth, but a new way of life for man, viz. the Kingdom of God; cf. Mark 9: 2. The electric storm on the mountain-top is an outward sign of the mystery of the divine presence and power, picking up from 19: 18, where it formed the background to the making of the Covenant. It is now also a necessary link with Moses' return down the mountain at 32: 15. It 'settled', RSV, on Mount Sinai. This is an important verb, and it came to exhibit great theological significance. It described the 'resting' of the special presence of God at a chosen spot. The post-biblical noun *shekhinah* is formed from it. Its three consonants are S-K-N. These are also the three consonants of the Greek verb *skenoō*, to 'tent'. Using this coincidence the NT draws a parallel between the Word of God 'tenting' *with* us, John 1 : 14, and the Glory (or Word) 'tenting' on Mount Sinai. The Glory of God is thus to be understood neither meteorologically nor phenomenologically, but essentially, and in terms of God's moral Being and saving purpose. In the NT it appears on the Mount of Transfiguration, Mark 9: 7, 'after six days' (cf. above), Mark 9: 2.

18   Forty days and forty nights is not a calendar period. Chapters 25: 1 to 31 : 17 that now follow form a long inset. We return to the narrative only at 31: 18, and thus must allow ourselves 'a good long time', as the phrase means, to understand and appreciate the significance of the inset; for it would take 'forty days and forty nights' for God to 'dictate' the contents of these chapters to Moses. Ex wants us to understand that, theologically speaking, the Sanctuary in the Wilderness was constructed at the direct command of God.

CHAPTER 25

THE TABERNACLE

Chapters 25–31 are a separate section of the book. They deal with ordinances on Sanctuary and Ministry which form aids to the upholding of the Covenant. Our concern is not with details of construction. Yet we should note that till quite recently scholars doubted the possibility that Moses could have ordered the construction of such an ornate building along with its many implements and the clothing of the priests. Scholars suggested that the description here is a reading back into the days of Moses of the magnificence of Solomon's Temple. But archaeology has revealed many beautiful artifacts from the Tell-el-Amarna age. Also we know that the climate and vegetation of Sinai were more amenable than they are today, and that the indigenous people, like the Aborigines of Australia, could wrest riches from the desert in a way that surprises us today. We need not question where all the gold and silver and rich material appeared from in a barren desert. Some of it was clearly the 'spoil of the Gentiles', the gifts of the Egyptian people to the departing Israelites. *Time* Magazine for Jan. 13, 1975, reported on the find of what it calls 'The Oldest Mine?' This was being worked in the Negev before Moses' day, and at that period produced ingots of copper, 97–98% pure, for which they used iron as a flux. And N. Glueck has excavated several other mining establishments in that area from the days of Moses.

So this ornate Tabernacle built in the Sinai desert is no more incredible than a European cathedral was in the thirteenth century, towering hundreds of feet above the flat sea of mud-brick hovels occupied by inarticulate peasants.

8   The building of a 'sanctuary, that I may dwell in their midst', is to be done by men and women working together in equality of opportunity, and willingly, almost, as the word means, excitedly. 'Sanctuary' means 'holy place' and so refers, not just to the Tabernacle, but to the whole sacred area. Holiness is that reality which Moses discovered about God at the Bush, 3: 5. At this place, then, Yahweh will not only be with Israel, 3: 12, his holy Presence will actually *reside* in her midst. With this language, then, Ex successfully links God's Covenant with Abraham, Gen. 17: 8, which had come down to him in a separate tradition, with that which God had made with Israel at Sinai, Ex. 19, showing them to be two 'moments' in the history of the one and only Covenant.

9   That Moses was to work to a divinely revealed plan is not a late Hellenistic reading into the Pentateuch of the Platonic idea of 'forms'. In fact it is the reverse. The Platonic 'form' reflects the material substances of earth. But God is now present with Israel in person, so that the Tabernacle and its accoutrements are to reflect, through the revelation made by the uttered Word, v. 1, the pattern that the *immanent* (3: 12) God has in mind.

10–15   *The Ark*. Thus when we read that the Ark was to be overlaid with gold, we are to lay the stress not on a precious metal but on what is precious in the sight of God. That is why we are not basically interested in discussions of length and breadth, of the nature of the various precious stones or animal skins, but rather in their significance for an understanding of the mind of God.

The Ark is described first, for it is the most important of the Tabernacle furnishings. It is not intended to 'contain' God. God is free of man, free even over his own revelation and instruction. This is symbolized when the Angel goes *before* Israel, 23: 20, or when it is not God, but the Name, the Face, the Word of God that dwells in the Tabernacle, according to the various traditions. As Israel travels, the Tabernacle is to travel too. Some tribes in Arabia used to carry just such a sacred box into battle; this fact argues for the ancient nature of the tradition. Being portable, the Ark is not left behind like an ancient monument as happens to many church buildings when the population moves from city centre to suburbs. Ex was obviously making this point in his day, when his friends were determined to build a fixed Temple in Jerusalem. He was also pressing that the new Temple should not be more ornate than the Tabernacle had been; for it was not to become a museum of culture as some old churches and abbey buildings are now.

'I will become with *you*', God had said to Israel, you, a people. Thus when God says, 'I will reside (from time to time) in the Tabernacle' he is not repeating what he had said at 3: 12. The *ekklesia*, as the LXX calls the congregation of Israel, is not composed of bricks and mortar, but of human beings who are to obey God by continuing to be on the march towards the future. Yet this does not preclude man from worshipping God through beauty and order according to God's plan for him. 1 Chron. 28: 12 uses this word 'plan' as late on as 300 B.C. There is to be a continuity of purpose in the continuing nature of the worshipping people of God. So 2 Chron. 29: 25 speaks of king Hezekiah as a link holding together the new world of the Jerusalem-centred cult of his day with the revealed plan of old which had come down from the age of Moses. It is fitting that Moses joined in building the Ark with his own hands, as Deut. 10: 3 says.

16 The beauty of the outer shell is to express the value of what the Ark contains; for it is the 'mummy' within which Moses is to place the two tablets of stone on which 'the finger of God' had inscribed the Decalogue, 31: 18. That is to say, wherever Israel goes, the moral law is to go too. Israel cannot escape the Word that has been spoken in her midst, as it is the cement of the Covenant binding her to God. Thus, while the Ark has to do with 'religion', with worship and the expression of the cult, unlike Israel's neighbours who recognized no relationship between religion and morals, 'the Ark of the Testimony' keeps reminding Israel that the two are one.

17–22 Paradoxically, the *Mercy Seat* was not there at all. It was more nearly a point of tension. It was that *place* where the wing tips of the cherubs only just met, only touched each other over the centre of the box. The cherubs were human or perhaps divine powers in the employ of Yahweh. They were not angels, 'messengers'. They were more like the sphinxes of Egypt which had the task of guarding holy places; cf. Gen. 3: 24, etc. At this *place* the Word was uttered, in and through the moral life, in and through the worship of Israel, in and through the co-operation of the powers that be. It was that *place* where God 'came down' to meet his covenant people, and where, as later generations believed, God forgave them and atoned for their sin. It was the *place* of the *mysterium tremendum*. It was the *place* where Israel rejoiced in the grace that had brought her out of slavery and had offered her the Covenant. This then was the real 'pattern' of what God had revealed to Moses, not an artifact of wood and precious stones. Such material things are necessary, for they clothe the revelation in space and time. But this *place* is that point in space and time where all these gifts of God meet together. In fact, in one tradition, the Tabernacle is known as the Tent of Meeting, 33: 7.

Note: 'Mercy seat', RSV, 'cover', NEB and *Tor*, from *kapporeth*. The root K-P-R means 'to cover over'. But 'to cover one's face' came to mean 'with a gift', and so 'to appease', and even 'to provide atonement', 32: 30. *Kopher*, the noun, could mean 'a ransom price'. Its verbal form described God's covering over a human act of rebellion with his hand, so that he could no longer see it. In this way the LXX saw the noun 'cover' to mean 'place of atonement', *hilasterion epithema*. So the verb came to mean 'forgive'. Martin Luther then translated *hilasterion* by *Gnaden Stuhl*, which renders into English as Mercy Seat.

Pauline language is frequently impossible to translate into languages which have few or no abstract terms, words such as propitiation, atonement, justification and such like. The expositor can often reveal the content of Paul's ideas, however, by drawing upon the word-pictures that are expressed in everyday language that our theologian, Ex, has so aptly given to the world.

23–30   *The Table.* Its measurements are quite small. It was about 3 ft. by 1½ ft. by 2¼ ft. high. Again the LXX lays stress on its meaning rather than on its structure, for it alters the original 'acacia wood' to 'pure gold'. It too was transportable. 26: 35 tells us where it was to be placed. Its purpose was to be a place handy to the Altar that could hold the sacred vessels, dishes, bowls, etc. These are to be described later. Yet the most important item that it held was 'The Bread of the Face'. Later generations gave it other names, embellishing it as the years continued; see Lev. 24: 6; Num. 6: 20; Ezek. 41: 22; 2 Chron. 4: 19.

The Bread, called the 'Face-Bread' here, was in later centuries put on the Table in 12 golden pans (the number of the tribes of Israel) with a golden saucer on the top of each. These contained the frankincense which smoked continuously. Ex only informs us of the plain fact that Bread was put on the Table. At 35: 13 and 39: 36 the wording is different and can lead to the English translation 'Bread of the Presence'; cf. Matt. 12: 14; Mark 2: 26; and see 1 Chron. 9: 32; Neh. 10: 33. Lev. 24: 8 says that it must be set forth 'before Yahweh', evidently meaning 'in his presence'. And so we meet an idea close to that of the Angel in 3: 2 and 23: 20. Israel is to 'remind' God that he in turn must 'remember' his Covenant by means of this symbolic meal, daily. 1 Sam. 21: 6 regards it as 'holy' because it was presented to the 'Holy One'. The KJV-AV calls it 'shewbread'. The Syriac Version expands with 'The Bread of the Table of the Lord'.

We know what was done in later years. On each Sabbath 12 fresh loaves were placed on the Table, Lev. 24: 8; the old loaves were then eaten within the Sanctuary. With the help of 16: 16–19 we discover that each loaf was a day's ration for two people.

The Bread is here clearly a symbol of what sustains human life, in this case the life of all Israel. It has come from God and Israel gives it back by laying it before his 'Face'. Yet God does not keep it. Unlike the gods, he does not eat food presented to him. He says: 'Through your priestly representatives *you* are to eat it, now that you have thanked me for it. It is for you'. Israel is to remind herself weekly of the grace of the holy God. The eating is therefore an act of communion with him whose Face was 'with' Israel. This communion was consummated, not at the Altar, but at the (communion) Table.

31–40 *The Lampstand.* Over the centuries the AV has given English readers the wrong impression by calling this artifact a Candlestick. The *menorah*, as it came to be known by synagogue worshippers, was composed of a central, vertical lampholder, with three other holders on each side, all seven being on the same plane. The seventh day is the Sabbath, the day of *light* and joy. Its decoration, as we read, was highly elaborate. No doubt the first model was simpler than the elaborate Menorah described here. A thousand years after, Zechariah described a very intricate article, one that was fed with oil by gravity from outside through seven pipes, one for each lamp, Zech. 4: 1–3. The lampstand stood on the left as you entered the Sanctuary.

Its purpose is obvious. It is to give light within the dim recesses of the Holy Place. For they possessed no windows. At 33: 14 its purpose is expressed by the Hebrew word 'light-giver'. This word is the same word as is found in the story of creation in Gen. 1, where at v. 14 God says, 'Let there be light-givers. . .'. At Gen. 1: 3, on the other hand, when God says, 'Let there be light . . .', the word used is different, it is the basic word for light. It is the Light that the Word utters within himself. But the sun, moon and stars are not that light. The seven planets seen by the naked eye are only lamps lighting up God's creation, even as the seven lamps on this Lampstand light up the special place of the presence of God's Face. And just as the lights in the sky come on each evening for the period of darkness only, so these lights are to be lit each evening for the period of darkness only. However, they are to be tended to all perpetuity – like the age of the sun, moon and stars, 27: 21; 30: 8. This symbolism illumines the close parallelism that obtains between special revelation and natural revelation.

CHAPTER 26

GOD'S DWELLING-PLACE

1–30   *The Curtains.* We visualize what the Curtains of the Tabernacle were like when we see a picture of a modern bedouin tent. Such a tent is rectangular, not round, as is a modern bell tent. The sides of the Tabernacle were a series of curtains hooked together. These were all held up by wooden poles at strategic positions. In other words, the Tabernacle was really only an empty space curtained off on four sides. It had no roof. For this reason it was not a 'little Temple in the Wilderness', as some scholars have presumed. Rather it was God's 'home on earth'. The Israelite families lived in similar homes, or bedouin tents, and now God also resided in one! God asks for this Tent to be built so that he might join the family of Israelite tent-dwellers. When the families strike their tent for a day's march further on, God's tent too comes down, and moves on with the common people to the evening site. Then when they re-erect their family homes God joins them in their midst in his. Yet God does not tie himself to earth. His tent has no roof. God is always free of man. He does not 'dig in', as we say today, nor join us as we pour our resources into 'ceiled houses' (Haggai 1: 4), and turn what should be temporary residences to last only three score years and ten into castles instead of tents. We might see this chapter, then, as a rebuke addressed to Cain, our prototype ancestor, natural man before the days of the Covenant, who 'went away from the presence of the Lord; and dwelt in the land of Wandering', Gen. 4: 16. There his son Enoch actually 'built a city' – in the land of Wandering! But Israel was now wandering *with* God, or rather, as we saw at 3: 12, God was wandering with Israel to the end-point of the Plan.

31–35   *The Veil.* Within the holy Tabernacle was a specially holy place, and God was specially present there. It was separated from the Holy Place by curtains, called the Veil, hanging down from a wooden cross-pole of acacia wood. Within the curtained area the Ark was placed. The Table and the Lampstand were outside of it. The effect was to divide the Tabernacle into two unequal cubes, the one cube now called the Holy Place, and the other the Holy of Holies. This was the *debhir*, the place of the Word, *dabhar*, the place where God will from now on speak his mind to Israel, 35: 22. The Holy of Holies formed a perfect cube. Its symmetry was therefore as meaningful to people then as is the circle of eternal life upon a Celtic Cross today. It represented the counterpart in the invisible of the life that Israel lived here and now. Man cannot see through the Veil. But its very presence represents the hope, simply because the inner cube is *there*, that in God's good time worshipping Israel will one day no longer see through a glass darkly, but then face to face. It is interesting that all the Synoptic Gospels connect the rending of the Veil (or its successor in the Second Temple) with the death of Jesus; Mark 15: 38, etc. Also Heb. 6: 18; 9: 3, 10: 20.

36–37   *The Screen.* Similar to the Veil, a curtain hanging from cross-bars formed a screen at the front entrance to the Tabernacle.

No representation whatsoever of the Holy God is to be found within this sanctuary – no animals, fish, reptiles, or even man, as was the case with all Israel's neighbours. The only representation God planned to produce was the likeness of himself in the life of a people so wedded to him that they would come to exhibit in their life together that beauty of holiness which could derive from God alone.

CHAPTER 27

AIDS TO WORSHIP

1–8 *The Altar* was to be square, 7½ ft. by 7½ ft. by 4½ ft. high. It was called *the* Altar, as against the later Altar of Incense or Bronze Altar. It carried horns at its four corners. These were of one piece with the Altar, just as a bull's horns are one with the bull. For practical purposes these horns were handles used when shifting the Altar's position. It was also supplied with rings through which poles could be pushed when the Altar had to be carried, as in the case of the Ark. In the cult some of the blood was allowed to run over these bull's horns, 29: 12; 30: 10; Lev. 4: 7, 18; 16: 18.

The Altar was not a table. Like the Tabernacle itself it had no top. It was an open wooden box, lined with bronze; for the sacrificial fire burned inside the Altar, its bronze lining taking the heat. The ashes of the fire, thick with animal fat, could be raked out at a grating low down, and were then carried right outside the encampment, Lev. 4: 12; 6: 11. The Altar must have looked something like a large square garden incinerator. There were to be buckets to carry away the dead ashes, and shovels, basins, forks and fire-pans, all of bronze, to serve the flames inside the Altar.

The word 'altar' means 'place of slaughter', and so 'place of sacrifice'. Nothing is said about the religious significance of sacrifice. The purpose of an altar was taken for granted by all ancient peoples. But throughout the centuries its theological significance deepened, a fact which we can trace throughout OT history. In the meantime we note, however, that sacrifice is at the heart of Israel's relationship to Yahweh. The Altar is a most sacred artifact. The horns kept even the priests from drawing too close, as did the rim around its middle; later descriptions speak of a step below the grating probably to prevent the priests from kicking the pedestals even inadvertently.

Yet while the priests, who must sanctify themselves before

undertaking their tasks (see later) kept a respectful distance from the Altar, any sinner *in extremis* could force his way into the Holy Place and grasp the horns of the Altar. For there he found refuge in the mercy of God, 1 Kings 1: 50, just at that point where the blood of the sacrifice had been dashed. Yet even there, paradoxically, a man's treachery might place him beyond the pale, 21: 14; 1 Kings 2: 28–34.

9–19   *The Court* was built right round the Tabernacle and enclosed it. Like the inner sanctuary it too was a rectangle consisting of two squares, and it too, naturally, was open to the sky. It was about 150 ft. by 75 ft. in size. The entrance, protected by a screen, was at the east, facing the rising sun. The east side of this area was divided into three 'rooms'. Just as the Ark sat at the centre of the 'Holy of Holies', so the Altar sat at the centre of this large 'Holy Place'. (We should note that no one is fully satisfied that we understand exactly what Ex's measurements all meant.) The long walls were to be beautifully embellished with the finest of woven material decorated by the needlework of an army of women, and held up by hooks of silver on bases of bronze. These curtain walls were about 7½ ft. high, just high enough to give total privacy to those within. Here the ordinary man could feel that he belonged in the fellowship of God. For the open court was virtually an invitation to all Israel to come and worship; and there a man would recognize that the beauty of the place represented the reality of the Glory of God, to be found *there*.

20–21   *The Lamp Oil* is only the best available, and is a gift from the people. The passage presupposes the election of Aaron and his sons to office, described later; cf. Lev. 24: 2–3. These were to light the lamp *regularly* each evening, rather than tend it *continually*, RSV; see at 25: 31 ff. So the man-made lamps witnessed to the great reality that God himself is Light, and in him is no darkness at all.

CHAPTER 28

THE PRIESTLY VESTMENTS

To create this chapter Ex has woven several traditions together; this is more evident at v. 6–30.

The Priesthood. Ex recognizes the priestly tradition, and how it was the plan of God that the Sanctuary was to be administered, not by Moses (at least one of whose descendants turned out to be an apostate, Jud. 18: 30), but by Aaron and his family 'for ever'. At an early point in Israel's story the tribe of Levi must have become a priestly class, Gen. 49: 5–7; Num. 1: 47–54; Deut. 33: 8–10. Moses and Aaron both belonged to this clan, Ex. 2: 1; 6: 16–25. We find in later history, however, that the direct descendants of Aaron are given the most privileged positions at the central shrine, both at the Tabernacle in the Wilderness and in the Temple of later centuries. The Levites as a group were then relegated to subordinate tasks. The whole issue is highly complicated and difficult to define. The emphasis, however, is not upon some kind of 'apostolic succession' amongst them, but upon the real fellowship and brotherhood of the priestly group. Moses then is to 'bring near', that is, ordain to office the males in the Aaronic family. The ordination of these representative individuals means of course the ordination, ipso facto, of all Israel; for all Israel is already claimed as a 'Kingdom of Priests', 19: 6.

2–5 It is interesting that Aaron needs special clothing to lead the cult. Moses wore no special dress to meet with Yahweh. In fact God clothed him with his own divine radiance when he 'talked with Moses his servant', 34: 29. God's relationship with man through the revelation of the Word takes precedence over any relationship gained through the cult. In modern phraseology, the Sacraments are to be the Sacraments of, and dependent upon that which must always come first, the Word. Aaron and his sons need therefore to be supplied with vestments 'for glory and for beauty', and once again

many men and women seem to have offered their services for
this purpose. We note with interest that the emphasis is laid,
not on the skill of their hands, but on their mental alertness
and their creative ability; the latter phrase is literally 'spirit
of wisdom'. This means that man-made vestments are really
inspired by God, because the spirit in man throughout the OT
period is a divine 'in-blowing' that integrates or incarnates
itself within the total human *nephesh* or personality; see at 1: 5.

6–14   *The Ephod* was a highly decorated garment, woven
from various coloured materials; it was to be worn by the
officiating priest. Some scholars see the colours as those of the
heavens from sunrise to sunset. 'The heavens declare the glory
of God', Ps. 19: 1. For in light of the later rabbinical teaching
the High Priest had to intercede for the whole cosmos. Across
his chest the priest was to wear a 'breastplate', and a belt
around his waist. Over these went an outer garment. Over
everything again there was a coat. On his head he wore a
turban.

The modern reader is puzzled by aspects of the Ephod. It
was obviously the most important vestment of all, for it was
used in delivering an oracle, 1 Sam. 14: 3; 23: 6–12. But some
descriptions show it to have been a kind of stiff mask, like a
'coat-of-mail' that could stand without collapsing when set on
the ground, Jud. 8: 27; 18: 14. Accordingly it contained
within it a certain mana, an aura of sanctity, apart from its
association with the priest who might wear it. Its importance
here is that it carried two onyx stones on which were engraved,
six at a time, the names of the twelve tribes of Israel. Thus
just as Moses represented all Israel when God promised, 'I
will become with *you*', 3: 12, so too Aaron bore all Israel upon
his shoulders like golden filigree epaulettes when he entered
the holy place. These engraved stones were to make Israel
keep remembering God's redemption. Yet Aaron was to carry
them into God's presence to *keep reminding God* of Israel! These
stones had the function of signet rings. A king would 'sign' a
letter by pressing his signet ring upon it in wax. The stones
were thus symbols of the divine authority or signature upon the
cult, upon the priesthood, and upon the deep covenant
relationship between Yahweh and his twelve tribes. But as the
priest had always to remember, he himself was only a rep-

resentative of Israel, and was in no way 'holier' than the ordinary man. He possessed a special function, but not a special status. He had to recall that he was himself the creation of that Israel, the People of God, whom God had chosen long before his day, to be his priestly instrument to the world of men.

15–30   *The Breastplate of Judgment* was a highly decorated and clearly beautiful piece of work. Its very name could mean 'lovely object'; but here it is obviously a technical term. We take it that it describes a breastplate, square, that hung down back and front over the wearer's head. In its turn the breastplate carried, not two, but twelve precious stones, representing again the People of God; cf. Rev. 21: 19–20. Actually ten verses are required to describe the magnificence of the vestment.

The judgment issue arises from what is mentioned at v. 30. In a pocket over the heart Aaron was to carry into God's presence at all times two objects here called *Urim* and *Thummim*. In the Babylonian epic poem on Creation, Marduk, the head of the pantheon, and judge of all the earth, carried the fate of the peoples on tablets in a pocket on his breast. The explanation of these two objects has always been a mystery. The very meaning of the words is vague. *Urim* may derive from *ōr*, 'light', with the plural suffix *im*, and *Thummim* likewise may derive from *tum*, 'complete', with a similar suffix. But what would these words mean? Even in Moses' day they might have been as meaningless as the Tibetan words *Om Mani Padni Hum* are now. On the other hand, they would certainly bear some reference to God, who in Hebrew is *elohim*, a plural noun. So they *might* mean, 'God is Light' and 'God is Perfection'. In Num. 27: 21; Deut. 33: 8; 1 Sam. 14: 41–42, however, the two objects seem to be in the shape of dice. The priest, in the presence of Yahweh, casts the two dice, or at least one of them, Num. 27: 21, to discover the mind of Yahweh upon an issue put before him. Because of this, most scholars believe that the one dye would convey the answer 'yes', the other dye the answer 'no'. While we cannot dogmatize on their significance we are clearly meant to see that *Urim* and *Thummim* express the judgment, not of any wise man, but of God himself. And so this vestment became known as the 'breastplate of judgment', to remind Israel that God is Judge, and that his Word is always the last word in human affairs.

31-35   *The Robe* of the Ephod, evidently of lesser significance than the Ephod itself, was a garment that slipped over
the head. It was originally a layman's uniform, 1 Sam. 18: 4,
just as was the 'seamless robe' of Jesus, John 19: 23. It was
wholly of blue, the colour of the heavens above. *The Pome-
granate,* which decorated its skirt, was an ancient symbol of
fertility. Possibly Moses had in mind to recall Israel to the
promise which God had given to each of the Patriarchs in turn
about the multiplying of the people to become God's blessing
to humanity. *The Bells* would tinkle as Aaron moved in and out.
And though the use of bells may originally have had an apotro-
paic purpose, that of frightening away evil spirits from the
holy place, the old custom would now keep reminding the
ordinary man, as he stopped his daily labour to listen, that he
had an intermediary in the holy presence who even then was
interceding on his behalf. The fact that the privilege of entering
into the aweful presence of the all-holy God was the priest's
alone is expressed as a matter of life and death importance.
Clearly our human worship should never be entered upon
carelessly or lightly, but always in the tone of the biblical
phrase, 'Holy, holy, holy'.

36   This reality is to be exhibited to Israel by sewing on
to Aaron's turban a *Golden Flower* in the shape of a signet with
two Hebrew words on it, 'Holy for Yahweh', or, more accurately, 'Holiness belongs to Yahweh'. Thus, through this
one man's repeated activity, all Israel remained a holy people,
19: 6, apart from all common and unclean usages to be a
nation of priests for the holy God. It was under the shadow of
this sign, therefore, that Aaron bore into the presence of God
the sin of the people, 'that they may be accepted by Yahweh'.
There is no reason to suppose that their sin at this early period,
as some commentators assume, was merely a series of inad-
vertent errors in the ritual God had prescribed. For it remained Israel's great hope that the day would come when her
whole life, whether in the shop, on the farm, or in the kitchen,
would exhibit this same divine holiness which was already to be
found in the Holy of Holies, Zech. 14: 20-21. Her hope remained that her *moral* guilt would one day be borne into the
presence of God in an effective and not merely a symbolic
manner, Isa. 53: 4.

39-43 Other less significant garments are now patterned. *The Coat*, RSV, 'tunic', NEB and *Tor*, was what we might call a cassock. It became common to all levels of the priestly hierarchy. When the High Priest in later centuries entered the Holy of Holies on that one day in the year when he had to celebrate the rites of the Day of Atonement, he stripped himself of all other vestments except the *Coat*. In this way he entered as an ordinary priest, not as some kind of arch-priest superior to his brethren. Having been once revealed, Ex finally declares, these ordinances of God must never be set aside.

CHAPTER 29

ORDINATION TO THE PRIESTHOOD

There are three steps towards ordination: (1) The ceremonial approach, making use of the materials now in the Tabernacle. (2) The investiture. (3) The anointing, symbol of consecration.

Physical washing with water, or lustration, was accepted in the ancient word as a symbol of washing off cultic impurity. For it is only a ritually clean body that can wear the special garments; cf. John 13: 10; Heb. 10: 22.

6 The word for 'crown', RSV, has not been used before. NEB explains it with the phrase 'symbol of holy dedication'. This word *nēzer* allows later generations to make play with forms like Nazirite and Nazarene.

9 Ordination is a 'perpetual statute', that is, the priesthood is to be hereditary. The whole ceremony is amplified at Lev. 8, parts of which seem to precede our passage. Anointing is (1) to the priesthood, (2) to the kingship, and as the verb shows, (3) to make a man a 'messiah', cf. 28: 41; and see 25: 6; 40: 9; 1 Sam. 9: 16; 2 Kings 9: 3; Ps. 132: 17; Isa. 45: 1; 61: 1, etc. We are given no information about the wording to be used at the ordination ceremony. But we know the significance of the action 'to fill the hand of the ordinand'. Like the modern minister into whose hand a Bible is placed it shows that he is now authorized to be the servant of the Word, and not merely the exponent of a theology of his own. The action, in a word, means 'This is your authorization'.

10 These animals, objects and garments are to be 'brought before' the Tabernacle. This is a technical, cultic term meaning to bring from the unholy into the holy. We note the unholy use of a bull in chap. 32. But they also symbolize God's will that all human possessions should be brought into his Plan.

11   Laying the hands on the head symbolized the identification of the priest with the death of the bull. To approach the Almighty is a life and death matter, which can be done only in 'deadly' earnest. When the bull died, the priest, 'died' too. So the Altar became associated with the death of the animal, another way of saying that God is worshipped through the shedding of blood. The blood flows over the Altar onto the horns, and then runs onto the ground. This is thus a 'total' act that is taking place, and by no means mere play acting. It is Moses who performs this first act, since Aaron is not yet consecrated. We now know that the Canaanites of the period used such cultic acts to seek forgiveness for wrongly-executed cultic acts. Israel on the other hand regarded such as sacramental signs by means of which she claimed the forgiveness of her sin.

13   The best substances go up to God as a gift. The unclean elements are buried outside the settlement of the 'holy nation' 19: 6. The entrails that near eastern nations used for purposes of Hepatoscopy (foretelling the future by examining the liver of a newly killed animal) are by Israel dedicated to God.

14   'Sin offering' is simply 'sin' in Hebrew. This explains what Paul meant at 2 Cor. 5: 21. His Jewish readers would all know that he was referring to this verse.

18   Since sin is not an evil attribute of man, but represents his total orientation to life, the sin-offering must be equally total to be of any use. God is pleased to recognize it as such. This rite is the basis of the later 'whole-offering' that 'went up' to God in fire and flames.

19–21   Whereas in the case of the sin-offering all the blood was thrown upon the Altar, now in this 'integrating act' (see at v. 28) some of it, as a *pars pro toto*, touched the persons of the priests, and then the rest was dashed upon the Altar. Some of this latter blood was then retrieved to be sprinkled upon both the priest and his vestments. In this way he was identified with the sacrificial acts, sharing in the sacrifice himself, and thereby rendering his life and the life of Israel a life of sacrifice; cf. Rom. 12: 1. We note that the oil of consecration must have mingled with the blood of the sacrifice on the priest's clothing, the significance of the one thus interpreting the significance of the other. For, as Lev. 17: 11 explains, 'The blood is the life'.

The blood of the slain beast was now smeared on the horns
(of the Altar of the Almighty) and then transferred to the
priests who represented Israel, from top to toe. The total
forgiveness of Almighty God is thus revealed through pain and
death. None of these ideas is dogmatically stated here. But
since the 'law of Moses' is filled with the living Word of him
who has chosen to 'become with' Israel, that 'law' cannot
escape growing in depth and meaning, and keep on adapting
to every new situation that Israel will need to face. How
completely other then is Israel's view of the life committed to
God from that of the religions of the east. The OT has no truck
with an escape from the realities of the life of this world into a
mystical union with God here and then into some kind of a
nirvana beyond death.

22–25   These bits of the animal were the most prized
delicacies. So understandably they went to God. They reached
him by being 'waved' before him, in a literal sense of the word.
The NEB obscures the significance of the act by translating as
'special gift'. What the exact movement was we do not know.
But since it was done 'before the Lord' Yahweh could see not
only what they were doing but also the intention of the heart
behind the action. It is blessed to receive as well as to give!

26–28   But God gives back a choice portion to Moses
and other portions to the priests. First he accepts what man
gives him freely and gratefully; and then man eats what God
graciously returns to him. In this way they eat the meat *together*. Their meal, which is to be a 'perpetual' one, is thus a
perpetual holy communion between God and man. It is a
'peace' offering, originating from the free gifts of the people.
Shalom means 'peace' only in a very secondary sense. The root
of the word is 'wholeness', 'completeness', 'integration'. So
we can see, as at v. 19 above, how *shalom* can be used as a
name for this basic act of union in communion.

33   This verse infers that the sacrifices described were
already regarded as effective for those within the Covenant.
They gained for Israel at-one-ment with God. The Hebrew
word behind 'atonement' bears a different meaning from the
English word. The original speaks of the act of 'covering-over'
sin at the 'mercy-seat' described at 25: 17. It is thus equivalent
to forgiveness; cf. Isa. 38: 17.

34   We may feel that here there is a great waste of animals. But God's providence in nature is prolific. Man too therefore is to give back to God just as open handedly. 'The Lord loves an hilarious giver', 2 Cor. 9: 7.

35   The creation of a priest to serve God took seven days, the same length of time as the creation of the world; it too was created to serve God. Did Ex notice the parallel? Did he expect us to notice it too? If so, then he is saying that the spheres of the natural and the supernatural are one.

36–42   To offer sin offering for the Altar was to disinfect it from any pollution, to decontaminate it from the contagious infection of sin. At 42b we are unexpectedly reminded that all this is a divine speech. In it the ordinary man is forbidden to enter the Holy Place. But he may meet with Yahweh at the entrance curtain of the Tabernacle, 'I will meet with you', plural. But it could be that God speaks to Israel only *through* Moses in that the following verse 'to speak there to *you*' is this time in the singular. Targ. Onk. reads here 'My Word will meet with you, by my Glory'. By this complicated expression later generations sought to express the reality of the paradoxical immanence of the transcendent God. The point to emphasize, however, is that the Presence is there *first*; worship is only man's response to God's initial approach within the Covenant.

43–46   In the form of a postscript the Covenant relationship expressed at 19: 5–6 is now finally confirmed in a sacramental act. Consecration to the priesthood is thus not an end in itself; it is a channel for the continual flow of the Word into Israel's life.

46   The climax of the whole movement of God's purpose from Egypt is now disclosed. It is 'that they may know that I am Yahweh, who brought ... that I might *dwell* among them', that is to say, that the immanence of the loving, saving, purposeful, transcendent God might become a historical reality. Yet, as Ex knew, there is this question to face, arising from the reality of the sacrificial flames at the Altar – 'Who among us can dwell with the devouring fire? Who among us can dwell with everlasting burnings?' Isa. 33: 14. It is by grace alone, then, that Israel can continue to exist, chosen as she is out of all the nations of men, to dwell *with* and *in the fires of God*.

CHAPTER 30

MORE FURNISHINGS

1–10   *The Altar for Incense*. This table seems small to our way of thinking. Its top was only 18 in. square, and it stood only 3 ft. high. It was made from the common tree of the wilderness – acacia wood. It too had 'horns', and it too could be carried on poles when Israel travelled; cf. 25: 27. The whole was overlaid with gold.

This altar may not have been original to Moses' day, however. For one thing it ought to have been described earlier; for another, the annual act of atonement seems to reflect a later development in the cult in the time of the Second Temple. In fact, all chaps. 30–31 may stem from a later period. On the other hand, there are scholars who are ready to believe they represent a true memory of contemporary events.

Incense was used as far back as the days of the Patriarchs in Mesopotamia, and was certainly employed by the Canaanites in Moses' day. Basically the ascending sweet smell and smoke are an outward sign of men's prayers ascending to heaven.

11–16   *The Poll-Tax*. There are several points to notice in a matter that might be passed over as mundane.

(1) Taking a census was at some periods considered a foolhardy thing to do. Originally it was considered an insult against the gods. Later on, if you published the figures of your adult males you were informing an enemy of your strength; cf. 2 Sam. 24. That was an act of disloyalty to your own national god. Moses here upsets all such notions.

(2) This poll-tax was a ransom. By paying it each adult was buying himself off from a judgment that would show itself like one of the plagues of Egypt.

(3) The half-shekel was to be *offered* to Yahweh, and so was more of a gift than an exaction.

(4) As an offering it marked the egalitarian nature of Hebrew society. Even the poorest could afford 30 cents a year.

The rich were not allowed, just because they were rich, to give more than the poor. The tax symbolized that each and every Israelite was equally precious to God.

(5) The offering was an instrument by means of which the *service* of God might continue in order that Israel might *remember* that they needed atonement.

17–21 *The Bronze Laver.* This curious object speaks of the divine love of cleanliness. The Tabernacle was to have an ample supply of water. Yet of course the Laver must have reminded Israel also of man's desperate need of moral cleansing, as we see from the language of the great prophets, e.g. Isa. 1: 16. The priests were to wash at the Laver daily. It is interesting to note that the Laver was fashioned from the brazen mirrors which the women-folk must have handed over as part of their share of the construction costs of the Tabernacle. Thus objects used for self-admiration were given freely in order that Israel might remember her uncleanness in the sight of God.

22–33 *Recipe for the Sacred Anointing Oil.* The four main ingredients were obviously very costly. The archaeologist has revealed that in Moses' day there was more trade with the east, where the spices originated, than we might have expected. Israel would have to pay for these luxuries by barter in exchange for those valuables she had brought out of Egypt. That the eastern nations should contribute to the Glory of God is a recurring theme of the whole Bible, e.g. Isa. 61: 5 ff; Matt. 2; Rev. 21: 24.

The oil was used for many purposes. The anointing both of the sanctuary furniture and of the persons of the priests was a sacramental act. It was a 'sign' of anointing with the grace of God. At this period it was not used on laymen. But later on even the sick were anointed as well as kings and prophets. The oil had a pleasant, 'happy' smell. So even the recipe for this trivial material is 'revealed'!

34–38 *Recipe for Making the Incense.* The various ingredients are to be seasoned with salt. This is 'the salt of the covenant with your God', RSV; Lev. 2: 13. In the culture of desert peoples eating salt together has always been a bond of covenantal friendship; cf. 24: 11. But if the salt has lost his savour. . . . Matt. 5: 13.

CHAPTER 31

THE INSPIRED CRAFTSMEN

G. von Rad suggests that this chapter should follow 35: 9.

1–11   God himself selects Bezalel; he calls him 'by name', just as he had called Moses, 3: 4. The artisan is thus as much elect to serve God's Plan as is the prophet and the priest. This is an important insight lost and regained more than once in history. Then 'more men of ability' are called to work with these obviously highly skilled craftsmen. v. 3 tells us that God filled them with his own Spirit, and that this showed itself both in their intellectual powers and in their practical abilities.

In the OT generally we discover that man's higher endowments of spirit come from God – Samson's unusual strength, David's skill, Solomon's wisdom, the prophets' insight; cf. Gen. 41: 38; Isa. 42: 1, etc. So God himself desires that the arts and crafts should reflect and serve his Glory.

12–17   *The Sabbath.* Even before the giving of the Decalogue, as have seen in earlier chapters, the basic significance of the Sabbath had been set forth. This new material from P now picks up the theological emphases Ex has already made and underlines them, as in 16: 22–30; 23: 12; 34: 21.

(1) God himself speaks of 'my Sabbaths', v. 13.

(2) The Sabbath is a sign between Yahweh and Israel in order that Israel may know experientially that Yahweh alone can sanctify her, and that she cannot sanctify herself.

(3) Since God himself is holy, the Sabbath too is holy.

(4) Therefore it is a day for holy, creative rest.

(5) The Sabbath rest has belonged in the Plan of God since before the world began. Thus it is understandable only in terms of creation and of the divine satisfaction and refreshment, v. 17, at seeing work that is 'good'.

(6) It is a perpetual covenant.

(7) Being a sign 'for ever', it points forward to an inevitable Sabbath rest for the People of God still to come.

(8) Being a sign, it is virtually what we today would call a means of grace.

14   This verse exhibits the vivid language of the Semite, that is not necessarily meant to be taken literally. We recall the words of Jesus, 'If your right eye offend you, pluck it out', Matt. 5: 29.

18   Ex skillfully places this verse here to link together his several chapters of divine instruction with the resumption of the great saga he is recording. No human language could convey more dogmatically Ex's belief that the Word is absolute and immutable. The two tablets are as much a covenant sign as is the Sabbath. But Israel has other ideas on the subject, as we discover in the very next verse.

CHAPTER 32

THE GOLDEN BULL-CALF

Chapters 32 to 34 form a unit; they follow from 24: 14. The problem of the relationship between law and grace within the Covenant is now explored in narrative form. Numbers of exegetes have supposed that the story that follows originated from the days of king Jeroboam I and was propagated in order to counteract the bull worship which Jeroboam introduced, 1 Kings 12: 26–33. Others have suggested that Jeroboam never abandoned the worship of Yahweh; the bulls he set up in Bethel and Dan were meant, they declare, to 'hold up Yahweh' – an idea that a simple worshipper would surely find hard to grasp. On the other hand I would suggest that this chapter is the memory of a real incident. Ex then reminds his readers that the period of Jeroboam when Israel similarly apostatized lay mid-way between Moses' day and their contemporary post-exilic period. What he implies is that if this apostasy has happened once, and even twice, then it could happen again.

1 Several individual words are important here. *To* Aaron is really *against* Aaron, implying the first rumblings of a threatening popular movement. 'They gathered themselves together'; this may be read as 'they formed themselves into (a parody of) a congregation'. 'Make us gods' could of course be 'make us God', *elohim*; but since Ex would have Bethel and Dan in mind, the word is more likely meant as a plural. 'Who shall go before us' is a parody of 23: 20, a passage, as we have seen, of deep theological import, cf. Acts 7: 40. 'This Moses' is an expression of scorn, uttered despite all that he had done for the people.

2–4 Aaron does not prevaricate. This incident could scarcely have been invented, any more than could that where Peter betrayed Jesus. Aaron is a coward. Moreover he forgets that in himself he is a nobody; for apart from Moses he has no authority. Yet he calls for any golden rings that have not yet been given for the service of Yahweh. The masses of men do not, generally speaking, understand their faith intellectually. That is why, in the eyes of God, the *leader* of any faith bears a terrible responsibility. This incident happens, let us remember, when Israel had no human security left at all to fall back upon. Israel was therefore defying the only security she had, that of her covenant relationship with Yahweh.

We are now acquainted with many features of the Canaanite deities. The most imposing of these gods was Baal, mentioned frequently in those biblical books that handle the period of the monarchy. Baal was worshipped under the guise of a Bull (cf. the god Apis the Bull of Egypt). In one of the Canaanite epic poems Baal mates with a heifer which then bears a calf. The Canaanite religion was basically the worship of man, strong man, virile man, sexual man. Baal, the male, and Ashera the female goddess, were ultimately sex figures, the apotheoses of man's natural lust of the flesh. In many other cultures, the bull was the very symbol of sexual prowess. The thousands of figurines of Ashera now in the world's museums all show her with exaggerated sex features. We have only to recall how attractive Baal worship was to later generations of Israel, as reflected in, say, the book of Hosea, to see how easily people slip into a syncretistic mixture of faiths. Israel still ostensibly worshipped Yahweh, but obviously preferred to practise the permissiveness which the Canaanites enjoyed. This 'worship' took place particularly in August–September of each year, when the people of the Fertile Crescent awaited the rains that were essential for a new beginning. By means of ritual prostitution and through a belief in imitative magic, human beings hoped to force sexual union between Baal and Ashera, and so to bring about the rebirth of the cycle of the year. The story follows neatly after Ex's calendar of the plagues that we noted in earlier chapters.

It is both curious and sad that human beings may at times become so irrational that they believe what they want to believe even when they know it to be false. 'These are your gods, O Israel, who brought you up out of the land of Egypt'. Yet Israel did not really want *another* God; Israel wanted Yahweh, yet a Yahweh whom they could get to do *their* will, but whom they did not have to obey. Till this day men have supposed that they were religious when all they really wanted was a God who would serve their ends and desires.

5–6   NEB here follows an interesting variant. Instead of 'Aaron saw', it reads, 'Aaron was afraid'. Aaron had clearly gone too far. He had cast a mould and out had come a Frankenstein; and this monster now demanded the worship of man. So to counteract this horror he proclaimed, 'Tomorrow shall be a feast to Yahweh'. But the people paid no attention. Next morning they held a high holiday in honour of – Yahweh? the god of sex? By now they would neither know nor care who it was; see Ps. 106: 19–210 1 Cor. 10: 7. The words 'They rose up to play' refer to a bacchanalian orgy. At this festival otherwise self-controlled men and women threw all restraints to the winds as at some kind of Mardi Gras, and indulged in alcohol, promiscuous sex, and probably in narcotics produced from plants that grew in the Sinai wilderness.

How satisfying it must have been to possess something tangible to believe in, a god whom one could touch and feel, a god whose nature was sensibly toned down to the level of one's human instincts. There are movements current today which seek the worship of fellowship, personal satisfaction, group dynamic activity, and such like, all of which Elijah of old would have called Baal worship. Yahweh is a jealous God, and any attempt to make the worship of a god made in the image of man serve his glory is doomed to judgment.

Why is this embarrassing incident recorded here? We only ask that question if we forget that the OT is not the story of unfaithful Israel but is the history of the faithfulness of God.

7–10   Yet it is no longer possible for God to continue in the same relationship to Israel as before, just as if nothing had happened. This is because sin and apostasy *matter*. To use human language, God can only be speechless with wrath when he meets with such intolerable insolence as his *own* people have just shown him. 'They are no longer *my* people', says God to Moses, 'they are yours'. 'God's nose grew hot', says Ex, literally, hot enough to *consume* Israel – the same word as that used of the Bush that was *not* consumed, 3: 2 (and cf. discussion at 29: 46). Yet the purpose of God's election of Israel must necessarily go on; the Word of God cannot return

unto God void. God informs Moses that he will now make
Moses' descendants his elect people, since all the others have
broken his Covenant. But to do that, Moses recognizes at
once, is not a possible alternative for God to pursue. Moses
was right in this thought, in that his grandson (as we noted
above) became an idolator, Jud. 18: 30. Indeed Moses had not
been called to be a new Abraham. So what we read now is
theology as it is thought through in the mind of Moses who
handles the various issues that God puts in his mind actually
in the hearing of all readers of the book of Exodus to this day.
We actually overhear him conversing with God as if the two
were equals!

11–14   For it is Moses who reminds *his* God, waiting
upon God in hope, that Israel is still *thy* people, whom God
has newly rescued from Egypt 'with a mighty hand'. He even
suggests to God that it would look bad in the eyes of the Egyptians if on his part Yahweh were to be disloyal to the Covenant
at the moment when Israel needed his loyalty most. For doubt
of God's providence would then destroy all hope for man. In
fact God would be threatening Israel with the ultimate horror
of the negation of his love. Yet God must be both I AM, that is
to say, wholly independent of his creation, and remain answer-
able to none but himself; and on the other hand he must
allow Moses to think through the ultimate significance of his
promise 'I shall become *with* you'. It dawns upon Moses that
this reality can be maintained by grace alone. So Moses begs
God to 'repent of this evil *against* thy people', that is, he asks him
to change his plan to destroy Israel and so to remain loyal to
the revelation of himself which he has made to Israel through
his Name, which is 'I shall become with you'. For the world, as
we know today, would lose all meaning if Israel disappeared.

Moses' temerity in calling upon God to *shubh*, 'repent', is
underlined when we discover the very same word being used
by the great prophets to backsliding Israel! Moses reminds
God of his essential nature, how he is the God who *swore* 'by
thine own self' to be loyal to his people's ancestors; and that
he is the God who *promised* them the land towards which Israel
was now moving stage by stage. Moses refers back to the days
of Egypt when God had already *remembered* his people, 3: 8, his
inference being that Yahweh, having now *come down*, should

once again deliver them, this time from the hand of their baser instincts. Clearly 'law' does not save a man from captivity to his own self-interest. In fact Israel had 'turned aside quickly from the Way which I commanded them'. Only grace can now avail. And so in Ex's masterly piece of theological writing this reality is made manifest by the device of showing how God allowed one of our fellow human beings to reach this conclusion himself. The conclusion which Moses reaches is one that our own human mind finds to be a fantastic notion, viz. that the living God, unlike the gods of Egypt and Canaan, not only forgives, but forgives actually by suffering himself as he identifies himself with the sinner, 3: 8. We are to remember that at this point Israel has now broken the 1st, 2nd, 3rd, 5th and 7th Commandments.

15–20   A strong contrast is now made. Moses comes down from the mountain with the revealed Way in his hand, 24: 12, and meets with his own people who have now chosen their own 'way'. Having been with God, Moses' mind understands why Yahweh's 'anger burned hot'. The wrath of Yahweh is expressed equally in both Testaments as the necessary action of the God of love when confronted with human insolence; e.g. in the first Gospel alone we meet with it at Matt. 8: 11; 10: 28; 10: 34 ff, etc. The two men hear 'the sound of shouting', 'the sound of the cry of defeat', 'the sound of singing', and the LXX, knowing the dangers of alcohol, adds 'and of wine'. The suggestion is that the sound they heard is too terrible to describe. It was no less than a roar rising from the abyss.

On God's behalf, therefore, Moses smashed the *sign* of the Covenant, as witness to Israel's deliberate decision to break her side of the agreement, 19: 5. God is the God of justice, and so of judgment too. The Decalogue is now superfluous. It had represented a revealed absolute, the content of the divine-human relationship within the Covenant. Outside the Covenant human morality knows no absolute; it reflects only the changing social mores of a given nation, relative to the contemporary social standards of that society. To demonstrate the truth of this Moses grinds the calf to powder and makes the people drink their god. Even as they drink the mixture the elixir becomes their poison, cf. Jer. 25: 27–28. One commentator calls this 'making the punishment fit the crime'. Yet this cannot be the final end of God's purpose and plan for Israel, as we shall see. Even the Covenant, like a seed, must fall into the ground and die before new life can spring forth from it. God brings resurrection out of the *end* of what rebellious man can do.

21–24 The weakness of Aaron's character is again apparent. He squirms before his brother, actually calling him 'sir'. He does not see that the responsibility for what has happened lies with himself. Instead he passes the responsibility on, even suggesting that the people are essentially evil. Finally, with the naivety of a child Aaron puts the blame on the fire – 'I threw (the gold) into the fire, and out came this calf'!

25–29 'Broken loose', 'gone wild', 'to their shame', 'an object of derision to their enemies'. To 'go wild' is a form of ecstasy. We meet with it in the NT also even in the case of genuine believers. But ecstasy as such is denounced by the great prophets. The English word comes from the Greek *ek-stasis*, 'standing-out' of one's body. The Hindu, the Muslim, the Christian sectist may do so, but he who is true to the biblical revelation may not. As we have seen, 1 : 5, man is not a soul living within a body. If and when a man is moved by the Spirit of God, as were the prophets, e.g. Micah 3: 8; Isa. 61: 1, then the whole of his person is moved to rational speech or action. This reality had to be learned in Israel. For Israel did not see it in the behaviour of the Canaanites. The original meaning of the verb 'to prophesy' was 'to behave as an ecstatic'; and we have portraits of such activity in 1 Sam. 10: 5–13; 18: 10; 19: 20–21; 1 Kings 22: 10–12; 1 Chron. 25: 1; 2 Chron. 18: 11. These prophets used wine and music, and possibly drugs, and even cut themselves with knives, to induce the ecstasy. They misused the power of the Holy Spirit to talk gibberish. A sober-minded but wholly dedicated man like Amos had thus to repudiate their abnormal behaviour, Amos 8: 14.

Moses now stands 'at the gate of the camp' (the traditional place of judgment) and cries 'Come unto me all you who are willing to commit yourselves to the Lord. Come out and stand with me'. This does not mean 'Come, if you are intellectually convinced about Yahwism over against Baalism'; but it does mean, 'Come, if you are willing to enter with Yahweh into *his* mighty Plan for the salvation of the world'.

Ex now employs a legendary story to bring out the theological truth he has already enunciated. In it the sword is the
'sign', the visible evidence, that the people died of drinking
the judgment of the God of wrath. And once again, like the
Semitic emphatic language Ex has used before (cf. 9: 6)
'every man' slew 'everyman his brother', about 3000 men in
all. Moreover, to show that it is saga we are reading and not
history, we find that the people do not even try to defend
themselves!

The story is told in this way to focus on the silence of Israel
at Moses' call to faith, a silence that is worse than the orgies
from which they have just been awakened. 'Their silence shows
that the elect wish to repudiate their election; and election
repudiated will be the end of their liberation', writes Miskotte,
op. cit. Silence in the face of a call to decision must necessarily
bring about a never-ending Last Judgment; cf. 1 Peter 4: 17.

Then follows the strange biblical emphasis that the Levites
who took the sword 'ordained themselves' by their action for
the service of Yahweh. Clearly we are being told that a man
may become a priest of the Lord only at great cost, a cost which
others too may have to bear; cf. Matt. 10: 34–36. In fact,
loyalty to God may have to come even before loyalty to family.

30–35   Having given the people a night to lick their
wounds, Moses informs them that he will seek to intervene
with Yahweh in the matter of their apostasy. Their apostasy
might be symbolically described as 'putting first the kingdom
of this world', 'making gods of gold', or as we say today,
'worshipping success, comfort and ease'. But once Moses
goes back up to meet with God, acting again as intermediary
between God and man, he takes one further step in his argument. He now actually offers to take upon himself the effect
of Israel's sin so that Israel might go free. We read at v. 7–13
the argument that went through his mind in response to the
seriousness of the situation. If Israel had in fact gone 'too far'
in disrupting the Covenant, then Moses sees that he must
offer to die in place of his people; Num. 11: 15.

Nowhere is the greatness of Moses more clearly depicted; cf.
John 15: 13. It is clear that he lived close to God, 24: 15–18;
32: 7–14; 33: 12–23; 34: 6–9, 29; and in that way he grew
to know what God is like in himself, what is his nature, his

purpose, his plan. But Moses had not yet learned all that God had in mind to reveal. He had still to learn that forgiveness does not wipe out the guilt, far less cancel the effect of sin. The basic principle of 'an eye for an eye', 21: 24, cannot be set aside unless something else is put in its place. For God is the God of justice: 'Whosoever has sinned against me, him will I blot out of my book', Moses has still to learn. It is only much later in history, with the help of Deutero-Isaiah, who flourished when Ex was still young, that the ultimate truth can not only be explained but also acted upon, viz., that it is only he who is 'God with, *in*, Israel', Isa. 45: 14; 53: 1–12 who can by *his* 'death' when united as one flesh with the Bride Israel, carry away and so atone for Israel's sin.

Yet the greatness of Moses is this that he is able, under God, to live with the tragedy of the situation of the moment – still unresolved – and simply *go on*. He is still to be the leader, the Angel, the personalized Presence of the living God, 23: 20, howbeit with the awful promise of judgment hanging over the heads of all.

Finally the judgment fell. It took the form of a plague upon the elect people. For they had now become pagans by choice, even as the Egyptians had been such by nature. But once again we meet, not with judgment, but with grace. For God, like a wise father who chastises his son for his own good, Prov. 19: 18, 'gets it over quickly', so that the loving relationship can be restored, and the past forgotten. For God is always eager to begin again, 32: 10; cf. Isa. 43: 25. Omniscience is ever willing to forget!

With what effect upon Israel, however? Till now Israel has been delineated as a self-willed people, as demanding the right to say when *she* wants to advance or retreat, even if that should lead back to slavery in Egypt or slavery to self. Bread from God has been regarded as an insult – Israel has wanted cake, not bread. Israel has feared her neighbours only because they are strong, yet has been glad to learn debauchery from them. The feasting and dancing round the calf have been a caricature of the feasting and joy Moses and the elders had known in the presence of God, 24: 9–11. All this then has happened *in history*. Yet God will not let his people go, *in history*.

The Covenant between God and Israel is like the covenant of

marriage, Hos. 1–3. It is therefore meant 'for all generations', Deut. 29: 14–15. Yet Yahweh must now define his relationship to Israel in new and different terms – but still within the bonds of the Covenant that *he* will never break, even though Moses has now smashed the tablets. So now we read in chaps. 33–34 that Yahweh, again of course of his free grace, donates to Israel certain mediating institutions. These are each and all signs of his wrath, since his holiness might on any provocation destroy his own people; yet at the same time they are each a proof of Yahweh's will to save. Yahweh now protects Israel from herself and from any annihilating encounter with the divine; and he takes precautions in order that his design to 'give Israel rest', 33: 14, may achieve its end. Yahweh has therefore now turned the awful curse into a blessing.

The exodus from Egypt is clearly not yet complete. The saving purpose of God that has been revealed step by step in historical situations must necessarily lead to a total fulfilment. A new act of God must still be looked for, one that must also take place in history. That is why, as the Christian under-stands the historical process, this new act did in fact begin to happen when 'Moses and Elijah appeared in the "glory", 16: 10; 24: 16; 33: 22, and talked with Jesus (on a new mount Sinai) about the exodus which he was concerned to *complete* at Jerusalem', Luke 9: 30–31.

CHAPTER 33

THE FACE OF GOD

1–3   Although Israel has apostatized God has not changed, for God does not break covenant for any reason, Jud. 2: 1. Neither has he revoked the promise he gave to the Patriarchs. This is a fact about God which some Christian groups have not realized when they consider God's relation to the Jews of today. God is still going ahead of Israel *in* his Angel (LXX, 'my angel', 14: 19; Jud. 2: 1) 'for my Name is in him', 23: 20. Israel is at once both the forgiven people in that the Angel has authority to forgive sins, 23: 21; but she is also still the disloyal people. We note therefore a significant variation in the mode of revelation. At this point the Angel is *not* Yahweh. Instead Yahweh *sends* his Angel; for Yahweh himself has withdrawn his presence from Israel's midst.

Yahweh acts thus because of his compassion. He is the zealous God, whose 'nose grows hot' against disloyalty, 20: 1. If he were to come too close now, Israel would be burnt up; cf. Isa. 28: 16–22; Matt. 3: 12; 13: 40–42. The great prophets later on are deeply aware that Yahweh, for his love's sake, may withdraw for periods of time from his own elect people; and that this withdrawal is for Israel's education in the knowledge of himself. Here then is a new revelation, that God's wrath is the inevitable sign of his love.

4–6   Man does not appreciate this action of God. He calls it 'evil tidings'. He is too petty to understand God's mind. Part of the discipline that God enjoins upon Israel, therefore, to help her understand, is declared symbolically, cf. Isa. 54: 7. Since men and women put on their finery only when they rejoice, they are now to strip off these ornaments. When God withdraws, life is drained of joy. Is this then an aspect of the Plague that God sent upon his people, 32: 35? God forgives, he enjoins a new beginning, but the guilt remains. Not to have God *with* us (cf. the name Immanuel,

Isa. 7: 14) is to carry a plague in the heart, is to know devasta-
tion of soul. God could depart altogether. God is wholly
self-sufficient and does not need man. But then, were he to do
so, he would not act 'in character', that to say, in accordance
with his Name. So God chooses still another course in his re-
approach to Israel, 'that I may know what to do with you'.
We learn presently what this is.

7–11   *Another Tent.* This short passage seems to be rooted
in the E tradition. Its memory of the Tent is different from
P's, who placed the Tabernacle in the *midst* of the camp, 25:
8; Num. 2: 17. Possibly there were two stages in the growth of
the Tradition, in that this Tent was really the first to be erected
and hallowed, and so came prior to the Tabernacle complex we
have studied. Unlike the Tabernacle this Tent is quite simple
and unadorned, just like Moses' own home in the desert – and
just like the tents of all the simple families of the people.

We noted that God is planning a new course. Ex has woven
in this E material after v. 6 to reveal what the plan is. First,
Yahweh will still be *with* Israel, but will only travel parallel
with them, so to speak, outside the camp. Secondly, in order
that, paradoxically, he may still be *in* Israel, he proposes to
make fuller use of Moses as his intermediary. Moses is now
(1) priest, (2) seer, (3) guardian of the Tent, all basic functions
of the later prophets and priests. But in this other Tent there
is no Ark, no Altar, no Incense. It is the place of direct *meeting*,
v. 7, with the divine. In this tradition Moses is the representative of all Israel, v. 8; and God replies to him alone. Moses
learns that Israel must still carry her guilt and continue to
suffer separation from God. So Moses' intercession now represents the only 'way', v. 13, by which Israel can return to God.
The whole apparatus of reconciliation described in chaps. 25–
31 is now null and void.

No sacrifice takes place here, no worship, only the hearing
of the Word, the sign of which was given at 13: 21, etc., viz.,
the pillar of cloud that united heaven and earth. The narrative
however shows us God eagerly waiting behind the door of the
Tent, so to speak, to utter his Word. Communion between
God and Israel has therefore been maintained after all, despite the disruption caused by the incident of the golden calf,
by means of the Word.

The English Versions speak of God's *presence*, as at 33: 14.
But this word translates the Hebrew *face*. It occurs at both v.
11 and v. 14. There are those who say that the Priestly writers
give us a 'Theology of the Presence', of the 'Face' of God
indwelling in the midst, but that E as here is concerned only
with the Word. Yet it would seem that Ex has woven the two
theologies together.

A rabbinical tradition declared that the great prophets saw
God variously through ten, down to two, *specularia*; but that
Moses saw him through only one. By this argument they
avoided a crude literalism that would destroy the mystery of
the holy otherness of the biblical God; cf. Num. 12: 7–8;
Deut. 34: 10–12. But they also meant that Moses had an
'immediate', intuitive understanding of God's will, whereas
that of the later prophets was 'mediated'. Their insights in
other words depended upon what Moses had first 'heard'.
For they in their turn were living in that Covenant which
Moses had first brought into being. In conformity with this
view Jesus can make the important distinction, 'Moses *and*
the prophets', Luke 16: 29. Ex actually gives us in this chapter
the most sophisticated theology of the divine immanence of
any in the OT, by showing that the immanent Word is one of
affection and love. For by now Moses has penetrated beyond
and through awe into fellowship. Then, by bringing in the
priestly service of Joshua, a layman, Ex widens the area of the
revelation of God's love beyond that attained by P's theology.
For, represented by the person of Joshua, all Israel now *sees*
that the Word is with Moses.

12–16   The verb 'to know' occurs six times in this passage.
So 'seeing God face to face' evidently means coming to know
him intuitively and thus to know his will. Moses, however,
cannot attain to this yet, even though God knows his 'name',
that is, knows Moses through and through, and has elected
him to service, and even though Moses has found grace in
God's eyes, v. 12. For to be elect does not mean to have full
knowledge. Moses longs to know just what his real task is. He
says to God, 'This nation is thy people'. Here he uses the term
goi, normally employed for 'Gentile'. Is that *all* that Israel is
now in the sight of God? he asks. Is Israel no longer the *'am*,
'people' of God, as Hosea too wondered in later years? cf.

Hos. 1–3. Please 'show me thy ways', he continues, 'that *I* may know thee' (again this verb of intuitive understanding and not of esoteric knowledge). Yet in this he makes the mistake of asking for an 'experience' of God, instead of for faith in God. So Yahweh replies with a phrase so astonishing that the Versions greatly differ in translating it: 'My Face will go' (there is no 'with you') 'and I will give *thee* rest' – spoken in the singular to Moses alone.

Till now God has not provided Moses with a scout who knows the terrain. That is to say he is pressing Moses to ask if faith has value without personal knowledge. So at last Moses recognizes his own need of God's guidance if he is to lead God's people forward (and now he returns to the word '*am*): for, as we saw at 11 : 7, God's people, eschatologically speaking, is 'distinct' from all the nations of the earth. Yet Israel does in fact possess God's grace, Moses says within himself, 'for he has been "going with us" all along the way', 3 : 12. In all this flurry of argument, then, we overhear Moses thinking through the meaning of the revelation and the redemption he has met in face of human apostasy.

We set certain expressions in parallel which Ex has used to describe God's Presence within the Covenant without seeking for dogmatic definitions. We possess the phrases (1) *Face*, 23 : 15; Deut. 4 : 37; Ps. 21 : 10; 80 : 17; (2) *the Ark*, Num. 10 : 29 ff; (3) *the Angel*, 33 : 2; (4) *Glory*, 33 : 18, 22; (5) *Goodness*, 33 : 16; (6) *Hand*, *Back*, 33 : 23; (7) *Way*, 33 : 13. All these are pictures which Ex paints where we would use abstract terms.

17–23   Moses goes back up to Sinai for a last communion with God. We overhear his thoughts on the way up. On top God grants him a private theophany. Being obedient now to the heavenly vision, Moses listens to the Word that God *says* in his heart, what he had asked for in v. 13. He has realized that the faith he now possesses stems from the fact that God had elected him before he believed. Yet he asks to know more than man should know, v. 18. God's reply is important. 'He said . . .' and this occurs three times; for this is a great moment of revelation through the Word, through 'saying', cf. Eph. 4 : 18; 5 : 14. It is made in several clauses:

(1) As we saw at 2 : 2 and 7 : 14 'good' means 'good for'. God's goodness is his essential love and care for Israel; cf.

Deut. 10: 13. So Moses is to contemplate the whole story of God's saving love for his people and through them for the whole world of men. God will make all this 'pass over' before his eyes, as at 12: 33.

(2) God will exhibit once again the meaning of his Name YHWH, that word which expresses the nature of his essential Being.

(3) God has already revealed his election love, his grace, for those whom he has called; now he declares that he will have compassion upon those needing compassion, that is, upon 'whosoever calleth upon the Name of the Lord'. Incidentally we note that 'I will be gracious ...' uses the same grammatical construction as 'I will become what I will become', at 3: 14. Moreover, the word for 'compassion' seems to be connected with the noun for 'womb'. It *may* therefore carry in it an overtone of mother-love; cf. Isa. 49: 14–16; Rom. 15–16.

Here God is declaring, 'Once again you will see that my very nature is love, and will come to understand that I have already forgiven my people her terrible sin'. In this way, from an incident in history, Israel will *see* that the grace of God flows *out of* her apostasy and stiff-neckedness and travels on as God's Face *with* Israel into the unknown future. Once again then these two great realities are expressed, that God is God and man is creature – God in his absoluteness cannot be 'seen' by finite man, yet, paradoxically, that grace bridges the gap; and secondly that grace takes up and works *through* the sin of man.

Evidently the words 'stand upon the rock' mean more than the obvious. The noun carries the generic article; it is *the* rock. We have seen that the name *shaddai*, which we translate by Almighty, probably derives from the idea that the Supreme Being is mountain, rock of ages, or such like, 6: 3. First man needs a 'place'. The Hebrew word means really 'room to stand up'. Then we are to remember that as man reaches for God from there he is to discover that faith only comes second. First he must stand upon the Rock which is itself faithful, reliable, always the same, as the word means in Hebrew. We note that this figure is picked up more than once in the Psalter, e.g. Ps. 18: 2. For it is only when a man sets his feet upon the Rock that he can understand; yet not all, for a man cannot see

God's face and live. By grace, though, he may see God's 'back' (interpreted as 'Word' in Targ. Onk.), that is to say, he may see the meaning of what God has done *in history*, after God has 'passed by', or 'passed over' an historical situation (clearly a direct reference to the theology of the Passover, chap. 12). God is not visible, in that he has hidden (protected) Moses from himself, to preserve the latter from the awful nature of his presence. For God must always remain the Hidden God. We noted at 3: 1, 16–17, however, how the word 'back' could be used to express what we today call the eschatological outcome of an event. And so here Moses is to discover the third great reality that the significance and the magnificence of what God has made known to man is in what he has *done*.

Moses now meets with a miracle of love. The Plan of God which Israel had lightly tossed away, as we read in chap. 32, is now to unfold all over again.

CHAPTER 34

THE COVENANT RENEWED

1–5a   It is told of Handel, the composer, that he drafted the whole score of *The Messiah* in two weeks. Scarcely taking time to eat or sleep, he reached a level of heightened consciousness such as few ever attain. Moses is now experiencing a heightened insight into the very mind of God. The story of this 'new revelation', 34: 1–28, is expressed in parallel with that already described in chap. 24; for Moses has gone up again onto the Mount to receive a new Word from God, 33: 17.

Moses has to present himself before Yahweh, that is, he must be there in person, prepared in heart and mind. This is to be no casual encounter. 'Be ready', as Abraham Heschel puts it, 'for a Word may come'. 'Come back up to Mount Sinai', for this is to be a *re*-newal of the Covenant. And 'be alone'; for Moses is now the only true Remnant of Israel. The whole scene is clothed in an air of utter sanctity, v. 3, every action being performed at the command of God, v. 4. The MT does not tell us who cut the new stone tablets; the English Versions all copy the insertion of 'Moses' found in the Sam. Pent. But the Hebrew 'he' leaves the proper sense of mystery about the incident. The mystery continues with the divine descent in the cloud; God is still the I AM, the wholly other.

5b–7   From out of the darkness comes forth the Word of Life, for the fourth time now in the book of Exodus – 3: 14; 20: 5–6; 33: 19, even as it was in the beginning, Gen. 1: 3; and as it was when, having put Abraham into a deep sleep of darkness, God spoke with this the first recipient of the Covenant in all history, Gen. 15: 12–21. So with this *re*-construction of the Covenant. After Moses has symbolically smashed it to pieces, 32: 19, it is again emerging from the mists of God's hiddenness, but being made intelligible to Moses in that he hears it as the Word. Moses hears the ineffable Name. And as he hears it he understands afresh that the unexpectedly gracious content of the Name which he has already met with at the Bush is the ultimate Reality about both God and man. What he sees is not the essence of God, but the beauty of God, yet even then such beauty as can only be understood 'humanly'.

'The Lord descended and stood *with* Moses', as he had promised to do at 3: 12, not confronting him, not challenging him, not accusing him, but standing alongside of him in grace at this terrible moment. 'And (he) proclaimed. . .'. Who is 'he'? Did Moses call out the name 'YHWH'? Or did Yahweh utter his own Name? In v. 6, on the other hand, there is no doubt that Yahweh is the speaker.

God's own exposition of the meaning of the Name is one of the peaks of biblical revelation. Israel had sought a sensual revelation before, chap. 32. God's reply is not given in terms of Omnipresence, Omniscience or Omnipotence. Such knowledge of God would not have answered man's deep need of forgiveness for his rebellion and apostasy. As K. H. Miskotte (*When the Gods are Silent*, p. 400) puts it: 'In these philosophical apriorisms lie the deepest cause of the ambivalence of religion and the rise of the atheistic reaction and the nihilistic rebellion of the human spirit'. Israel never forgets the words of self-revelation here. And later in the OT reference is made to them again and again; cf. Num. 14: 18; 2 Chron. 30: 9; Neh. 9: 17; Ps. 86: 15; 103: 8; 111: 4; 112: 4; 116: 5; 145; 8; Joel 2: 13; Jonah 4: 2. What Yahweh does is to 'pass by' once again, as he did at the Passover, but this time he makes himself intelligible to Moses' mind in terms of a direct, loving, personal relationship. So Moses need hide no longer in the cleft of a rock, 33: 12; 2 Kings 19: 9–18.

'Merciful' is a word used only of God. We saw at 33: 19 that it may be connected with the word for womb. 'Gracious', though derived from the common noun for 'grace', in its form as an adjective is used also for God alone. 'Slow to anger' is literally 'long of nose', that is, it takes a long time for the snort of anger to come through God's nose. A strikingly anthropomorphic picture then to show that wrath is not primary to God, but has to be motivated and developed in response to the sin of man. 'Abounding in steadfast love' is literally 'great of *ḥesedh*'. This Hebrew noun has no English equivalent. The AV (KJV) translates it, so it is said, by 46 different English words;

and the RSV still employs, we believe, some 16 words to express what it means. Obviously it speaks of something unique in the nature of God that man does not possess by nature. Hosea expounds it by employing it for the *content* of the Covenant, for the loyalty-in-love that is the cement of the marriage relationship. H. Wheeler Robinson spoke of it as the 'nut' within the 'husk' that is the Covenant. It is most important for the reader of the NT to remember that no Greek word can express its meaning. This means that when the early Church adopted the pagan noun *agape* to express the concept of love, Hebrew speakers would include within it the many facets of meaning that the OT word *ḥesedh* conveys. Thus the only way to understand fully the meaning of the NT word for love is to look back and see how God handled Israel, both here at this moment, and in all successive moments in her history.

'Faithfulness' means 'reliability', 'unshakeableness'. The word 'Amen' comes from it. God is the Amen, the same yesterday, today and forever, an idea that is pictured at 33: 22 and elsewhere when he is called 'the Rock' which cannot be moved. The LXX translates by 'true', 'real'; cf. John 14: 6.

'Watching, guarding, keeping *ḥesedh* for thousands', that is to say, preserving intact his loyal-love for the masses of humanity. 'Forgiving iniquity', or 'lifting away' human guilt, as in Zechariah's parable, Zech. 5: 5–11; lifting away man's twistedness, his in-equity and transgression; removing man's 'rebellion', forgiving his 'missing the mark' in life. All these pictorial terms are aspects of the OT concept of sin.

'Who will by no means clear the guilty', or better, with the NEB, 'not sweeping the guilty clean away'.

8–9 Moses now puts his finger on the main issue. In humility and awe, and within the context of worship, he challenges Yahweh, declaring that if Yahweh is really like what he says he is, then, despite the stiffneckedness of Israel, he *can* forgive his people 'our sin'. He *can* return from walking in parallel with 'the army of the Lord' outside the camp, 33: 7, and revert to walking in its midst. And he *can* remember his promise to make Israel his inheritance on earth, 19: 5.

10 God's reply is what 'seeing God face to face' ultimately means. For here the Face is revealed in the Word. We have now reached the climax of the whole book of Exodus.

God shows his comprehensive forgiveness by remaking his Covenant with Israel, all over again. He offers his people in love a new beginning within the profound relationship of the Covenant. The remaking of the Covenant will be accompanied by 'marvels' such as have occurred before, that is to say, it will be of equal eschatological significance. But more, this time it will be 'a terrible thing that I will do'. Israel has now seen, as a result of her own folly, chap. 32, that it is a terrible thing to fall into the hands of the living God. The reality of this terror, of which there was no mention when the Covenant was first made (chap. 19), will however be 'built into' the content of the new covenant.

11–16 The danger of a contemptuous mishandling of the Covenant is 'terrible', especially the danger of 'going awhoring after other gods'. It is within such a context that the significance of God's zeal or jealousy becomes vividly clear. Israel will now have to do terrible things such as, for example, the tearing down of altars, if they are to understand fully that this covenant is an exclusive one. For it has been offered out of the pain and sorrow and searching forgiveness of the living God. God's Name even is Jealous, well rendered in *Tor* by 'Impassioned', for such is the true picture of him as Lover – so loving, so passionately in love with his Bride Israel (as Hosea expounds the idea) that he will permit her to give her charms to no one but himself. And this, as Ex understands it from the later prophets, was because the great Lover had planned to use her constancy, devotion and loyalty for his own ends, for his own glory, even as he moved forward *with* her to the redemption of the cosmos. In other words, God's creative purpose now advances through forgiveness and renewal.

17–26 Ex inserts here another 'Decalogue'. Some suggest it was originally a Kenite Code (see chap. 18). It is possible to find 13 clauses in it. The first Decalogue, however, has not been annulled. This other one is more concerned with ritual than with faith and morals. It differs starkly from the Decalogue of chap. 20. By placing it here Ex declares that it is only secondary and derivative; for first come the primary apodictic Words of God. We should compare its contents rather with the Code found at chap. 23.

27–28 That Moses has to rewrite the words of the

Covenant himself is the 'sign', visible to Israel, that God has acted to forgive his people and is initiating again his unique relationship with this one nation from out of all the nations of the earth. Moses writes because under God he is actively the Mediator of the covenant. He is completely committed to his task (he neither ate nor drank). So he himself is now the finger of God, 34: 1; Deut. 10: 2; and cf. 2 Cor. 3: 7–18. The period of 40 days and 40 nights witnesses to the re-newal of the original Covenant, which also required that period of gestation, 24: 18; Deut. 9: 9, 18. And so the Ten Words are now revalidated for all time.

29–35   The true saint is humbly unaware of his saintliness. Moses did not know that the people could see the Glory of God reflected on his face: 'The skin of his face shone'. [The traditional rabbinical interpretation was 'sent forth beams'. The verb is *qaran*, found only here and at Ps. 69: 32 (Heb.). The Vulgate confused *qaran* with the noun *qeren*, meaning a 'horn'. That is why we have medieval painters showing Moses with horns protruding from the front of his head.] Moses has humbly accepted the fact that he was only a *pro-phetes*, that he was only an instrument that spoke *for* God, chap. 4. He had asked to see God's Face, 33: 18. God had now answered his prayer by letting *Israel* see God's Glory on *Moses'* face. Such glory reveals unwitting concern, not for self, but for others. After 40 days Moses had come to know and to reflect the God of compassionate concern for *people*. Moses was now 'crowned with glory and honour', as Ps. 8: 5 can say of elect man – a witness to grace alone. Yet Moses promptly bridges the gap between Aaron and himself by talking normally with him and with the leaders of Israel. He rejects their view that somehow he is specially holy. Instead he passes on to them what God has said to him, doing so in a natural manner, in human terms, and not in some charismatic eccentricity. Nor does he exploit the fact of his manifest charisma when finally he becomes aware of it, and flaunt it like some popular evangelists have done this century. His role as mediator remains. It is interesting that Professor G. von Rad admits to the authenticity of as few facts about Moses as Professor Bultmann does about Jesus. Yet both characters emerge as greater than their 'historians' can paint them.

35   The veil which Moses puts over his face may have been a priest's mask. Only with it on could he endure the awful encounter with the holy God. The verbal tenses are iterative. From now on, they imply, Moses continues to go in and out of the Tent, 33: 7, each time receiving further instructions from the Lord. By this verbal usage Ex is expressing what, as an educated man, he knows to be a fact, that the Law of Moses grew and developed over a long period, as any law code must do even as the circumstances of a nation's life develop and change. Using narrative form, in other words, Ex declares that the later additions to the 'Law of Moses' are as truly 'inspired' as is the original Decalogue.

The last words of the chapter are 'to speak with him'; yet the Vulgate may be right in reading 'with them', in the spirit of the previous statement, thereby emphasizing the on-going revelation to the whole People of God even after Moses' death.

We have reached the end of Moses' long conversation with God. At last, therefore, the Tabernacle can be built.

THE FELLOWSHIP RESTORED

'These are the things (words?) which the Lord has commanded you to do', 35: 1, 4. For the Word of God is a thing; cf. Matt. 21: 28–31. Thus we note the movement of the Word to becoming 'thing' in this chapter: (1) God said to Moses; (2) Moses said to the people; (3) The people built. The primary 'sign' of the Covenant is God's gift of the Sabbath. This is now the sixth time that Ex has recorded the command to keep that day. So it is now sufficient to refer to it in condensed form. It is only after that matter has been cleared away, the command that Israel is not to build on the Sabbath, that the people are even to begin to collect material. Clearly their health and welfare come before even the worship of God. They are now to 'undo' the blasphemous misuse of their silver and gold, chap. 32, by donating their treasure, this time to Yahweh. For they are now in a renewed relationship to Yahweh brought about by his grace and forgiveness alone. In fact, the basic meaning of the first verb in 35: 1, viz. 'called', NEB, emphasizes that 'the people of Israel' are being 'recalled' by God to be his witnesses. All are now to set to and build the Tabernacle along with the various sacred objects that God had commanded before as recorded in chaps. 25–28; for these would now become 'means of grace' for upholding Israel in continuing fellowship with God within the Covenant; cf. Rev. 21: 3.

The response is what one would expect, 35: 21–22; 36: 6–7. We note at 35: 30 how the work of the untalented is as acceptable as that of the talented. We also note that this time God *elects* Bezalel, in the theological sense of the term, as well as empowers him to do the work. Work is now an aspect of worship. That is what 'calling by name' means. So Moses informs the people that Bezalel is now to 'teach' his fellow-artisans. Ex uses for this verb the root which in noun form is the word Torah. And then we read of Bezalel and the others actually doing the work, 35: 30–36; 2, 5. An interesting memory of women functionaries is preserved in 38: 8. These would be given office only in later years once the Tabernacle had come into being; cf. 1 Sam. 2: 22.

CHAPTER 39

THE PLACE OF THE PRIEST

1–31   The priestly vestments symbolize the special task of the priest. The priest deals in holy things; and he belongs in a great procession of ministers to Yahweh that is part of the continuity of the People of God. Israel was originally adopted as God's 'son', 4: 22, more than 3000 years ago. The People of God must remain in that filial relationship for ever. The priest helps them to do so. So it is not the continuity of the priest that guarantees the continuity of the Church; it is the Grace of God bestowed in covenant upon all the People of God including the priest.

32–43   People are more important than ecclesiastical utensils. It was the people who completed the work that God had commanded; it was the people who brought all their handywork to Moses; and it was the people whom Moses then blessed, not the Tabernacle and its fittings, nor the vestments of the priests.

This chapter is in 7 paragraphs. The phrase '. . . as the Lord commanded Moses' occurs in it 7 times. The Rabbis were quick to note the parallel this offers with the 7 days of creation, which was also 'at the Word of the Lord'. The Tabernacle took 7 months to build, and Solomon's Temple 7 years.

CHAPTER 40

THE END OF THE BEGINNING

1-15   The consciousness that we have reached a new beginning is expressed by the phrase 'On the first day of the first month'. On that day Moses was to erect and set in place all the furnishings that the people had made. He was to begin with the holiest of all, with the place of God's Presence, and thence was to work outwards. Next, and still on the same day, he was to consecrate Aaron, that is to say, he was to initiate the priestly succession which was then to be 'perpetual', 29: 9; Num. 25: 13; Heb. 5: 6.

16-29   One year has now passed since Israel crossed the Sea, 19: 1; 24: 18; 34: 28. It has been a tumultuous twelve months. But now, with the Tabernacle erected, the Ark in its place, the two tablets of the Decalogue laid within the sacred Box, all the auxiliary sacred items laid out in order, and the screens set up to preserve the sanctity of the whole, Moses is in the position to offer the first sacrifices. How often, even in this chapter, have we met the phrase, '. . . as the Lord had commanded Moses'. Israel may therefore face the future in confidence, since all that has happened to her has been at the Word of the Lord.

At 39: 42 we read that 'the people of Israel' had completed their share of the work, the 'service' of God. This word means also 'worship'. Then at 40: 33 we read that *Moses* finished the work, a different word, the 'physical labour' of erecting the Tabernacle. The two actions complement each other. So now we have reached the End of the Beginning.

30-33   Yet a note of sadness remains. The Tabernacle continues to be a perpetual witness – to the inability of its ministry to open the way for worshippers to enter Yahweh's Presence. That is why sacrifices, whether daily or annual, must go on and on, for Israel's sinfulness still forms a barrier between herself and God. On the other hand we must not

forget the other emphasis that is made in this chapter. Apart
from the daily sacrifices, each day the presence of the Glory
in the midst is a reality. The Targum on Lev. 26: 11 reads:
'Yahweh delights to make his Shekhinah dwell in his holy
Temple' (in oral form from about 100 B.C.). The *Sayings of the
Fathers*, also about 100 B.C., declares: 'Whenever ten men sit
together and occupy themselves with the Torah, the Divine
Presence abides with them; and the same applies even to one,
because it is said, "In every place where I cause my Name
to be rememered I will come unto thee and I will bless thee" '.

34–38   To conclude his description of the whole cycle of
divine activity Ex now brings together several of the pictorial
theological categories he has used before; cf. 3: 1–17; 13: 21;
16: 6–7; 24: 9; 25: 8; 17: 29; 43–45; 33: 16. In Egypt Israel
had been alone, abandoned, hopeless and helpless. Now the
cloud, the symbol of God's 'otherness', 'abode' (the root we
discussed at 33: 14; and see 1 Kings 8: 10–11; 2 Chron. 5:
14; 7: 2; Ezek. 44: 4; and cf. Matt. 17: 5 with parallels Luke
1: 35; 2 Peter 1: 13; also 2 Cor. 5: 1, 4 for a 'heavenly tent',
and Luke 16: 9; Rev. 7: 15; 21: 9) at that spot at the heart of
Israel's life where man might meet with the Word; for the
theological significance of the Tent described at 33: 7–11 has
now been integrated with the theological significance of the
Tabernacle, 39: 33. The 'Glory of the Lord' has now returned, in forgiveness and grace, to dwell in Israel's midst.

And so Israel, by grace, and in fulfilment of the divine
promise at 20: 43, 45, steps out of the old aeon of pain, sorrow
and disgrace, and goes forward on this New Year's Day into the
unknown future of the new aeon; but now she is no longer
alone.

As we learn from Deut. 34: 5, Moses dies and enters the
silence. He who had walked with God, was not, for God took
him, Gen. 5: 24. We do not hear of his finding personal salvation. But we do know that he had completed the work which
God had given him to do, and in the doing of it he had found
fullness of fellowship with God.

So here we leave Israel, stepping out on the march *with* God
and *by* God (cf. Isa. 43: 5a; Matt. 28: 20b), bearing with her
the promise, through the very nature of the Word, of still more
revelation to come.